THE
POLICY FACTOR

Agricultural Performance in Kenya and Tanzania

Michael F. Lofchie

D1732676

Lynne Rienner Publishers, Inc.　•　Heinemann Kenya Ltd.
Boulder & London　　　　　　Nairobi

This book is included in the Food in Africa *series*.

Published in the United States of America in 1989 by
Lynne Rienner Publishers, Inc.
1800 30th Street, Boulder, Colorado 80301

and in the United Kingdom by
Lynne Rienner Publishers, Inc.
3 Henrietta Street, Covent Garden, London WC2E 8LU

Published in Kenya by
Heinemann Kenya Ltd.
P.O. Box 45314, Nairobi, Kenya

Library of Congress Cataloging-in-Publication Data

Lofchie, Michael F.
  The policy factor.
  (Food in Africa series)
  Bibliography: p.
  Includes index.
  1. Agriculture and state—Kenya.   2. Agriculture and
state—Tanzania.   I. Title.   II. Series.
HD2126.5.Z8L64   1989   338.1'86762   88-18396
ISBN 1-55587-136-4 (alk. paper)

British Cataloguing in Publication Data

A Cataloguing in Publication record for this book
is available from the British Library

Printed and bound in the United States of America

The paper used in this publication meets the requirements of
the American National Standard for Permanence of Paper for
Printed Library Materials Z39.48-1984

THE
POLICY FACTOR

For Kelly, Carl, and Jim

Contents

Contents

Tables and Graphs

———

Graphs accompany Tables 4.1–4.12 and 6.3.

Tables and graphs for Tables 4.1–4.12 and for Table 6.3, and Table 5.2–5.8 were prepared by Marcus Catlett and Steven Mattas.

Preface

The study of African agriculture has become a daunting enterprise. This is due partly to the fact that the costs of sustained field research are prohibitively expensive, partly to the fact that reliable statistical information is exceedingly difficult to obtain, and partly to the fact that African political processes are so complex that to develop a plausible perspective requires the continuous support and nurturing of countless colleagues both in this country and in Africa. This study has benefited especially from such support. The list of those whose assistance has been indispensable is so long that it is impossible to thank them all by name; to those whose names do not appear in this necessarily brief thank you, I offer the assurance that their help has not been forgotten.

As the statistical materials in Chapter 4 reveal, this book would not have been possible without the generous assistance of the Africa/Middle East Branch (AF/ME) of the U.S. Department of Agriculture. Indeed, the book began, in early 1983, as a study for AF/ME of the impact of policy factors on agricultural trade. Cheryl Christensen, then branch chief, initiated and funded the original study (to the utter bewilderment of an academic whose work to that point was exclusively on the "soft" side of our discipline). Lawrence Witucki, desk officer for eastern Africa, made available not only his encyclopedic personal knowledge of agriculture in Kenya and Tanzania, but an unmatched library of research materials and a bibliophile's knowledge of the relevant literature on this region. Although Cheryl and Larry would scarcely recognize that study in its present form, their input has been determinative through the several drafts that have taken place since. Financial support for the three years' additional work required to turn the study into a book was generously provided by the Presiding Bishop's Fund of the Episcopal Church and by the Academic Senate and African Studies Center of the University of California, Los Angeles.

Scholars at the University of Dar es Salaam and the University of Nairobi have been unstinting in their hospitality and support. In Dar, Jumanne Wagao offered a resolute and implacable counter to the arguments this book puts forward. Similarly, Gelase Mutahaba, Benson Nindi, Samuel

Wangwe, Lucian Msambichaka, Gaspar Munishi, and Immanuel Bavu demonstrated by personal example that exceptional research can take place under arduous circumstances, and that the bonds of friendship transcend analytic differences. In Nairobi, the same kind of sustenance was provided by Michael Chege, Shem Mighot-Adhola, and, especially, Peter Ngau, whose personally guided tours of agriculture on the slopes of Mt. Kenya were a high point in the field portions of my work. My deepest thanks go to all of them, as well to the staff members of the Harvard Institute for International Development projects on agricultural and district planning in Kenya: John Cohen, Malcolm Hall, Judith Geist, Stephen Peterson, David Lewis, Michael Roemer, and Michael Westlake.

The list of Africanist scholars who provided advice and counsel is all but impossible to limit. Robert Bates and I have shared ideas since we coedited a book on African agriculture in 1980. David Leonard was willing to sit down and patiently explain the basic impact of class factors in Kenya and Tanzania; Chapter 7 would not have been possible without him. Stephen Commins, now the president of Immaculate Heart Foundation, was not only an intellectual companion at UCLA, but also created the Development Institute, which attracted graudate students whose sole obsession was to study African rural development. Richard Sklar offered constant encouragement through his belief in the value of a study that, although employing the structural adjustment paradigm, would also show that some African governments do get their policies right. Frank Holmquist provided a manuscript critique that should be published independently as a commentary on agricultural policy formulation in East Africa.

Any academic who has ever tried to combine administrative and scholarly roles knows all too well that, to do so, one must inevitably cheat a little bit on both. Therefore, a note of apology here to the colleagues whose meetings I did not attend and whose phone calls and letters went unanswered for too long; also, to the students whose appointments were not kept and to the African Studies Center staff members who rose to ever greater heights of imagination to explain why the center director was not at the meeting he was expected to attend. And a note of thanks for the patience of friends who managed to pretend that maize pricing policy in Kenya and Tanzania was well worth a full evening's discourse.

Many research assistants have also provided fundamental support. Special thanks to Geoffrey Bergen and Jamie Monson. And an overwhelming statement of gratitude to Marcus Catlett and Steven Mattas for their virtuoso work with Lotus 1-2-3 and Perspective 3-D, used to produce the tables and graphs in the book.

The usual disclaimer is probably unnecessary. I am certain that all of these friends are well aware that the shortcomings of this book appear despite their best efforts and are the sole responsibility of the author.

Michael F. Lofchie

· 1 ·

The African
Agricultural Crisis

Africa is in the midst of a generalized agricultural crisis, the most visible symptom of which is the continent's intermittent inability to feed itself. The problem of widespread agricultural decline first came to public attention during the Sahelian drought of the early 1970s, when acute famine conditions focused international attention on the underlying weaknesses in a number of West African agricultural systems. The Sahelian tragedy demonstrated that these systems had little or no reserve productive capacity with which to respond to a temporary deterioration of climatic conditions. It also demonstrated that, on their own, these countries lacked the financial capacity to import sufficient volumes of foodstuffs to avert starvation. Although the most extreme conditions of drought and famine were confined principally to western Africa, comparable agrarian weaknesses could also be discerned in such dissimilar eastern African countries as Ethiopia and Tanzania, which also experienced severe food shortfalls during this period.

By the mid 1970s, chronic food deficits, growing out of inadequate agricultural performance, had begun to affect nearly half of sub-Saharan Africa's forty-five independent countries. The Food and Agriculture Organization (FAO) of the United Nations estimated at one point that countries affected by food shortages might need to import as much as 7 million tons of food per year during the 1980s. This figure might have been substantially greater had not an adequate pattern of rainfall returned to East Africa.[1] The World Bank suggested an even higher figure; one report indicated that Africa's food imports had climbed to nearly 10 million tons per year by the early 1980s, an amount adequate for virtually the entire urban population.[2] Current trends are such that Africa can be expected to remain a food-importing region for the foreseeable future. As early as 1981, a major study by the Africa/Middle East (AF/ME) Branch of the U.S. Department of Agriculture (USDA) documented a pattern of diminishing per-capita food availability for a large and growing number of African countries. Of twenty-five countries surveyed, about two-thirds (seventeen) had experienced a measurable decline in per-capita food production during the 1970s.[3] Africa had dramatically emerged as the only major world region to have suffered a

1

decline in per-capita food production since the early 1960s, a pattern with ominous implications not only for human nutrition but, because of the high cost of food imports relative to national resources, for Africa's overall development.

The degree to which intermittent famines and food deficits reflected a pattern of long-term agricultural decline was portentous. Africa's food shortages could no longer be understood as the outcome of short-term episodic events—such as droughts, civil wars, or crop blights—but, instead, had to be analyzed as the consequence of fundamental structural factors— such as inappropriate agricultural policies on the part of African nation-states, and adverse features of the international economic system. The beginnings of Africa's agrarian crisis were visible as early as the immediate postindependence period in the 1960s. The continent had already become a net importer of grains, though, as the 1981 USDA report notes, this was not a matter of urgent concern. Import volumes were relatively low, and adequate low-cost supplies were readily available from donor countries prepared to make grain shipments on concessional terms. Foreign-exchange reserves were relatively plentiful, so there was sufficient hard currency to finance both food imports and the importation of other economic necessities.[4]

Toward the end of the 1960s, however, the level of food imports began to become a matter of major concern. Not only did the volume of food imports double during this decade, but the cost of grain imports increased nearly sixfold. Even before the Sahelian drought of the early 1970s, it had become clear that the poor agricultural performance of a large number of African countries was also at the root of a broader and more diffuse economic crisis, beginning, for example, to diminish the prospects of urban industrial growth. A large number of countries had embarked upon costly programs of industrialization based on import substitution. The need to allocate larger and larger amounts of hard currency for food imports competed directly with the fledgling industrial sector's need for capital goods and raw materials. Poor agricultural performance threatened other important values as well. Africa's newly independent governments were profoundly committed to expanding their level of social services, but there was simply no way to finance the growth of medical and educational programs while scarce funds had to be diverted to the purchase and distribution of imported foodstuffs.

Although drought spotlighted weaknesses in Africa's agrarian economies, it could by no means be held accountable for them. The continent's need for imports has continued to escalate in both favorable and adverse weather conditions. This escalation has ominous implications: The international donor community, whose patience had already become strained by an extended period of poor agricultural performance, has begun to show signs of increasing reluctance to provide concessional or humanitarian aid, a phenomenon sometimes termed "donor fatigue." There is a growing conviction on the part of many donor countries that Africa's food deficits are the product of poor agricultural policies. The appropriate remedy, therefore, is policy reform, not food assistance. Donor policymakers have also become sensitive to the extent to which food aid contributes to the continent's crisis, whether through a disincentive effect on agricultural prices or by providing a substitute for agricultural reform. Many donor organizations have been offended by the tendency of some African governments to use food aid for political purposes or as a basis for elite corruption.[5] Although no major donor agency has suggested a termination of food-assistance projects, the donor nations are likely to take steps that will increasingly shift the cost burden of food aid to recipient countries.

Food deficits, however, reflect only one dimension of Africa's agrarian crisis. Often overlooked, because of the high visibility of the food crisis, is the fact that export-oriented agriculture has also performed poorly. These two dimensions of the continent's agrarian problem are directly intertwined, for export-oriented agriculture, which could have provided the foreign-exchange earnings necessary to finance food imports, has been unable to do so because of stagnating production. There is one line of argument that suggests that the continent's food crisis would not exist if there had been more robust performance in the production of exportable agricultural commodities. Since food grains such as wheat, corn, and rice are easily available on the world market at prices that are deeply depressed because of oversupply, Africa might have been able to finance the necessary level of food imports out of the foreign-exchange earnings derived from agricultural exports.

The principal symptom of Africa's poor export performance has been its failure to maintain a world-market share. Africa's share of the world market for major agricultural exports (such as coffee, tea, cotton, bananas, and oilseeds) has been falling steadily since the early 1970s.[6] Because world demand for these commodities is projected to grow only slowly at best between now and the end of this century, Africa's prospects of developing an adequate foreign-exchange earning capacity must necessarily lie in the introduction of agricultural policies that will enable the continent to recapture its former share of world trade. This will require a major and politically difficult diversion of national resources to the countryside, away from urban industries and services.

The faltering performance of export agriculture has already imposed a serious constraint on the performance of Africa's urban industries. Since much of sub-Saharan Africa's industrial sector is based on import substitution, it depends heavily on the hard-currency earnings of other economic sectors, principally agriculture, to finance the importation of needed inputs. As the earnings from export agriculture have stagnated, and as the diminishing reserves of foreign exchange have been used to finance the acquisition of other necessary imports (such as food and energy), Africa's industries have begun to suffer from the lack of replacement capital goods, spare parts, and raw materials. The most conspicuous symptom of these shortages has been a falling rate of capacity utilization, already as low as 25 percent to 30 percent in some countries. Other symptoms of the problem are to be discerned in such phenomena as high rates of inflation (caused by the scarcity of consumer goods), increasing rates of urban unemployment (caused by industrial closures), and a falling real-wage rate (caused, in part, by the fall in labor productivity).

The ramifications of agricultural failure reflect the extent to which this sector has been required to be the basis for achieving a number of major developmental objectives. At least four such objectives can be identified:

1. Agriculture has been expected to provide African countries with a high degree of food self-sufficiency, not only as a means to minimize the foreign-exchange costs of food imports, but as a way to avoid dependency on Western countries for food relief.
2. Agriculture has been expected to generate a high level of foreign-exchange earnings to finance importing both consumer goods and the whole range of inputs necessary to sustain a steady expansion of public-sector services and import-dependent industries.
3. Agriculture has been viewed as the source of a high rate of savings, the essential economic precondition for domestic capital accumulation.
4. Agriculture has been consistently regarded as the largest source of expanded employment opportunity—the employer of last resort—to help provide economic livelihood for the continent's rapidly growing population.

Employment opportunities in agriculture are a great concern. Today, there is an urgent need for African countries to create the basis for an expansion of smallholder agriculture. The continent's cities seem increasingly unable to provide economic opportunity for displaced members of peasant society, who migrate to urban centers in a desperate quest for livelihood. With the absolute decline of industrial activity in many countries, rates of urban unemployment of 40 percent or more are by no means uncommon; even this figure does not include those persons whom economists technically designate as "underemployed." Even Africa's better-off countries confront a social crisis as the number of school-leavers exceeds the number of new jobs being created. In societies where stagnation of export agriculture has caused a decline in the industrial sector, annual job-creation in the modern sector is a negative number. It is not likely that Africa's informal sector, vast as it is, can provide employment opportunity on the necessary scale. The buoyancy of this sector is heavily dependent on the purchasing power of urban middle and working classes, whose capacity to act as consumers for goods produced in informal industries has been sharply eroded by inflationary trends. Despite the fact that the agricultural sector holds the major prospect of employment generation, few African countries have made systematic efforts to develop smallholder-based systems of agricultural production.

Food deficits, industrial decline, and urban unemployment are only the most conspicuous outcomes of Africa's agrarian malaise. Africa has also become a continent of generalized political and social instability, which is, at one and the same time, cause and effect of the deterioration of the agricultural sector. One of the most tragic indicators of the continent's chronic economic problems is the extremely high number of refugees. Although sub-Saharan Africa hosts only about 10 percent of the world's population, it now accounts for about 25 percent of the world's refugees, approximately 2.5 million persons. A high rate of infant mortality has emerged also as one of the effects of pandemic economic difficulties. Africa's infant-mortality rate is now approximately double that of other developing regions. There is increasing evidence that among children who survive, chronic food deficits are beginning to take an additional toll in terms of such ratios as height or weight to age. Because life expectancy in developing countries is closely related to per-capita income, it is not at all surprising that Africa's poorest countries also rank among the lowest in the world in this regard.

Unless there is a major reversal of current trends in the agricultural sector, there is little basis for optimism about Africa's economic future. Major economic indicators seem to point to a further worsening of the present situation. During the past decade, for example, African countries have accumulated an enormous debt burden, which diminishes the prospects of economic recovery because debt servicing is an enormous drain on dwindling foreign-exchange reserves. As late as 1974, the total outstanding debt of Africa's low-income countries was only about U.S. $7.5 billion, and the debt-service ratio for these countries (total debt servicing as a percentage of export earnings) was only about 7 percent. Within just a decade, foreign debt has increased nearly fourfold, to approximately $27 billion; the debt-service ratio has increased almost four and a half times, to almost 31.5 percent.

Africa's debt-service ratio is now substantially higher than that for the Latin American-Caribbean region, generally regarded as the world's principal debtor area, where the debt-service ratio in 1983 was approximately 26 percent. Indeed, if the debt burden is figured on the basis of the ratio of total debt to annual export earnings, Africa's low-income countries have a debt burden nearly three times as great as that of Latin America and the Caribbean.[7] The debt burden has grim implications for Africa's socioeconomic future. Since debt servicing competes for foreign exchange with imported agricultural and industrial inputs, the debt problem has a direct and negative bearing on the prospects for an economic recovery of the agricultural sector.

Policy analyses of the causes of Africa's agricultural crisis often omit one of the most important long-term factors: the degradation of Africa's physical environment. The omission is singularly regrettable, for damage to the continent's ecosystems has become so severe in some areas that the prospects of agroeconomic recovery would be extremely poor even if appropriate policy reforms were to be introduced. The agricultural effects of environmental damage have been dramatically stated by Antoon de Vos:

> It is a frightening fact that the quality of the African environment today is deteriorating at an unprecedented and accelerating rate. Many ill-advised, unproductive and destructive practices, such as deforestation, one-crop farming and strip mining, are steadily contributing to an ecological imbalance which has already had catastrophic effects in some areas and will have long-ranging ones in others.[8]

These problems are most conspicuous in the Sahel, where vast regions of once-arable land have been converted to desert wasteland within the last century. But damage to the continent's physical base can also be discerned in a number of countries throughout the eastern, central, and southern regions of the continent.[9]

Agricultural systems introduced during the period of European colonialism have contributed greatly to Africa's environmental difficulties. To understand the genesis of this process, it is useful to recall that much of Africa's land is not well suited to intensive agricultural development. The soil cover is typically thin, and therefore highly fragile, deficient in vital nutrients, and low in organic content. In addition, Africa's rainfall patterns are characterized by extremes of high and low precipitation, and by a frustrating degree of unpredictability from one season to the next. As a result, African soils are susceptible to a rapid depletion of their capacity to sustain intensive cultivation. Methods of agricultural production that were developed in temperate latitudes, where the soil base is denser and rainfall patterns more regular, have proved to be highly destructive under these conditions.

In Africa's tropical regions, preservation of the soil base typically depends on the presence of a perennial ground cover, consisting of forests or grasses and shrubs. This ground cover performs a number of ecologically vital functions. It helps to preserve the moisture content of the topsoil by forming a protective mulch of leaf litter and fallen grasses. This mulch shields the topsoil from direct exposure to the baking sun and from the potentially erosive bombardment of heavy tropical rains. The protective mulch provided by a perennial tree and grass cover also replenishes the nutrients in the soil: Through the process of microbial decay, the mulch decomposes into organic material that penetrates the soil beneath. In addition, the root systems of perennial trees and plants are a major stabilizing factor for the soil. Africa's physical environment may have been able to sustain a relatively dense green cover during the precolonial era, but this was only possible through a highly delicate balance of organic decomposition of surface vegetation and the growth of new plant materials.

Colonial agricultural practices frequently required clearing the original ground cover, in order to introduce crops that have an annual harvest cycle. Crops such as cotton, groundnuts, and tobacco have proved to be especially harmful, for they have required that vast amounts of land be cleared of its original cover, thereby interrupting the natural cycle of organic replenishment. Once such annual crops have been harvested, moreover, the earth is laid bare and exposed to the baking action of the sun. Desiccated soils have virtually no capacity to store moisture; when rain does fall, even in modest amounts, it typically causes erosion and gullying. Deprived of the stabilizing benefit of tree- and shrub-root systems, the soils are easily washed away, leaving behind a barren terrain wholly unsuited to agricultural production.

It would be incorrect to place the entire responsibility for this sort of environmental destruction on colonial agricultural systems. Certain rural practices of African peoples have also proved harmful. As Africa's population has expanded, communities have been forced to abandon such traditional agricultural practices as shifting cultivation, which allowed for long fallow periods during which the soil could regenerate. In addition, Africa's rapid population growth has been accompanied by a rapid growth in the size of the continent's herds of domesticated animals. This has resulted in widespread overgrazing, further stripping the soil of its protective cover of grasses and shrubs. Deforestation also persists because wood continues to be Africa's most common cooking fuel and construction material, and because for some countries, such as the Ivory Coast, timber exports are a critically important source of foreign exchange.

The cumulative effect of these factors is to render agroeconomic recovery extraordinarily difficult. The most likely scenario is a gradual but inexorable deterioration of agricultural performance, punctuated by intermittent recovery during brief periods of adequate rainfall, and when other factors, such as international commodity prices, are momentarily favorable.

THE ANALYTIC ISSUE:
EXTERNAL AND INTERNAL FACTORS IN AFRICA'S CRISIS

For the past decade or more, the causes and effects of poor agricultural performance have been at the center of developmental analyses of the African continent. The subject first gained prominence during the Sahelian drought, when the famine the drought helped induce spurred an outpouring of official and academic research on the causes of pervasive agricultural decline and the means of arresting it. Although African agriculture had been the subject of considerable research throughout the colonial and immediate postindependence periods, much of this early work was highly localized in scope and focused either on technical agroscientific questions or on matters of local government and administration. There was little sense of an urgent or impending crisis. The new generation of research was of an entirely different character, reflecting a profound sense that a desperate continental emergency was at hand.

The first efforts to develop a systematic, continentwide profile of agricultural performance were not undertaken until the late 1970s. Two major studies appeared in 1981. In that year, the World Bank published its widely read and controversial report, *Accelerated Development in Sub-Saharan Africa*.[10] Commonly referred to as the Berg Report, after its principal author, Elliot Berg (then at the University of Michigan), this study launched a major international debate about the causes of Africa's agricultural difficulties. Because of its provocative conclusion, which placed principal responsibility for the crisis on the inappropriate economic policies of African governments, the Berg Report elicited a highly critical response from African political leaders. The African reaction to the World Bank's viewpoint was officially embodied in the Lagos Plan of Action, a document adopted by the Organization of African Unity. While acknowledging that African governments had committed serious mistakes, the Lagos plan tended to stress multiple causes, including the continent's colonial legacy and an adverse international economic environment.

Almost simultaneously with the Berg Report, the USDA published a massively documented study, *Food Problems and Prospects in Sub-Saharan Africa*.[11] Although less controversial, this study shared many of the conclusions reached in the Berg Report. Both provided compelling statistical documentation of virtually all-pervasive decline in per-capita food production, and of stagnation in the production of exportable crops. Like the Berg Report, the USDA study tended to place the principal responsibility for this decline on the economic policies of independent African states. Its principal argument focused on the disincentive effects of pricing and marketing systems common throughout the continent.

The sponsorship of these reports says much about the reasons for the long delay between the Sahelian famine and the first appearance of research reports with continentwide scope. Assembling statistics covering forty-five or more independent countries is a formidable and extraordinarily expensive undertaking, one far beyond the financial and organizational resources ordinarily available to individual academics. While private scholars have been able to produce studies describing agricultural conditions in one or perhaps several countries, financial factors alone typically have ruled out the feasibility of any project conceived on a more ambitious scale. As a result, defining an intellectual paradigm for understanding African agriculture has largely passed out of the hands of academics, to be taken up by governmental or quasi-governmental bureaucracies directly involved in the continent's agricultural development.

Each of these bureaucracies had a somewhat separate institutional agenda. The World Bank needed to understand African agriculture because it was clear to major bank officials that previous lending policies, centering principally on individual projects, had not been well informed by a broad economic understanding of the continent as a whole. Indeed, many of the bank's large-scale projects had failed for reasons that had less to do with project design than with the fact that the surrounding economic environment had become badly distorted, an effect of the economic policies of the host government. Development economists at the World Bank became deeply concerned that projects, the feasibility of which had appeared highly promising on paper, simply failed when located in economies characterized by inappropriate exchange rates and by inflationary monetary and fiscal policies.

The USDA was motivated by a different consideration: As a major provider of food grains to famine-stricken countries and regions, it required an economic model that would help forecast agriculture performance over large areas over extended periods of time, thus providing some way to assess the extent to which domestic production might satisfy food requirements. The AF/ME branch of the USDA's Economic Research Service (ERS) was mandated to conduct research that would help anticipate the extent of Africa's need for grain imports, during both times of drought and more normal periods. Both the USDA and the World Bank were in a position to devote massive human and financial resources to African agricultural research. Cheryl Christensen, chief of AF/ME, initiated the compilation of its continentwide data base. She has estimated that, by 1987, nearly seventy person-years had been devoted to the compilation and tabulation of African agricultural statistics.

The best-known academic study to venture onto the research terrain of continentwide generalization is Robert Bates' seminal volume, *Markets and States in Tropical Africa,* which also appeared in 1981.[12] The differences between this study and those by the World Bank and USDA make it immediately clear how differently a university-based scholar had to operate with respect to this subject matter. Bates' volume, the outcome of his period of residence as a visiting scholar at Stanford University's Food Research Institute, is of a different genre than the Berg Report or the USDA study. It is less concerned with generating a continentwide statistical profile than with developing a theoretical paradigm, which would effectively combine political science and economics in a unified approach to Africa's agrarian difficulties. As a result, its statistical materials are somewhat more eclectically drawn than those of its two contemporaries and its intellectual focus views economic policies as the outcome of political forces.

The striking feature of these three studies is their analytical consensus: They are in substantial agreement that the principal source of Africa's agricultural difficulties is the disincentive effect of economic policies pursued by African governments since independence. While differing in nuance and in the degree of emphasis on particular policies, these three studies concur that African governments have intervened in their nations' economies in ways that create disincentives for agricultural producers, thereby reducing aggregate agricultural production. The studies by the bank and the USDA stop at the point of outlining the patterns of economic policy that harm agriculture.

Bates' volume seeks to identify a causal factor, finding it in the political imperative of urban bias. Bates found that African governments must deal with the high potential for political volatility of their urban constituencies. They respond to these political demands by formulating and implementing policies that extract resources from agriculture and transfer them to urban populations. The clearest example is cheap food. Urban populations, which are consumers, want food to be as inexpensive as possible. Governments can accommodate this demand by imposing controls on prices and by using these controls to reduce producer prices to levels below those that an open market might make available.

Broadly speaking, then, the academic and institutional participants in the debate over Africa's agrarian crisis can be divided into two schools of thought: internalists and externalists. Internalists tend to believe that the basic causes of agrarian breakdown in Africa can be found in the economic policies pursued by African governments since independence. Internalists are joined by the view that economic recovery is effectively within the political grasp of governments prepared to undertake serious efforts at policy reform. While acknowledging the relevance of such external factors as terms of trade, internalists are basically convinced that internal policy reform can make it possible for African nations to attain the all-important objectives of food self-sufficiency, improved balance-of-payments performance, and considerable employment generation.

Externalists, on the other hand, tend to place their principal emphasis on the adverse features of the international economic environment facing countries that depend on primary agricultural exports. Adverse features include the nature of Africa's colonial heritage, its high degree of dependency on external markets, and the activities of multinational corporations and donor agencies.[13] In this intellectual genre, there is a strong presupposition that unless the international economic environment can be made more hospitable, internal policy reforms will fail to trigger economic recovery. Externalists argue that countries dependent on the export of primary agricultural commodities will inevitably continue to suffer low per-capita incomes, extreme balance-of-payments difficulties, foreign-exchange shortages, and acute deterioration of public- and private-sector services that depend on imported inputs.

The externalist position has been developed principally by scholars who do not have access to the massive research resources of powerful economic institutions such as the World Bank or the USDA. As a result, there is an intellectual asymmetry in the literature on Africa's agricultural crisis. Whereas the internalist viewpoint has been abundantly documented by voluminous institutional studies drawing on a rich and highly diversified array of statistical materials, externalist treatments have been principally of a historical nature and have consisted mainly of case studies of individual countries or regions. There is no single study that corresponds to the Berg Report in demonstrating the salience and impact of external factors on the continent as a whole.

One of the earliest externalist treatments was published before the appearance of the World Bank and the USDA reports. Richard W. Franke, an anthropologist, and Barbara H. Chasin, a sociologist, published their volume, *Seeds of Famine*, in 1980.[14] Franke and Chasin find the immediate cause of famine in the widespread problem of environmental deterioration in the West African Sahel. The source of this deterioration, in their view, lies in West Africa's colonial legacy, specifically in the agricultural policies pursued by colonial administrations motivated to develop large-scale, export-oriented agricultural production. Franke and Chasin also place considerable emphasis on the extent to which dominant political elites in the Sahelian countries act as the implementers of foreign-instigated projects, with the principal motivation of short-term profit rather than preservation of the social and environmental fabric.

The classic statement of an externalist viewpoint appeared two years later, in 1983, with the publication of Michael Watts' *Silent Violence*.[15] In his book, Watts demonstrates in detail the way in which the introduction of capitalist methods of agricultural production undermined the social fabric of traditional society in Northern Nigeria. Watts argues that exogenously introduced capitalism changed existing social systems in ways that left large segments of the population vulnerable to food deficits. He argues that famine conditions are the inevitable outcome of social changes that have eroded long-standing institutional methods for handling social crisis, thereby placing larger and larger proportions of the population at risk during periods of low production.

Although the externalist literature has no single counterpart to the continentwide studies by the World Bank or USDA, it is extensive. In 1979, for example, the British journal, *Review of African Political Economy* (ROAPE), published a double issue, "The Roots of Famine," which included articles on the external source of agricultural decline in seven African countries.[16] These articles, like the works by Watts and Franke and Chasin, exhibit a common theoretical core generally termed the theory of underdevelopment. According to this theory, the principal cause of food deficits in contemporary Africa lies in the fact that colonial powers changed existing economic systems, integrating them into the world trading system.

The authors of this issue of ROAPE are unanimous in their conviction that the root of Africa's present crisis lies in the colonial administrations' transforming of traditional agricultural systems in ways that reduced their capacity for food self-sufficiency. If a single causal factor were to be identified in this literature, then, it would most certainly be European capitalism and the socioeconomic changes it induced in indigenous systems of agricultural production.

The broad distinction between internalist and externalist schools of thought inevitably involves an unfortunate element of oversimplification. Very few academic observers or policy analysts fall unambiguously into one or the other of these categories. Even the most critical readers of the Berg Report have been compelled to acknowledge its sensitivity to such external factors as terms of trade and features of the colonial legacy over which African governments have no control. Similarly, analysts whose principal focus is the external environment tend almost invariably to point out that part of the problem for African agriculture has been urban bias in the economic policy of the vast majority of independent states.[17] There is some occasion, then, to regret that these schools of thought are posed so often as alternative interpretations, for each sheds valuable light on some of the complex causes of the present crisis.

This book seeks to deal appreciatively with both internal and external explanations for the agricultural difficulties presently experienced by so many African countries. Each of these interpretations has directed our attention to certain ineluctable realities. Externalists have established the fact that the international economic environment is deeply inhospitable to the long-term growth prospects of small agricultural countries. Since the early 1970s at least, the international economic system has been experiencing a pronounced and sustained tendency toward the oversupply of agricultural goods, a situation commonly referred to as the commodities crisis. Because of this crisis, the prices of agricultural commodities have been generally on a downward trajectory, especially in comparison with the international price levels of manufactured goods produced by the industrial countries. Agricultural countries tend to receive lower and lower real prices for the goods they export: hence the widely discussed decline in the terms of trade for agricultural countries and the concomitant deterioration in their balance of payments. In the commonplace metaphor, the end result is that agricultural countries must run faster to stand still; that is, export larger and larger volumes of their products merely to afford the same market basket of industrial imports.

The externalist perspective has one critical shortcoming: It does not enable us to understand extraordinary differences in economic performance, particularly among countries that have a fairly similar assortment of exportable commodities and food staples. The international economic environment is, by its very nature, common to entire sets of countries.

Therefore, it can help us to understand why agricultural exporters face acute balance-of-payments difficulties and foreign-exchange shortages. But it cannot help us to understand why individual countries have been more successful than others in avoiding these difficulties. Similarly, the externalist point of view can help us to understand why a particular group of countries may be experiencing a debt crisis of such severity as to require negotiation and eventually a traumatic settlement with the International Monetary Fund (IMF). But it cannot help us to understand why individual countries of a similar nature manage their debt burden with relative ease and can negotiate with the IMF on a more collegial basis. As a theory about the impoverishment of agricultural countries, the externalist perspective provides us with only modest guidance as to why some are able to enjoy prolonged periods of economic growth.

The strengths and weaknesses of the internalist perspective mirror those of its theoretical counterpart. By focusing on the specific policies of African governments, internalist thinkers can provide highly persuasive explanations of the widely differentiated patterns of economic performance among states. Individual African governments vary enormously in their approach to such macroeconomic policies as exchange-rate management and money supply, and to a host of such microeconomic policies as commodity pricing and the treatment of agricultural producers. If externalists have established the fact that Africa's agricultural producers confront an inhospitable international environment, internalists have established that different policies have predictably different outcomes. Governments that overvalue their exchange rates, pursue inflationary monetary and fiscal policy, and suppress producer prices can expect stagnant or deteriorating agricultural performance. Governments that take a more prudent and realistic approach to these policy areas can expect to be rewarded with a positive rate of agricultural growth.

The principal shortcoming of the internalist approach is that it treats the international economic environment as a neutral factor, when, in fact, external market conditions pose a sharp limitation on the economic prospects of agricultural countries. The internalist perspective could be dramatically improved if its proponents were more prepared to address, as a basic question, the limits of economic growth for agricultural countries. It is well to bear in mind that, among the world's developing areas, those countries that have gone furthest in bridging the huge economic gap between the First and Third worlds are those that have been able to create an industrial sector with the capacity to export on world markets. Even the most casual overview of the World Bank's 1986 atlas reveals a pattern of huge per-capita income disparities between the world's industrial and agricultural countries.[18] This is especially true of Africa.

With very few exceptions, even the most successful of Africa's agricultural exporters exhibit per-capita incomes that are not only alarmingly static but among the lowest of the 180 or more countries surveyed.[19] The conclusion to be drawn from the World Bank's figures is that even the most robust agricultural performance may not provide sufficient overall economic growth to curb the widening disparity between per-capita income levels in industrial and agricultural societies. This may provide the best way to interpret the impact of the external economic environment, which sets the outer limits of economic possibility for agricultural exporters. But those limits do not become clear so long as part of the economic predicament of these countries can be accounted for on the basis of poor domestic policy.

These observations bear directly on the central purpose of this book: to compare the economic performance of an agriculturally successful country, Kenya, with that of an agricultural failure, Tanzania, and to demonstrate that Kenya's success and Tanzania's failure are largely attributable to differences in their agricultural policies. To that extent, the book is internalist in its analysis of Kenya and Tanzania, but it is also intended to offer a broad discussion of both approaches to Africa's agricultural crisis. The purpose of Part 1, in which these differing perspectives are set forth, is to clarify the contours of the intellectual debate within which the detailed discussion of Kenya and Tanzania that follows in Part 2 is situated. The essential argument in Part 1 of this volume is that the externalist paradigm, though having many important strengths as a delineation of the difficult international environment within which countries that depend on agricultural exports must operate, does not fully enable us to explain the dramatic differences in economic performance among African countries.

It would be unrealistic and ahistorical to dismiss altogether the importance of external factors. The present economic circumstances of every African country are, to some degree, a product of the impact of exogenous forces, including European colonialism, on that society. It is impossible to understand modern Kenya without reference to the pattern of British colonial rule, and in particular, to the way in which it established a European settler community that used its political influence to acquire ownership of a vastly disproportionate share of the country's best arable land. The political and economic privileges of British settlers have a clear modern echo in the land and agricultural policies of Kenya's African governing elite. Similarly, it would be equally difficult to understand the politicoeconomic trajectory of contemporary Tanzania without reference to its colonial status, first as a League of Nations mandated territory and after World War II as a United Nations trusteeship. International oversight was profoundly important in limiting the political and economic role of European settlers but also in lowering the incentive for European investment in the agricultural sector.

While important, these factors simply do not loom as large analytically as the postindependence policy choices of the two governments. The second part of this volume seeks to validate that viewpoint by dealing specifically with modern agricultural policy in Kenya and Tanzania. Its purpose is to illustrate the extent to which different approaches to agricultural policy can result in widely differing patterns of agricultural performance. In Part 3, this book speculates briefly about why these two countries may have adopted such different policy frameworks. The thesis it advances is that the critical variables are land policy and, more specifically, the degree of tolerance for or encouragement of private investment in land by members of the political elite. Elite investment in land has made an enormous difference in Kenya's agricultural policies, contributing greatly to the evolution of a political environment favoring producer welfare. Tanzania's political elite has tended, on the other hand, to cut itself off from land ownership. As a result, concern for producer welfare, while part of the country's official ideology, has not been clearly manifested in its policy framework.

This book treats Kenya as an agricultural "success story," and there is abundant evidence to affirm that judgment. As the statistical figures presented in Chapter 4 demonstrate, Kenya has attained dramatic successes since independence in increasing its production of export crops. Despite a limited supply of arable land, Kenya has also scored well in regard to food production, and though there have been occasional periods of grain imports to meet drought-induced needs, its overall record has been one of food self-sufficiency. The result is that its foreign-exchange earnings from agricultural exports have been available to capitalize the ongoing infrastructural development of its agricultural sector, to finance the importation of consumer goods for its rapidly growing middle and upper classes, and to provide for the capital needs of its rapidly expanding industrial sector.

Tanzania is treated as a case of policy-induced agrarian decline. The figures in Chapter 4 corroborate this judgment. Tanzania's agricultural exports have deteriorated precipitously since independence, causing crippling shortages of foreign exchange and an acute balance-of-payments crisis. Its record with respect to food production is somewhat better, showing steady increases since the mid-1970s in the production of all major grains. Despite this, Tanzania has remained heavily dependent on food imports, mostly in the form of food aid. Despite a natural endowment that most observers consider adequate for prodigious increases in output of a wide variety of agricultural commodities, Tanzania has surrendered its once-important position as a prominent actor in the world's agricultural trade. Because the foreign-exchange crisis resulted in severe constraints on the country's industrial sector, there were no discernible sources of growth in the economy. Tanzania in the mid-1980s was locked in a seemingly inescapable economic crisis, characterized by rapidly falling levels of both production and consumption.

By 1986, Tanzania's economic crisis was so great that there was no alternative to an agreement with the IMF, a settlement that all but doomed the country's cherished experiment in socialist development. This settlement, the Economic Recovery Program, provided for a set of policy reforms, including drastic currency devaluation, the implementation of sweeping measures for trade liberalization, a sharp curtailment of the role and powers of parastatal corporations, and much greater latitude for private entrepeneurial opportunity. Some of these reforms had actually begun several years before the IMF agreement. A modest program of trade liberalization, for example, was initiated as early as 1983 and a substantial currency devaluation took place in the summer of 1984. Policy reform was given additional impetus by the inauguration of a new president, Ali Hassan Mwinyi, in the late fall, 1985—a change that some observers consider the necessary political precondition for the IMF agreement. Although there is much reason to believe that policy changes have begun a process of economic recovery in Tanzania, the evidence is as yet too incomplete to sustain any such conclusion.

Today, these two countries present very different images to the world. Kenya has established itself as a thriving center for international commerce, finance, and tourism. Buoyed by a temperate climate and an astonishing diversity of service industries, its capital city, Nairobi, has flourished as the domicile for a large number of international agencies, private voluntary organizations, and multinational corporations. Tanzania, by contrast, has suffered badly from the long-term stagnation of its agricultural sector. Chronic shortages of foreign-exchange, occasioned principally by the collapse of its former major agricultural exports, sisal and cashew nuts, and by the stagnation of such exports as coffee and tea, have resulted in severe shortages of all imported necessities. As a result, its capital city, Dar es Salaam, has deteriorated visibly since the early 1960s. Today, Dar es Salaam's physical decrepitude offers a constant reminder of the country's unenviable status as one of the world's twelve poorest nations.

Kenya today is a "threshold" country, poised at the edge of an industrial revolution. The standard of comparison for its economic performance is no longer that of the vast majority of African societies, but rather, the economic achievements of the smaller of the world's newly industrializing societies, such as Singapore and Taiwan. The critical questions for Kenya's future have less to do with agricultural performance than with whether its industrial sector, currently based principally on import substitution, can convert to become competitive in international markets. Tanzania's immediate future is more uncertain. The critical questions do not have to do with industrial performance, but with whether economic reforms initiated at the insistence of the IMF can stimulate an agricultural recovery.

Virtually since independence, Kenya's and Tanzania's cultures have stood counter to one another. From the standpoint of liberal Kenyans, disturbed by the social inequalities that have accompanied the country's prodigious economic growth, Tanzania remains an enduring symbol of socialist egalitarianism, an epitome of the conviction that economic development should not be pursued at the cost of social misery. For economically pragmatic and centrist Tanzanians, Kenya is a constant reminder of the opportunity cost of two or more decades of failed socialist policies, a living national embodiment of the sacrifices imposed upon an entire generation by political leaders unable to acknowledge the inadequacy of their socioeconomic model.

Although this volume is internalist in its intellectual orientation, then, it is not unabashedly so. The subject matter that follows does not exclude the possibility that the international economic environment poses ultimate constraints on the prospects for economic growth. The problem is that so long as a country's domestic policy framework is not growth oriented, these constraints are all but impossible to determine. Since Tanzania's agricultural decline can be immediately explained as the outcome of a set of inappropriate agricultural policies, it is premature to ask what its economic possibilities are under current world-market conditions. The answer to this question cannot become clear until its domestic agricultural policies are corrected and until the effects of these corrections have had time to ripple through the country's economic system, stimulating improvements in agricultural output.

Kenya poses precisely the same question in a slightly different way: Because its policy framework is basically favorable to the agricultural sector, it is butting up against growth limits posed by external market conditions. Since the early 1980s, Kenya has sought assiduously to implement the policy recommendations of World Bank and IMF advisors. Today, it is generally regarded with respect by both these international lending institutions for its concrete achievements in having adopted the sort of policy framework they advocate. Although some observers believe that Kenya might induce further slight improvements in its agricultural performance by additional refinements in its policy framework, there is general consensus that its latitude for doing so is extremely limited. For this reason, Kenya raises profound questions about the limits of growth of agricultural exporters. These questions pertain not only to Kenya's economic future but to the economic future of other countries that adopt its policies as a model.

Tanzania's current economic predicament exemplifies the worst fears of those who argue that bad policy can produce only bad results, while Kenya's economic success helps to validate the belief that appropriate policy can foster agricultural growth. Despite its agricultural success, Kenya has had the greatest difficulty during the past ten years in achieving an economic-growth rate high enough to provide significant increases in per-capita income. The reasons for this difficulty have little if anything to do with the economic policies it has adopted. They have far more to do with the sort of international environment that Kenya, like other countries dependent on agricultural exports, must confront. There is a sort of irony in Kenya's economic success: It not only helps to validate the internalist viewpoint of the relationship between economic policy and economic performance, its very success also makes it imperative to take seriously externalist arguments about the limits of growth for even the most successful agricultural exporters.

NOTES

1. UN, Food and Agriculture Organization, *Food Situation in African Countries Affected by Emergencies: A Special Report* (n.p., April 1985), pp. 2–5.

2. The World Bank, *Toward Sustained Development in Sub-Saharan Africa: A Joint Program of Action* (Washington, D.C., 1984), p. 10.

3. U.S. Department of Agriculture, Economic Research Service, *Food Problems and Prospects in Sub-Saharan Africa: The Decade of the 1980s*, Foreign Agricultural Research Report no. 166 (August 1981), p. 3.

4. Ibid., pp. 4–5.

5. For a discussion of the food-aid dilemma, see Raymond F. Hopkins, "Food Aid: Solution, Palliative or Danger for Africa's Food Crisis," in *Africa's Agrarian Crisis: The Roots of Famine,* ed. Stephen Commins, Michael F. Lofchie, and Rhys Payne (Lynne Rienner, Boulder, CO, 1986), pp. 196–209.

6. The World Bank, *Acclerated Development in Sub-Saharan Africa: An Agenda for Action* (Washington, D.C., 1981), p. 46.

7. The World Bank, *World Debt Tables: External Debt of Developing Countries* (Washington, D.C., 1985), pp. 6–7 and 158–159.

8. Antoon de Vos, *Africa, The Devastated Continent?* (Dr. W. Junk b.v., The Hague, 1975), p. 13.

9. For a treatment of this issue, see Lloyd Timberlake, "Guarding Africa's Renewable Resources," in *Strategies for African Development* ed. Robert J. Berg and Jennifer Seymour Whitaker (University of California Press, Berkeley and Los Angeles, 1986), pp. 111–128.

10. See n. 6 above.

11. See n. 3 above.

12. Robert Bates, *Markets and States in Tropical Africa* (University of California Press, Berkeley and Los Angeles, 1981).

13. An example of this literature is Richard W. Franke and Barbara H. Chasin, *Seeds of Famine: Ecological Destruction and the Development Dilemma in the West African Sahel* (Montclair, Allanheld Osmun, 1980).

14. Ibid.

15. Michael Watts, *Silent Violence: Food, Famine and Peasantry in Northern Nigeria* (University of California, Berkeley and Los Angeles, 1983).

16. *Review of African Political Economy* 15/16 (May–December 1979).

17. For a discussion of the areas of common ground between internalist and externalist approaches, see Robert S. Browne and Robert J. Cummings, *The Lagos Plan of Action vs. The Berg Report: Contemporary Issues in African Economic Development* (Brunswick, Lawrenceville, VA, 1984).

18. The World Bank, *The World Bank Atlas 1986* (Washington, D.C., 1986), pp. 6–9.

19. Of the world's twenty-five lowest countries in per-capita income, eighteen are in Africa and include at least two, Malawi and Togo, that are generally held out as agriculturally successful. See ibid., p. 17.

·PART 1·

·2·
External Considerations: Is Policy Enough?

The externalist viewpoint holds that the difficulties besetting independent Africa's agricultural economies cannot be adequately explained on the basis of internal considerations (such as inappropriate agricultural policy); they must also be understood in terms of the adverse impact of a host of exogenous factors. If this is so, it raises serious doubts about the extent to which the continent's agrarian crisis is amenable to solution through economic reform. The key question then becomes: Can policy make a difference between economic growth and economic stagnation? The case studies of Tanzania and Kenya in Part 2 of this volume suggest that the answer to this question is positive, that appropriate agricultural policies can make a substantial difference in the extent to which a country's agricultural sector makes a contribution to overall national well-being. To form a fully fleshed-out portrait of Africa's agrarian crisis, however, it is important to consider the external environment and the ways in which it affects agricultural exporters. Countries dependent on the export of primary agricultural commodities do confront an international system that is in many ways adverse to their long-term economic prospects.

THE THEORY OF UNDERDEVELOPMENT

The best-known and, by a considerable margin, most widely discussed version of an externalist approach to economic underdevelopment in Africa, and hence to the continent's crisis of agricultural performance, is the theory or, more properly, complex of theories known as the theory of underdevelopment. Sometimes termed "dependency theory," because it places great stress on the extent to which Africa's political and economic systems are dependent on Western capital, technology, and political support, the theory of underdevelopment argues that the root cause of Africa's economic problems, like those of other developing areas, lies in the nature of the international economic system and the ways in which developing countries are compelled to interact with it. For theorists who hold this viewpoint,

21

policy changes within African countries would, at most, have marginal effects on their economic well-being, because they would not alter the international patterns of trade, investment, and political control that pose ultimate barriers to economic growth. In the theory of underdevelopment, poor agricultural performance is but one manifestation of a far broader and more all-inclusive economic malaise, which can be seen in the lack of industrial and commercial development as well as in the weaknesses of political and social institutions.

Because the literature arguing this general viewpoint is of encyclopedic proportions, and because the debates it has engendered are equally voluminous, it is simply unfeasible here to discuss the theory. It would, in any case, be impossible to do intellectual justice within the brief confines of a single chapter to the ideas of such diverse and prolific theoreticians as André Gunder Frank, Samir Amin, Arghiri Emmanuel, Paul Baran, Immanuel Wallerstein, Irving Zeitlin, Benjamin Cohen, and a host of others.[1] A more feasible approach is to summarize this literature very briefly, in order to consider that portion of the theory that bears most directly on the problems of Africa's agrarian sector.

The starting point for most underdevelopment theorists lies in the proposition that the world's economies can be divided into two major categories: core and periphery. The core consists of those countries in Europe, North America, and (increasingly) Asia that, during the past five centuries, have been able to develop highly advanced capitalist economic systems, characterized by large and very powerful corporations, the extensive application of sophisticated scientific technology to the process of production, fluid capital markets, and the clear predominance of industrial over agricultural production. The periphery consists of those countries in Africa, Asia, and Latin America characterized by weak and underdeveloped economic systems, whose principal features include a high degree of dependence on trade with the core, especially the sale of raw materials and primary agricultural products. For dependency theorists, the products exported by peripheral countries are always of lesser complexity and value than those they must purchase from the industrial core. The periphery is also characterized by a far smaller role for the industrial sector (which is principally confined to the assembly of components manufactured overseas) and by weak, highly unstable political systems.

According to the theory of underdevelopment, the core countries have been able to attain high levels of national wealth and development in part because of their ongoing ability to extract wealth from the periphery, while peripheral countries are poor precisely because much of their wealth has been siphoned off to sustain the development of the industrial core. In a nutshell, the capital surplus that peripheral countries might have used to finance their own growth and development has been used, instead, to capitalize the industrial development of already powerful and well-developed

industrial societies. Although these theorists sometimes acknowledge a degree of economic interdependence between core and periphery, they view this as highly asymmetrical; core countries have far greater discretion over the terms of their participation in the international trading system. Peripheral countries, on the other hand, are compelled to accept the international trading system as a given over which they have little or no control.

The theory of underdevelopment also posits a particular conception of the nature of political leadership in peripheral countries. Theorists in this genre believe strongly that the political leaders of developing countries are subservient to the economic interests of international capital, and that the policies they pursue subordinate national development to the economic needs of Western capitalist nations. Using such terms as *comprador bourgeoisie* or auxiliary bourgeoisie, dependency theory states explicitly that the leaders of these countries are, in effect, the puppets of powerful external forces. Because they do not or cannot govern with a view to the development of their own countries, underdevelopment is all the more permanent and intractable. The susceptibility of political leadership to manipulation has great long-term relevance, since it means that the change from colonial to independent status will have no real effects on economic policy. Even after independence is gained, the basic economic structures of peripheral economies will continue to be shaped according to the contribution they can make to capitalist development elsewhere, not according to the needs of their own populations.

This theory has been subjected to a variety of criticisms, including serious exception to a grave problem of oversimplification inherent in the view that the world's economies are amenable to a bipolar division between core and periphery. As an alternative, it has been suggested that dependency is to some extent an attribute of all economies, so that degrees of dependency must be treated with far more discrimination. Critics of dependency have also faulted its conception of political leadership, suggesting that it is grossly inaccurate and unfair to the political leaders of many Third World countries to say that they are the puppet-like creatures of Western capitalism. It is also possible to question the historical accuracy of the view that the net flow of economic resources is uniformly and at all times from developing to developed countries. The directionality of international capital flows is far more complex than this and appears to vary widely both over time and between sets of countries. It would not be difficult to document that the world's developing regions and countries differ considerably in the extent to which they have been net exporters or importers of capital resources.

Agrarian Dualism and Export Dependency

Disputes over degrees of dependency and the role of leaders are not only beyond the scope of this volume, but, by their very nature, not easily amenable to empirical resolution. The preceding summary of the general contours of the underdevelopment framework is used here to introduce two aspects of one dimension of the theory, which bear specifically on the rural sector and the nature of its relationship to national development: the idea of export dependency and its kindred notion, agrarian dualism. Theorists of underdevelopment believe that the colonial experience left the vast majority of African countries with economic systems exhibiting a pronounced dependency on exports. This dependency is viewed as the root cause of the continent's high degree of vulnerability to external influences. Over-emphasis on the production of exportable items is sometimes blamed for the neglect of food production, and therefore for the growing crisis of food deficits; the same over-emphasis is invariably the major component in economic analyses that stress Africa's declining terms of trade vis-à-vis industrial and commercial exporters. Because of depressed price levels for agricultural products in world markets, it has been used to explain the continent's chronic balance-of-payments problems. Because the prospect of a future improvement in the world market for primary agricultural goods is extremely poor, dependency on these exports is also a key factor in bleak predictions for the continent's future.

Underdevelopment theorists have linked export dependency inextricably with another feature of colonial economies that depended on primary agricultural exports: the marked discrepancy between the pattern of production in the export sector and the production system that prevailed with respect to the cultivation of food staples for domestic consumption.[2] This discrepancy is sometimes referred to as agricultural bimodalism or agrarian dualism. For theorists of underdevelopment, agrarian dualism is the critical structural requirement for export dependency. It derives from colonial economic policies that placed the greatest emphasis on the development of the export sector and that, indeed, subordinated the needs of other economic sectors to the production of exportable commodities. The concept of agrarian dualism has been heavily utilized by scholars of East African agriculture. In an early treatment of agrarian dualism in East Africa, Roger Leys defined the idea in the following terms:

> This [dualism] is characterised by:
> (a) an *export enclave* in turn characterised by the production of a few raw materials for export and processing in the factories of the developed countries. The growth of this enclave is primarily determined by the growth of effective demand for these (mainly agricultural) materials in the developed countries.
> (b) a *hinterland* in which the majority of the population lives and works in the traditional agrarian economy. The main contribution of this hinterland to the export enclave is a flow of cheap, unskilled migrant labour.[3]

The concept of agrarian dualism suggests that the colonial era left Africa's economic systems so biased toward the production of export crops that other critically important economic sectors, such as industry, were badly neglected.

According to this theory, the export bias resulted from the commitment of colonial governments in Africa to the principle that their colonies should be financially self-sufficient and, indeed, ought to provide at least limited markets for manufactured goods. The precondition for these objectives was the colonies' capacity to earn hard currency on world markets, in turn requiring that great emphasis be placed on the development of a profitable export sector. As a result, the cultivation of Africa's key export crops (such as coffee, cocoa, tea, oil palms, groundnuts, and sisal) was heavily promoted by colonial governments. Production of exportable agricultural commodities was abetted by a variety of agricultural policies, including governmental sponsorship of intensive research on improved methods of crop husbandry. To insure that the results of this research would be easily accessible to export-oriented farmers, colonial governments expended considerable financial resources on their agricultural extension services, and on a whole array of vitally necessary "soft" services, such as market research and credit facilities.

Colonial administrators also took pains to see that export farmers had access to the most favorable agricultural land. Moreover, the land devoted to export crops was, in general, privately owned, and thus could be used as collateral for loans to finance capital improvements and the acquisition of inputs. More important still was the pervasive tendency of colonial governments to tilt the development of physical infrastructure toward the export-oriented regions. Road and railway systems, for example, were generally concentrated in these areas, as was the development of storage and processing facilities. For example, in his excellent study of the economic policies pursued by the British colonial administration in East Africa, E. A. Brett found persuasive evidence that railroad transportation rates were often set in such a way as to subsidize the producers of export crops at the expense of other economic sectors.[4] The development of irrigated agriculture in Africa has also been confined almost entirely to the production of export crops. Paradoxically, this may help explain why irrigation has been so rare on the continent: Since export-crop producers generally have access to naturally well-watered lands, the need to supply water artificially has been negligible.

The concept of agrarian dualism offers a structural explanation for the poor performance of the food sector of a number of Africa's agricultural economies. It suggests that the food-producing regions benefited from few governmental supports. Food production was generally carried out by peasant smallholders, whose farms were on communally held land that could not be used as collateral for development loans. The technological difference between food and export production was striking. The technology of peasant food production was practically prefeudal. Hand-held implements were the most common instruments of production; animal-drawn traction was exceptional, and energy-driven machinery virtually nonexistent. The posture of colonial administrators toward food-producing areas could best be described as one of neglect. Peasant food producers received almost none of the scientific inputs that were so common in the exporting regions. High-yielding seed varieties, chemical fertilizers and pesticides, and scientifically improved methods of husbandry were conspicuously absent.[5] Other vital supports, such as extension services, were also perfunctory at best. If any single explanation is necessary for the utter stagnation of productivity among African peasant food producers, it lies here, in the almost complete absence of technological and scientific inputs of the modern age.

The same is true with respect to physical infrastructure. Whereas the exporting regions have been given the benefit of ample road and railway networks, Africa's food-producing regions continue to be badly deficient even with respect to a minimal system of feeder roads. As in colonial times, today's farm-to-market route for a food staple begins with little more than a bicycle path. In many countries, the difficulties of transporting basic items from the countryside to the major cities are so great that large amounts of food languish and spoil in rural markets, where they can sometimes be purchased for absurdly low prices, while urban demand, though sufficiently strong to encourage greater production at a more reasonable price level, is either unmet or satisfied through imports. Often, rural storage facilities are so poor that the supply of locally produced food staples tends to go through an extreme cycle, ranging from high availability during harvest season to severe scarcity or utter unavailability during the agricultural off-season. Food that could easily be stored and processed locally is, instead, imported from abroad at great cost in foreign exchange while local food producers lack sufficient capital to improve their land or purchase more up-to-date equipment.

Radical observers of rural development in Africa have long suggested a direct politicoeconomic link between the technologically advanced pattern of agricultural production for export and the backward character of domestic food production. Rodolfo Stavenhagen, for example, has argued that the backwardness of the peasant sector is not merely the accidental by-product of benign official neglect or the unintended consequence of a misplaced overemphasis on the production of exportable crops.[6] It was necessary in order to insure the full development of the export sector, because, in addition to needing a high level of governmental support and a continuous infusion of modern inputs, the exporting farms also required an abundant and readily available supply of low-wage agricultural workers. There was, basically, only one sphere of society from which this labor supply could be obtained: the peasantry.

African peasants had to be forced to make themselves available, at least during periods of peak labor needs, as a pool of migratory workers. There is an entire school of African history that documents the various methods that colonial governments employed to compel potentially self-supporting peasants to become migratory agricultural laborers. These methods included various systems of taxation, such as the head tax, the imposition of legally obligatory labor requirements for adult males, and, in the Portugese territories, outright forced labor. Less dramatically visible, but at least equally consequential, was the complex set of colonial economic policies that so immiserated peasant producers that wage labor became the only alternative to starvation.

The notion of agrarian dualism also offers a partial explanation for some of the domestic policies pursued by African governments, thereby linking external and internal considerations. One example is the nearly ubiquitous tendency of African governments to control and suppress the prices paid to peasant farmers for domestic food staples. In Stavenhagen's analysis, suppression of producer prices to independent peasants was among the most effective methods of generating a plantation labor supply. The forcible imposition of a system of price controls provided both colonial and independent African governments with an effective method of reducing peasant income.

Suppression of the price levels of domestically produced food staples provided an important secondary benefit, also. Since food costs are a fundamental determinant of wage levels, artificially low food prices contributed directly to lowered labor costs on the export farms. In a broad sense, then, the suppression of food production was a historical precondition for the success of export agriculture, and hence for the attainment of other objectives of colonial administrations. But this policy set the stage for the growing food crises that were to begin within years of independence and that today occur as major episodes of famine.

Does Agrarian Dualism Explain East Africa?

The most systematic application of the concept of agrarian dualism to East Africa was undertaken by Ann Seidman, who published a series of articles in the *East Africa Journal* in 1970.[7] Seidman's articles sought to demonstrate the intense impact of the colonial experience by showing that it had left both Kenya and Tanzania characterized by agrarian dualism. There can be little doubt that both countries were heavily dependent on agricultural exports. Sisal, cotton, and coffee provided more than 55 percent of Tanzania's export earnings, for example; coffee, tea, and sisal provided more than 50 percent of Kenya's. Seidman further argued that since Great Britain's colonial strategy had been to develop these countries as sources of primary commodities (including industrial raw materials) and as markets for finished manufactured goods, both countries were also marked by extremely limited industrial development. The most conspicuous symptom of industrial weakness was the need, in both countries, to expend large percentages of foreign-exchange earnings on the importation of consumer goods: nearly half in the case of Tanzania and about one-sixth in the case of Kenya.

Seidman also sought to show that both countries suffered from the overdevelopment of an export enclave. The evidence for this argument is less persuasive; the two countries varied greatly in this respect. Kenya provided a clear case. Here, the export enclave consisted principally of the so-called White Highlands, approximately 7.5 million acres (more than 12,000 square miles) of the country's most fertile land, located in the relatively cool plateau regions to the north and west of Nairobi.[8] Since less than 50,000 square miles of Kenya is considered suitable for relatively intensive agriculture, the highlands amounts to about 25 percent of the country's best arable land. The White Highlands originated in Great Britain's determination to develop Kenya as a colony to be settled and ultimately governed by British immigrants. As early as 1902, the British government had begun to make determined efforts to recruit settlers to Kenya, principally by setting aside some of the country's best land for them. The vast majority of the roughly 60,000 British immigrants who eventually settled in Kenya did not involve themselves directly in agriculture, but by 1960, the eve of independence, there were approximately 3,500 settler families whose principal economic activity was farming.

The White Highlands hosted three distinct forms of agricultural production:

1. *Plantation enterprises* occupied just over 2 million acres. Plantations were owned largely by foreign companies and were operated in a manner essentially similar to plantation systems in other tropical regions. Kenya's plantations were devoted principally to the production of coffee, tea, and sisal.

2. *Mixed farms* occupied approximately 3 million acres and were the major source of livelihood for the settler community. Although some settlers produced modest amounts of exportable commodities, Kenya's coffee and tea crops were grown almost entirely on plantations. The settler farms were devoted principally to the cultivation of food crops and animal products for local consumption.

3. *Cattle ranches* accounted for the remaining 2.4 million acres. Kenya had approximately eighty large-scale cattle ranches, averaging about 30,000 acres, located in the drier regions of the highlands.

The development of settler farming in Kenya had a significant impact in transforming a segment of African society into agricultural workers. About 250,000 Africans were employed as wage laborers in these three forms of agricultural enterprise.

The average size of a European land unit in Kenya was about 2,400 acres, but, in fact, the vast majority of the European settlers resided in the mixed-farm areas, where farms were generally on the order of 400 to 600 acres in size. Here, they cultivated a wide variety of crops, normally combining a certain amount of coffee production with the cultivation of grain crops (such as wheat, corn, and barley) and the production of beef and dairy cattle. Mixed farms formed the political but not the economic core of Kenya's colonial system. Although it was widely maintained that their productivity was economically indispensable for the society, Colin Leys has demonstrated clearly that this was not the case. His analysis of the mixed-farm sector suggests strongly that the mixed farms were, in fact, economically weak and had to be subsidized through an elaborate system of colonial regulations that granted them both protection from African competition and a supply of cheap African labor. He notes further that, "if one systematically subtracts from the value of the mixed farms output the value of the further subsidies they received from the African population, in the form of services partly financed by the African taxpayer, one soon approaches a very modest if not negative figure."[9] In Leys' view, the myth of mixed-farm productivity was principally significant in convincing African political leaders that the structure of the colonial economy had to be maintained if Kenya was to prosper after independence.

The most important segment of the colonial economy were the plantations, which produced the vast majority of the country's coffee, tea, and sisal. These were not typically farmed by settler families, but owned and operated by foreign companies and corporations such as Socfinaf (Société Financiale Française), the country's largest coffee producer, or Brooke Bond (later Brooke Bond Liebig), a large owner of tea estates. During the colonial era, Kenya had approximately 55 tea plantations, averaging about 4,500 acres. As noted above, there were about 80 cattle ranches, owned by companies or private individuals, averaging about 30,000 acres.

The remaining three-fourths of Kenya's high- and medium-potential land area was occupied by small-scale African peasant households. Since Africans were legally prevented from engaging in the cultivation of export commodities, African farmlands were generally allotted to such crops as maize, peas, beans, millet, sorghum, and yams. The contrasts between the European farming areas and those held by Africans were monumental. European farms were large in scale, held on the basis of individual title, well served by physical infrastructure and extension services, and farmed using advanced agricultural methods. African farms were extremely small in scale, generally held on the basis of traditional forms of tenure that emphasized communal rather than individual entitlement, and, for the most part, poorly served by the country's physical and service infrastructures. Whereas European farm areas were financially buoyed by a variety of colonial policies—including their monopoly of export cropping, access to cheap African labor, and inexpensive transportation rates—African farmers were generally neglected by the colonial administration or made to bear the brunt of a tax system that effectively subsidized European agriculture.

The concept of agrarian dualism does not have nearly the same descriptive validity for Tanzania. Although various colonial administrations sought to develop Tanzanian agriculture along lines parallel to those in

Kenya, the policy had only limited results. The development of Tanzania's export enclave was initiated by the German colonial administration prior to the turn of this century.[10] But this policy did not show great success. Part of the explanation for this may have to do with the fact that the Germans placed their primary emphasis on industrial crops such as cotton, rubber, and sisal, rather than beverages such as coffee and tea. Since industrial crops tended to suffer from particularly intense international competition, the plantations devoted to them never flourished economically in the same way Kenya's coffee and tea plantations did. Tanzania's cotton, for example, competed on international markets with that produced in the United States as well as a number of other developing countries. Its rubber exports suffered greatly from competition with Ceylon, Malaysia, and Liberia. The only crop that became relatively successful for Tanzania was sisal, which emerged as the dominant export just after the turn of the century.

Another factor that slowed the pace of estate development in Tanzania was the changeover of colonial administrations following World War I. When the British government assumed colonial responsibility for Tanzania, it expropriated the German plantations and resold them to British, Italian, Greek, and Asian investors. Estate production of coffee and tea in Tanzania dates from the interwar period, but it seems clear that the British government was not anxious to develop large-farm production of these commodities to the point of competition with coffee and tea exports from Kenya. Thus, sisal remained Tanzania's principal export crop until well into the 1950s. After World War II, the British government intensified its efforts to develop Tanzania's plantation sector. The best-known experiment, perhaps, was the ill-fated groundnut scheme. Between 1947 and 1949, the British sought, at great expense, to develop about 220,000 acres of land as a source of groundnuts, in an effort to alleviate an acute national shortage of edible fats and oils. The calamitous failure of the groundnut scheme seemed to discredit the idea of plantation development in Tanzania, and afterwards, Britain's efforts in this direction all but ceased.

A comparison of agrarian dualism in Kenya and Tanzania, then, reveals striking differences. The most visible of these had to do with the sheer magnitude of the plantation sector. On the eve of independence, Tanzania's large-scale agricultural estates occupied only about 2.5 million acres, about one-third as much land area as in Kenya. This amounted to less than 1.5 percent of Tanzania's total land area. Since only about 1 million acres were actually under cultivation, Tanzania's estate sector was, in reality, only about one-seventh the size of Kenya's. Tanzania's large-scale estates accounted at most for only 5 percent of the total cultivated area of the country, only about one-fifth as much as had been given over to large farms in Kenya. And since Tanzania, unlike Kenya, does not suffer from a limited area of high-potential land, the creation of this sector did not entail the dispossession of large numbers of Africans from their farms.

The most important difference, however, was not one of magnitude, but of the role of African smallholders. German agricultural policy in Tanzania had differed significantly from that of the British in Kenya in that encouragement was always given to the development of African smallholder production. Even after Great Britain assumed colonial responsibility for Tanzania as a League of Nations mandated territory, there was a high degree of tolerance for African smallholder involvement in cash-crop production. Principally because of the constraints imposed by League of Nations supervision, the British colonial administration was not in a position to confer extraordinary economic privileges on the settler community. Where colonial policy in Kenya had sought to provide European settlers with monopolistic rights to the cultivation of export crops, colonial policy in Tanzania had imposed no such limitations.

As a result of these differences, the socioeconomic impact of colonial policy was far different in Tanzania than in Kenya. Whereas colonial rule in Kenya had effectively banned Africans from the cultivation of cash crops and had involved Africans in the export sector only as wage laborers, Africans had played an integral role in the development of the export sector in Tanzania from the very beginning of the colonial era. Peasants in Bukoba, for example, had grown coffee for export to the Arab countries as early as the turn of the century, and well before the outbreak of World War I, coffee was being grown extensively by smallholders in the Kilimanjaro region. Seidman estimates that, by the time Tanzania attained independence at the end of 1961, there were nearly 500,000 smallholder coffee producers in the Bukoba and Kilimanjaro areas, approximately 250,000 smallholder cotton producers, principally in the Sukuma area, and as many as 75,000 pyrethrum farmers. If African smallholder involvement in the production of other cash crops, such as cashew nuts and copra, is included, the total could well have exceeded 1 million households.

The theoretical significance of these differences is considerable, suggesting that the concept of agrarian dualism has both strengths and shortcomings as an approach to postindependence African agriculture. Its descriptive validity is highly variable. Kenya developed during the colonial era as an agriculturally dualistic society, in which there was a clear division of labor between large-scale export-oriented estates—controlled by expatriate economic interests—and the overwhelming majority of African peasant farms—systematically forbidden to enter the export sector. But in Tanzania, African smallholder production of key export crops exceeded that of the expatriate estates from the very beginning. And though an estate sector did emerge, it could not be said to have had very great economic significance.

Agrarian dualism has its greatest validity in directing attention to the vast developmental discrepancy between the export sector and the food-producing sector. Whether export production has been carried on by expatriate estate owners or African smallholders, it has nonetheless vastly differed from food production, in both technological style and the availability of modern approaches and inputs. Peasant food-producing regions in Kenya and Tanzania did tend to suffer from neglect and resource starvation, even where a significant portion of the peasantry was benefiting economically from its ability to involve itself in the production of high-value exportable commodities. In this respect, East Africa has much in common with the rest of the continent. The notion of agrarian duality thus does merit attention as a partial explanation of the particularly poor postindependence performance of the food-producing sector.

The idea of agrarian dualism does not, however, sustain itself as a statement of fundamental constraints on postindependence development. According to the theory, Kenya ought to have experienced far more difficulty in attaining postindependence development than did Tanzania. For Kenya's economy was, to a far greater degree than Tanzania's, structurally based on agrarian duality, and on the impoverishment and proletarianization of the African peasant majority. Since Kenya's agricultural sector has flourished since independence, the evidence suggests that neither export dependency nor a high degree of agrarian duality is an important constraint on postindependence development. Indeed, agrarian dualism may have provided important advantages for postindependence development. It helped facilitate the capitalization of the agricultural sector and contributed to the provision of a remarkably extensive infrastructure. As a result, Kenya on the eve of independence was already to a large degree possessed of a modern and highly productive agricultural system. The principal task for the postindependence government was providing Africans access to that system in ways that would not undermine its great productivity.

The theory of agrarian dualism has its greatest difficulty, however, in accounting for the agricultural experience of postindependence Tanzania. It seems imperative at the outset to distinguish between export dependency and the creation of an export enclave. The Tanzanian experience makes it very clear that a country can be highly dependent on a small number of agricultural exports without developing a structurally differentiated export sector. Indeed, Tanzania provides an excellent illustration of export dependency in the context of extensive indigenous smallholder cultivation of export crops. Second, there is a strong possibility that the very absence of an export enclave may have proved to be a considerable disadvantage in the postcolonial era. Lacking a well-developed export sector, Tanzanian agriculture remained relatively undercapitalized. Aside from the sisal estates, units of production were small; it was not easy to introduce intensive methods of cultivation. Contrary to the basic presupposition of the theory, the absence of large-scale export-oriented estates has proved to be more disadvantage than advantage in the postindependence era.

Comparative Advantage in Export Dependency

The most powerful critique of the theory of underdevelopment, and defense of Africa's export orientation, is to be found in a classical theory of international trade—comparative advantage. This theory, which is most closely identified with the eighteenth-century British economist, David Ricardo, states that countries engaging in international trade can maximize their material well-being by concentrating on the production of goods at which they are most efficient in terms of such inputs as land and labor. Although this concept was first developed nearly 200 years ago, it remains a persuasive argument for the concentration of a nation's resources in the export sector. Its reasoning is powerful and compelling: If given amounts of inputs can generate a greater amount of economic value when allotted to the production of exportable items than when allotted to the production of goods for domestic consumption, then these inputs ought to be allowed to move to the export sector and domestic needs be satisfied on the international marketplace. By maximizing its economic output in this way, a society avails itself of the highest possible value in commodities for its people.

Economists who accept the doctrine of comparative advantage acknowledge that specialization for international trade, when adopted as an economic strategy by agricultural nations, may require a lessened production of foodstuffs for domestic consumption. But there is a tendency to insist that this is not an economic problem since, if a given amount of land and labor can produce, for example, two to three times as much value when devoted to an exportable commodity, it makes compelling economic sense to import food items from countries that can grow them more cheaply. The difference between the value of the exports and the cost of the food imports could then be used to purchase other goods on the world market. According to this theory, it makes no economic sense for small agricultural countries to aim for economic self-sufficiency when, by orienting themselves to take advantage of opportunities in the world trading system, they can avail themselves of a far wider array of desirable goods. This notion has been put most succinctly by the economist William O. Jones:

> The great African production of cocoa, tea, peanuts, palm oil and cotton occurred because these crops could be sold; that is, because consumers in Europe, North America and elsewhere manifested an economic demand for these commodities, and because a marketing system was developed to communicate the character and magnitude of this demand to African farmers. As a consequence, African producers were able to enjoy more nonfarm goods, such as textiles and utensils, than they had before. . . . Incomes increased because of greater ability to buy the production of others.[11]

The key assumption underlying this argument is that poor agricultural countries are measurably better off trading in the international system.

The doctrine of comparative advantage has attracted a number of contemporary adherents. It is, for example, the operative idea in Elliot Berg's report for the World Bank, *Accelerated Development in Sub-Saharan Africa*.[12] It is central in the strategies of many of Africa's donor organizations, especially those that provide substantial funding for export-oriented agricultural projects. The principle of comparative advantage has also attracted a substantial number of academic proponents. In their recent volume, *Agriculture and Economic Development*, for example, Subrata Ghatak and Ken Ingersent have presented comparative advantage as the basis of a strategy for overall economic growth. They comment that

> many LDC's [less developed countries] have a comparative advantage in the production of agricultural goods. Given a trade regime which is relatively free from control and regulations, LDC's can use their comparative advantage in producing agricultural goods to raise their standard of living. Indeed, in an export-led growth model of trade, it would be to the advantage of many LDC's to especialize [sic] in the production of those goods where they have a comparative advantage and to export the surplus production. Such a policy will lead to the use of trade as an engine of growth.[13]

Ghatak and Ingersent cite Thailand and Malaysia as examples of societies that have used the revenues from agricultural exports to finance industrialization.

Very few economists today would take issue with the fundamental proposition that some degree of orientation toward the international marketplace is critically necessary. There is a whole range of goods and services that small agricultural countries cannot expect to produce for themselves, and that must therefore be obtained by selling commodities in the international trading system. These would include, for example, petroleum and its derivatives, medical equipment, capital goods, and raw materials for industry. Moreover, only the most powerful industrial nations are able to produce such highly technological commodities as buses, trucks, railway engines, electric generators, road-building equipment, or commercial aircraft. It seems utterly irrefutable that any country seeking to limit its involvement in the international marketplace in order to concentrate its productive resources on goods for domestic consumption would do so not only at great cost to its capacity to acquire these goods (and therefore to its ability to conduct a host of vitally important economic and social activities), but at even greater cost to the material living conditions of its population.

The critical issue, however, is not whether some degree of export orientation is essential, but whether the principle of comparative advantage can satisfy the broad claim set forth by Ghatak and Ingersent: that it can provide an effective strategy of broad economic development. On this point, there is reason for doubt, since in practically all of the countries of sub-Saharan Africa, specialization for export (the structural legacy of the colonial era) has failed to promote the sort of balanced economic development envisioned by these authors. Comparative advantage has enjoyed such widespread currency among analysts of development that few have analyzed its shortcomings as a theory of economic development. But a powerful critique has been put forward by Hollis Chenery (a Harvard University economist), who was formerly vice-president for development policy at the World Bank.

Chenery suggests that there is a major distinction between trade theory and growth theory. He argues that the doctrine of comparative advantage is one of trade maximization, with little relevance for overall economic development: For example, "the classical analysis [comparative advantage] focusses on long-run tendencies and equilibrium conditions, while modern theories of growth are concerned with the interaction among producing and consuming units in a dynamic system."[14] In a nutshell, the assumption that trade maximization will have important benefits for other sectors of a nation's economy is unproved. Chenery's analysis makes it clear that, contrary to the expectations of those who believed that the development of agricultural exports would have important spill-over benefits for other sectors of a nation's economy, it is perfectly possible for the export enclaves of agricultural countries to flourish without having such stimulative effects.

Chenery's analysis demonstrates that the allocation of resources prompted by the goal of export maximization is substantially different from that which would take place out of a concern with overall development:

> Growth theory either ignores comparative advantage and the possibility of trade completely, or considers mainly the dynamic aspects, such as the stimulus that an increase in exports provides to the development of related sectors, or the function of imports as a carrier of new products and advanced technology. With this different point of view, growth theorists often suggest investment criteria that are quite contradictory to those derived from considerations of comparative advantage.[15]

It would be naive to believe that the colonial administrators who planned and installed Africa's export enclaves were guided by any systematic theory of economic growth, much less by the principle of comparative advantage. But this concept has been invoked to defend the economic system they put in place. Chenery's analysis illuminates one major shortcoming—the failure to sustain broad-based development outside the sphere of agricultural exports.

ECONOMIC MODERNISM

It is regrettable that debating the theory of underdevelopment has been allowed to monopolize discussions of economic externalities and their impact on contemporary Africa, for the debate has obscured the fact that there are dimensions of the international economy that do act as deterrents to the economic growth of primary agricultural exporters and thereby help explain why it has been so difficult for African countries to achieve the sort of broad-based growth to which Chenery refers. These include declining terms of trade and low-demand elasticities for primary agricultural products, as well as externally induced balance-of-payments difficulties, such as neoprotectionism in the industrial world. The impact of international donor organizations must also be considered. To distinguish these factors from the theory of underdevelopment and to provide a generic rubric for their consideration, it may be useful to employ the term economic modernism.

Declining Terms of Trade

The most commonly cited of the outside economic forces that intrude on the African continent and affect the well-being of its peoples are the terms of trade. It is virtually an article of faith among innumerable observers that Africa has suffered severely in this respect, and that declining terms of trade can help explain the crippling foreign-exchange constraint that now figures so prominently as a root cause of broad economic malaise. For those who cite this factor, it is axiomatic that the real price levels of Africa's primary agricultural exports have not risen nearly as fast as the prices of industrial goods and other processed commodities that African countries must obtain through the world trading system. Thus, African nations must export larger and larger volumes of their principal agricultural commodities merely to afford a constant level of imported goods. Since Africa's imports include spare parts and raw materials for its industrial sector, the falling rate of capacity utilization may be attributed directly to the foreign-exchange scarcity brought about by falling terms of trade.

Although a fall in the terms of trade may have been harmful, it is important to approach this subject with great caution. The evidence is by no means unambiguous; the precise relationship between the terms of trade and Africa's current agrarian crisis is, therefore, by no means clear. The World Bank's recent series of studies on Africa provides one example of just how contradictory interpretations of the terms of trade can be. Bank economists have taken wholly different positions on this issue. In *Accelerated Development in Sub-Saharan Africa*, for example, Elliot Berg expresses doubt that changes in the terms of trade can be held accountable for the current crisis. He argues that "past trends in the terms of trade cannot explain the slow economic growth of Africa in the 1970's because for most countries—mineral exporters being the main exception—the terms of trade were favorable or neutral."[16] He insists, instead, that Africa's foreign-exchange difficulties are caused mainly by the continent's inability to expand export volumes.

To substantiate this position, Berg presents evidence that Africa's agricultural exporters enjoyed a positive shift in the terms of trade for the twenty-year period from 1961 to 1979. His figures indicate that the purchasing power of agricultural exports increased 4.9 percent per year between 1961 and 1970, and 1.1 percent per year from 1970 to 1979. The critical factor so far as balance of payments is concerned were stagnating export volumes. Whereas the continent's agricultural exports had managed a 4.7%-per-year increase during the 1960s, the decade from 1970 to 1979 saw export volumes drop by more than 2 percent per year. Berg's analysis implies that if agricultural exporters had been able to maintain their share of world trade, the balance-of-payments crisis would have been avoided.

The bank's follow-up study, *Sub-Saharan Africa: Progress Report on Development Prospects and Programs,* takes a substantially different position, arguing that adverse external circumstances have eroded gains that might have been achieved through increased export volumes. It cites, in particular, falling export prices for primary agricultural commodities as the principal source of Africa's balance-of-payments crisis. The Sudan offers an excellent illustration of this problem. As the bank's report notes:

> in Sudan, major changes in macro and sectoral policies have been introduced by the Government in recent years to improve cotton production for exports. These policy reforms contributed to a 24% increase in output in 1981 and a further 10 to 20 percent increase in 1982. However, due to the fall in the world market price, the increased foreign exchange earnings which could have been expected from increased cotton production have essentially been wiped out.[17]

Senegal suffered from a similar set of circumstances. Governmental efforts to improve its budgetary position through pricing reforms in the agricultural sector were badly undermined by a drop in the world price of groundnuts. While not taking direct issue with the report on *Accelerated Development,* the authors of *Sub-Saharan Africa: Progress Report* note that it covered only as far as 1979, and that the international economic environment confronted by agricultural exporters had deteriorated substantially since 1980.

The most recent bank study on Africa, *Toward Sustained Development in Sub-Saharan Africa,* documents a dramatic fall in the international terms of trade since 1980. According to this report, Africa's low-income countries (principally those not exporting oil) suffered a fall in their terms of trade of approximately 14.5% between 1980 and 1982; middle-income countries suffered a fall of about 11% in that period.[18] This study also states that between 1980 and 1982, the prices of non-oil primary commodities exported by African countries fell by 27%; for the low-income countries, this caused a loss in gross domestic product of about 2.5%. A severe fall in Africa's terms of trade since the early 1980s is further documented in the bank's *World Development Report 1984.* This study shows that there was a gradual drop of about 1.6% between 1965 and 1980, but a severe fall of more than 15% between 1980 and 1983.[19] The 1984 development report leaves little doubt that the economic effects of falling terms of trade provide a major explanation for Africa's agrarian malaise.

An additional problem arising out of the terms of trade is the tendency toward sharp fluctuations, often within short periods of time. The bank's African studies demonstrate that the price levels of primary agricultural commodities can change dramatically from one year to the next. This unpredictability is as damaging as the tendency toward long-term decline, for it makes long-term planning all but impossible. Effective planning requires that such critically important economic factors as foreign-exchange earnings be fairly predictable over a given time span. African countries face daunting difficulties in this regard. Even modest shifts in commodity prices can alter by tens of millions of dollars the foreign-exchange earnings of a country that exports hundreds of thousands of tons of a particular commodity. The country that plans cautiously on the basis of low world price levels runs the risk that it may not use its foreign-exchange earnings to the fullest for development purposes. Countries that plan more boldly, anticipating high world prices for their goods, may have to borrow capital at high interest rates to cover foreign-exchange deficits. Since agricultural countries have to deal with other unpredictable factors, such as the impact of climate on annual marketed production, long-term economic planning often becomes an exercise in futurism rather than an empirical analysis.

Low Demand Elasticities for Primary Commodities

Preoccupation with the terms of trade has somewhat obscured the importance of other features of the international economic system that constrain the development of primary agricultural exporters. Among the most important of these are low-demand elasticities for primary commodities such as coffee, tea, cocoa, and other agricultural products. African countries are in a double bind: World demand for their goods does not generally increase in response to lowered price levels, but it may drop if prices increase significantly. This factor alone may cast serious doubt on the feasibility of an export-led growth strategy for agricultural countries. It suggests that countries that seek to increase their foreign-exchange earnings by boosting export volumes may simply confront glutted markets, in which falling prices cause their net hard-currency earnings to fall. Although it may be possible for a single country (or very small number of countries) to improve its position by increasing export levels, this strategy is not available to agricultural exporters as a group since the increased supply of any given commodity would simply bring about an offsetting drop in price.

The reality of today's international marketplace is deeply unsettling for those observers who once believed that tropical agricultural exports could provide the basis for broad economic development. Implicit in their belief was an assumption that tropical agricultural commodities were comparable to the spices that were imported into Europe from southern Asia during the very first generations of international trade; that is, scarce, high-demand goods available from only a very small number of sellers, who possessed a virtually monopolistic command over supply and were able to choose from an extensive list of consumer nations. There was a strong expectation that such commodities as coffee, tea, and cocoa would continue almost indefinitely to be scarce, high-cost luxury goods. Instead, the international marketplace for tropical exports is enormously competitive, with new suppliers emerging even during periods when producer prices are falling. Today, many tropical products are available in such profuse oversupply that producer-price levels barely return the cost of production.

This situation is unlikely to improve in the foreseeable future. Indeed, the international factors causing a downward pressure on the price levels of tropical exports may well intensify between now and the end of this century. One such factor is the widespread introduction of artificial substitutes. Many African exports already compete with synthetic alternatives manufactured in the industrial world: For example, cotton competes with polyester and dacron; sugar with artificial sweeteners and, increasingly, with corn fructose (a sugar substitute produced in temperate-zone countries); cocoa with artificial chocolate; coffee and tea with soft drinks; and rubber with a synthetic alternative. In some cases, including sugar, cotton, and rubber, the price effects of synthetics and intense competition have been disastrous. Chronically depressed economic conditions in Liberia and the Sudan provide vivid evidence of the impact of weakened world demand in countries that had become dependent on one of these products. For many other tropical crops, the availability of artificial alternatives is a kind of background threat, forestalling any serious possibility of price increases.

A large part of the problem lies in the disappearance of some of the world's major agricultural markets. This is, perhaps, best illustrated with reference to the world's two largest countries, China and India. Until relatively recently (India through the 1950s and China through the 1970s), both were high-volume importers of a wide range of agricultural goods, especially grains. Within a short period of time, they have managed not only to achieve food self-sufficiency but to emerge on the world market as highly competitive agricultural exporters, adding to the oversupply of primary commodities. India, for example, is now the world's largest tea exporter, and, owing to the success of "green revolution" growing practices, one of the world's largest exporters of rice.[20] Following the introduction of important agricultural reforms in the late 1970s, China quickly became self-sufficient in rice and an important exporter of both rice and maize. Both countries are also self-sufficient in cotton; both export processed cotton products on world markets. Other traditional agricultural exporters, such as Thailand, Argentina, Brazil, and Australia, have sought aggressively to expand both their production levels and their share of world markets; their success helps account for Africa's diminishing share of world trade.

If African countries are to recover economically, two important conditions must be satisfied. First, world demand for such pivotally important commodities as coffee, tea, cocoa, sugar, cotton, and palm oil would have to increase substantially. Second, African countries would have to maintain or improve their share of world markets for these products. There is no apparent likelihood that either of these will occur. So far as demand is concerned, the most likely trend is for a steady but low rate of increase. The World Bank anticipates that world consumption of Africa's key exports will increase by an annual rate of only about 3% or less during the next decade; indeed, for the majority the rate of increase will be only about 2%.[21] Thus, for example, world consumption of coffee, sugar, and cotton will grow by only about 2% per year or less, and of cocoa and tobacco by between 2% and 3%. Only rubber, palm oil, and tea will enjoy a rate of increase in world consumption higher than 3%. As a result, oversupply of all these tropical exports can be anticipated and will continue to exert strong downward pressure on producer prices.

Africa seems unlikely to be able to maintain even its current share of world trade in these commodities. Of the eight commodities surveyed above, Africa's share of world trade is expected to decline for six (coffee, cocoa, sugar, palm oil, cotton, and sisal) and to increase for only two (tea and tobacco).[22] Some of these losses will be severe. Between 1970 and 1995, it is predicted, Africa's share of world trade in cocoa will decline from 67% to 41%; in palm oil from nearly 20% to less than 1%; in sisal from 63% to 44%; in cotton from 17% to 9%; and in rubber from 7% to less than 2%. Further, downward pressure on prices, arising from international competition, will lessen the earnings from those commodities for which the continent's share of world trade increases. Under these conditions, it is unlikely that agricultural exports will be able to provide sufficient revenues to finance programs for economic recovery.

The prediction of economic trends is a hazardous enterprise at best; the World Bank's estimates of the future prospects of primary agricultural commodities are not exempt from this qualification. The bank's estimates are based on a set of assumptions about the future economic performance of the industrial nations. Basically, the bank's economists developed their projections for developing areas on the basis of optimistic but modest hopes for positive growth rates of between 3% and 4% for the industrial world. The economies of Western Europe, North America, and other industrial regions are expected to grow at the rate of about 3.7% per annum between 1983 and 1990, and about 3.5% per annum between 1990 and 1995.[23] This is expected to generate very positive rates of economic growth for the developing world as a whole. Low-income Asian countries, for example, are anticipated to have growth rates of nearly 5% per year between 1986 and 1995, a figure that translates into annual per-capita income increases of between 2.5% and 3%.[24]

African countries, in contrast, may have the greatest difficulty in achieving rates of economic growth sufficiently high to match the rate of population increase. The bank forecasts that the economies of low-income

African countries will grow by only about 3% per year between 1986 and 1995, and—given a rate of population increase of about the same magnitude —that increases in gross domestic product (GDP) per capita will be marginal at best. Even this forecast may be unduly optimistic. Most observers now believe that Africa's rate of population increase is well above 3% per year. If this is the case, the rate of change in GDP per capita may be on the order of -1% per year. The critical question, then, is why Africa's economic performance will be so markedly different from that of other developing regions. The answer probably lies in the fact that growth for the developing world as a whole is largely accounted for by countries that have already attained a substantial industrial base, such as Brazil, China, and India. These countries will, in all likelihood, continue to develop along industrial lines, for they have internal markets large enough to sustain further industrial development.

African countries, on the other hand, have virtually no industrial sector; because of the very slow growth of their internal markets, their development will be almost entirely dependent on primary agricultural exports. This will impose major constraints on their prospects for economic development, for, as agricultural countries, they will confront an inhospitable international environment. The principal features of this environment will be not only falling terms of trade and low demand elasticities for their agricultural products, but an ensemble of other factors that, in recent years, have begun to create especially severe balance-of-payments difficulties.

Externally Induced Balance-of-Payments Difficulties

Failing a dramatic growth of commodities markets in the industrial world, and absent any significant likelihood that African countries will be able to recapture their former share of world trade in primary agricultural exports, the best prospect of economic recovery lies in the development of agricultural-processing industries. These would enable producer nations to achieve economic gains by increasing the value added to their exports. If the concept of export-led growth is to have any real meaning for less developed countries, it must include the establishment of a processing sector. Export processing offers the only feasible alternative to industrialization through import substitution. Since exporting industries generate their own foreign exchange, there is far less likelihood that they would encounter the hard-currency constraints that have so encumbered the development of industry based on import substitution.

Neoprotectionism in the Industrial World

The current structure of the international trading system militates strongly against the development of export-processing industries, being characterized by forms of protectionism that discourage the development of processing industries in agricultural countries.[25] Although it is commonly assumed that neoprotectionism is having its greatest effect on world trade in manufactured goods, industrial trade barriers are, in fact, far less common than those against primary agricultural products. Such barriers have had a sharply adverse effect on African countries. As Shamsher Singh has demonstrated, Africa's "exports of processed products face escalating tariffs and other barriers in the industrial countries."[26] Although Africa's losses from the new protectionism are not nearly as great as those of Latin American countries, they are considerable. In its 1985 *World Development Report,* the World Bank has estimated that protectionism in the industrial world against sugar alone cost African countries approximately $270 million annually between 1979 and 1981, and that this figure rose to more than $420 million in 1983. Trade barriers against beef exports were costing the continent approximately $100 million per year during this period.[27]

Protectionism has a number of adverse consequences. By reducing the value of exports, it adds considerably to the continent's balance-of-payments difficulties. Thus, it seriously impedes Africa's capacity to service its foreign debt, as well as its ability to acquire the goods and services needed to launch a development process. Even more importantly, protectionism sends a strongly negative signal to those countries prepared to consider seriously policy reforms designed to promote exports. Since protectionism also reduces the development prospects for secondary or tertiary industries (i.e., industries to service the export industries), it has virtually incalculable effects on the continent's capacity to attract foreign capital. Primary agricultural exporters seem destined to suffer indefinitely from problems of underdevelopment: Since their exports will not generate sufficient hard-currency earnings to finance the development of an industrial sector, they are condemned to remain at the lowest level of the world's low-income countries.

External economic shocks. Of the various external factors that impinge upon African countries and affect their economic prospects, some have a long-term structural quality: Their working out covers a period of years or even decades. Changes in the terms of trade or the effects of global economic recession have this quality. Their impact is not sudden, but gradual, and therefore almost imperceptible from one year to the next. Other changes occur with dramatic suddenness. The economist Bela Belassa has referred to these as "external shocks."[28] Three such shocks have had a particularly important recent impact on Africa: the overvaluation of the U.S. dollar in the early to mid-1980s; the oil-price increases in 1973 and 1979; and the quantum leap of world interest rates in the late 1970s and early 1980s. Belassa has summarized the overall effects of such shocks in the following terms:

> Adjustment to external shocks in low-income sub-Saharan African countries took largely the form of reductions in imports through decreases in the rate of economic growth and in the income elasticity of import

demand while these countries lost export market shares. Losses in export market shares and the extent of import substitution were smaller in the oil-importing middle-income countries of sub-Saharan Africa, which further accelerated their economic growth by utilizing additional net external financing in excess of the balance-of-payments effects of external shocks . . . . Compared to less developed countries in other regions, one thus finds greater reliance on import substitution and lesser reliance on export promotion in the oil-importing countries of sub-Saharan Africa and, in particular, in the low-income countries of the region.[29]

Belassa's analysis covers only 1973 to 1978, following the first of the oil-price increases, and thus does not explicitly include the effects of heightened interest rates or the second oil-price increase. But his evidence nevertheless provides stunning confirmation of the degree to which African economies can be buffeted by sudden, short-term changes in the international economic environment.

The overvaluation of the U.S. dollar offers an excellent illustration of this phenomenon. A number of international economic transactions of vital importance to African countries, including debt servicing and energy purchases, are reckoned in dollars and thus become more costly in exact ratio to overvaluation. Dollar overvaluation magnifies the effects of other economic factors—such as a decline in the terms of trade, an increase in the interest rate on foreign debt, or an increase in the cost of critical imports—by adding a sort of surcharge to each of them. It accentuates balance-of-payments difficulties by adding to the adverse shift in the terms of trade (dollar-denominated goods become relatively more expensive) and, by making economic inputs such as fuel and transportation equipment more expensive, can contribute to lowered export volumes. Although it has been possible for some African countries to compensate for dollar overvaluation by increasing external borrowing, this is at best a short-term response, and one not conducive to economic growth. The principal long-term effect of external borrowing is to add to the debt-service burden and thereby to lessen the amount of foreign exchange available for purchasing needed economic inputs.

Oil-price increases have a twofold impact: They affect the continent directly by requiring an immediate increase in the percentage of foreign-exchange earnings allotted to energy imports, and indirectly by triggering a recession, during which world demand for Africa's exports is lowered. Belassa has estimated that during the four-year period following the oil-price increase of 1973, Africa suffered an annual loss in its terms of trade equal to about 4.6 percent of GDP.[30] African countries had only just begun to recover from this extended recession, thanks to a momentary surge in the prices of key commodities in 1978, when the second oil-price increase occurred in 1979. Although Belassa's figures do not cover the effects of this shock, there is no reason to believe that its results were any less severe. Like the earlier oil-price increase, that of 1979 was followed almost immediately by a major global recession that had especially severe effects on Africa's key export markets in Western Europe and North America. Indeed, the post-1979 shock was, in all probability, of far greater consequence than the earlier increase, coinciding almost precisely with a surge in world interest rates. African countries were thus compelled to cope with the effects of two shock events simultaneously.

The effect of increased interest rates has been little short of calamitous. Between 1974 and 1978, African countries had managed to maintain a remarkably stable and very low debt-service ratio. This ratio had stood at 7.1% in 1974 and, despite heavy borrowing by middle-income oil importers, had risen to only 9% in 1979. Between 1979 and 1983, however, while the continent's total debt was increasing by only about 50% (from $19.5 billion to $27.1 billion), its debt-service ratio skyrocketed from 9% to 31.4%.[31] At one and the same time, African countries were confronted with a further tripling in the price of oil and a debt-service ratio that had more than tripled within a period of about forty-eight months.

Agricultural policies of developed countries. The global recession following the 1979 oil-price increase was so severe that it caused many Western industrial countries to reinforce the trend toward agricultural protectionism. In an effort to cushion the unemployment effects of the economic downturn, the European Economic Community, (EEC) the United States, and other industrially developed agricultural producers either adopted or strengthened a number of protectionist measures, including price supports and non-tariff barriers. These policies helped bring about vast surpluses, affecting the economic prospects of agricultural countries in at least two ways. First, surpluses have resulted in a sharp downward movement in world price levels for agricultural commodities. Second, surpluses have made it extremely difficult for African agricultural exporters to enter the European or North American marketplace. The end result of acute world overproduction of primary agricultural commodities is that debt repayment has become all the more difficult for African countries. Both African and Latin American countries have been driven to seek to increase their export volumes, adding to the global glut of primary commodities and depressing prices even further. Under current market conditions, timely debt servicing is virtually impossible for all but a handful of African countries. Nearly every African country has been compelled to enter negotiations with one of the major international lending institutions in order to arrange a manageable schedule of debt payments.

The Policies of International Donors

In the broad dialogue between externalists and internalists, the impact of donor policies on African agriculture is often omitted. The omission is regrettable since the international donor community is a vitally important actor in Africa's economic affairs, and donor policies often have an extremely significant effect on the process of African development. This is nowhere more conspicuous than in the rural sector, where the influence of donor agencies is sometimes so strong that it can have a determining effect on agricultural trends. A case can be constructed to the effect that certain policies of the donor nations have played an important part in contributing to Africa's agricultural crisis.

The rural policies of Africa's international donor community can best be viewed in historical terms. The concept of agrarian dualism, though imperfect, provides a useful starting point, for it calls attention to the relatively undeveloped state of African nations' food-producing sectors at the end of the colonial era. The legacy of underdevelopment has had a considerable influence on the perspective of donor agencies. From the standpoint of international donors interested in rural development, the critical problem was how to improve the productivity of the food-producing sector, so that food imports would not continue to be a drain on financial reserves needed for industrialization. The principal constraint on this improvement, as identified by these agencies, was the absence of agronomic or technological development among peasant food producers. In the economic argot of the time, food production was a "backward sector."

The challenge of rural development, as perceived by many professional experts and academic observers, was to complete the diffusion of modern agricultural practices throughout the countryside, allowing food production to keep pace with rising national needs. The policy commonly chosen to achieve this goal was the creation of large-scale farms, which could demonstrate scientific agriculture and the benefits associated with advanced agricultural practices. This strategy for rural development has generally been called the "project approach," and its hallmark is the allocation of huge sums of money to establish large farms, combining intensive research on scientific methods of crop husbandry with agricultural extension programs to diffuse these methods to individual peasant producers.[32] The operative idea underlying this strategy was that once peasant farmers had been made aware of the benefits to be derived from agricultural innovation, their traditional resistance to change would be overcome, and sweeping improvements in food production would take place.

The project approach achieved a few dramatic successes, but, in general, it failed by a wide margin to attain the ambitious goals its proponents had claimed. Indeed, it may even have contributed measurably to a worsening of economic conditions in the countryside. It is clear, for example, that the project approach rested on a highly questionable assumption about the nature of African peasantry: specifically, that peasant cultural conservatism was the principal obstacle to agrarian innovation. Today, observers of the African rural scene are virtually unanimous in their conviction that African peasants are not bound by cultural constraints; that they respond with alacrity to economic opportunity; and that when financial incentives are present, their production for the marketplace increases accordingly. The project approach failed to diffuse improved agricultural practices for reasons that had little, if anything, to do with peasants' cultural proclivity for traditional agricultural methods. It failed because it did not address colonially introduced systems of producer pricing that left the vast majority of peasant farm families with only the most meager cash income.

The project approach may also have contributed somewhat to the problem of declining per-capita food production. Food crops grown on heavily subsidized demonstration farms sometimes competed on the market with those grown by peasant producers, and this probably contributed to low price levels that drove marginal producers off the land.

Large-scale, capital-intensive projects are vulnerable to criticism on ecological grounds. Environmentally oriented developmentalists in Africa are seriously concerned about the impact of temperate-zone agricultural technologies transferred to tropical regions. Systems of cultivation requiring that large areas of land be cleared of their original cover of forest and perennial grasses and replacing indigenous farming systems that involved mixed cropping and long fallow periods are highly destructive of fragile tropical ecosystems. The annual harvesting of large land units leaves the harvested acreage exposed to the elements during the off-season, thereby contributing directly to the degradation of the soil base and making it progressively less suitable for agriculture.

The project orientation of the donor community has also had a major adverse impact on the financial stamina of African nations. The vast majority of donor agencies insist that the agricultural projects they have created become the financial responsibility of the host government after a certain period of time. This has proved to be an almost impossible burden. The demonstration projects tend to be expensive to maintain; they become a major drain on scarce economic resources. In a large number of cases, African governments have been forced by sheer financial pressures to abandon these projects, but not before some had expended invaluable resources and personnel in vain efforts to maintain donor good will by keeping the projects alive. Since donor projects were designed to be capital- and technology-intensive, the costs in scarce foreign exchange were invariably great. By the early 1970s, the African countryside was littered with the debris of countless failed agricultural projects. The costs of this policy to Africa, in financial and human terms, have never been fully calculated, but African governments must certainly have been compelled to divert hundreds of millions of dollars into projects that had little realistic prospect of success. It is more than idle speculation to ask what the benefits might have been if these funds had been allocated to the improvement of peasant agriculture.

Despite its shortcomings, the project approach remained extremely popular with the donor community, and even today is a cornerstone of donor strategy for developing the African countryside. The donor nations' reluctance to abandon the project orientation may be partially explained by the fact that it retains a certain amount of popularity among African governments, which welcome the resources that pour in and the opportunities for patronage created at the local level. The preference for large projects may also reflect the bureaucratic character of some of the donor agencies. Like other large-scale governmental bureaucracies, donor organizations are often committed by their budget cycles to expend very large sums of money within very short periods of time, and they therefore find it administratively impractical to fund numerous small-scale projects. In addition, many donor experts continue to believe that the principal reason for the failure of the project approach lies not in its intrinsic unsuitability, but in the cultural and educational inadequacies of African peasants.

CONCLUSION

The purpose of this chapter is neither to affirm nor to rebut the externalist viewpoint about Africa's agricultural performance. It is, instead, to establish the context within which Africa's export-dependent agricultural systems operate. The mere creation of an inventory of external factors that impinge on Africa suggests its own conclusion: The international economic system represents an environment that is deeply inhospitable to the developmental prospects of small agricultural countries. This much is beyond dispute. The difficult question is not whether the international environment is inhospitable, but whether it is *so* inhospitable that it will inevitably frustrate even the most carefully crafted efforts to achieve development on the basis of agricultural growth.

This volume attempts to answer that question in the negative, using Kenya's agricultural success to suggest that countries that implement policies favorable to the agricultural sector can overcome the constraints on development deriving from the international economy. But it is well worth remembering that even the most successful countries face daunting developmental prospects. The ability of individual countries, such as Kenya, to overcome international constraints cannot be taken for granted as a permanent given. It would not require a great deal of worsening in the international economic arena for that arena to become so inhospitable that failure must result.

NOTES

1. Those wishing to pursue the works of those mentioned here are directed to André Gunder Frank, *Capitalism and Underdevelopment in Latin America* (Monthly Review Press, New York and London, 1967); Samir Amin, *Accumulation on a World*

Scale, 2 vols. (Monthly Review Press, New York and London, 1974); Arghiri Emmanuel, *Unequal Exchange* (Monthly Review Press, New York and London, 1972); Paul A. Baran, *The Political Economy of Growth* (Monthly Review Press, New York and London, 1957); Immanuel Wallerstein, *The Modern World System* (Academic Press, New York and San Francisco, 1974); Irving Zeitlin, *Capitalism and Imperialism* (Markham, Chicago, 1972); Benjamin Cohen, *The Question of Imperialism* (Basic Books, New York, 1973).

    2. See, for example, Randall Baker, "Linking and Sinking: Externalities and the Persistence of Destitution and Famine in Africa," in *Drought and Hunger in Africa,* ed. Michael H. Glantz (Cambridge University Press, Cambridge, 1987), especially pp. 153–54.

    3. Roger Leys, "Introduction," in *Dualism and Rural Development in East Africa* (Institute for Development Research, Copenhagen, 1973), p. 7.

    4. E. A. Brett, *Colonialism and Underdevelopment in East Africa: The Politics of Economic Change* (Heinemann, London, 1973), pp. 92–95.

    5. The introduction of hybrid maize in Kenya during the late 1960s was one of Africa's great exceptions to this proposition.

    6. Rodolfo Stavenhagen, *Social Classes in Agrarian Societies* (Doubleday, Garden City, NY 1975). See especially Ch. 6, "Agrarian Changes and the Dynamics of Class in Black Africa," pp. 72–93.

    7. Ann W. Seidman, "Comparative Development Strategies in East Africa," *East Africa Journal* 7, no. 4 (April 1970), pp. 13–18; "The Dual Economies of East Africa," 7, no. 5 (May 1970), pp. 6–20; and "The Agricultural Revolution," 7, no. 8 (August 1970), pp. 21–36.

    8. Seidman, "Dual Economies," p. 5.

    9. Colin Leys, *Underdevelopment in Kenya: The Political Economy of Neo-Colonialism* (University of California Press, Berkeley and Los Angeles, 1974), pp. 36–40.

    10. Ibid., p. 9.

    11. William O. Jones, *Marketing Staple Food Crops in Tropical Africa* (Cornell University Press, Ithaca and London, 1972), p. 233.

    12. Published by the World Bank, Washington, D.C., 1981.

    13. Subrata Ghatak and Ken Ingersent, *Agriculture and Economic Development* (Johns Hopkins University Press, Baltimore, 1984), p. 279.

    14. Hollis Chenery, *Structural Change and Development Policy* (Oxford University Press, New York and Oxford, 1979), p. 273.

    15. Ibid., p. 275.

    16. The World Bank, *Accelerated Development in Sub-Saharan Africa: An Agenda for Action* (Washington, D.C., 1981), p. 19.

    17. The World Bank, *Sub-Saharan Africa: Progress Report on Development Prospects and Programs* (Washington, D.C., 1983), p. 3.

    18. The World Bank, *Toward Sustained Development in Sub-Saharan Africa* (Washington, D.C., 1984), p. 12.

    19. The World Bank, *World Development Report 1984* (Oxford University Press, New York, 1984), p. 24 (see Table 2.7).

    20. India imposed a ban on the export of tea during 1984 in order to assure a low cost supply for its domestic market. This resulted in a doubling of the world market price, vastly improving the export earnings of Kenya. India resumed its tea exports in 1985, thereby eliminating the possibility that Kenya and other African tea

exporters might continue to benefit from a scarce supply.

21. Shamsher Singh, *Sub-Saharan Agriculture: Synthesis and Trade Prospects,* World Bank Staff Working Papers no. 608 (Washington, D.C., 1983), Table C, p. 8.

22. Ibid., Table 17, p. 48.

23. The World Bank, *The Outlook for Primary Commodities,* World Bank Staff Commodity Working Paper no. 9, (Washington, D.C., 1983), p. 27.

24. Ronald Duncan, ed., *The Outlook for Primary Commodities 1984 to 1995,* World Bank Staff Commodity Working Papers no. 11 (Washington, D.C., 1984), Table 5, p. 18.

25. For a discussion of the forms of protectionism, see Douglas R. Nelson, *The Political Structure of the New Protectionism,* World Bank Staff Working Paper no. 471 (The World Bank, Washington, D.C., 1981).

26. Singh, *Sub-Saharan Agriculture,* p. 11.

27. The World Bank, *World Development Report 1985* (Oxford University Press, New York, 1985), pp. 40–41.

28. For a full discussion of this issue, see Bela Belassa, "Policy Responses to External Shocks in Sub-Saharan African Countries," *Journal of Policy Modeling* 5, no. 1 (1983), pp. 75–105. (Reprinted as World Bank Reprint Series no. 270).

29. Ibid., p. 101.

30. Ibid., p. 79.

31. These figures are taken from The World Bank, *World Debt Tables: External Debt of Developing Countries* (Washington, D.C., 1985) pp. 6–7.

32. For an excellent discussion of the project orientation, see E. Philip Morgan, "The Project Orthodoxy in Development: Reevaluating the Cutting Edge," *Public Administration and Development* 3 (1983).

· 3 ·
Internalist Explanations:
Policy Makes a Difference

Internalist analyses of Africa's agricultural crisis argue that African governments have intervened in rural markets in ways that pose fundamental disincentives to agricultural production. The most influential recent scholarship elaborating this position is that of Elliot Berg and Robert Bates.[1] Their work and the analysis in this book owe much to the seminal research of Michael Lipton.[2] All three of these authors are linked by a belief that, since independence, African governments (as well as those of many other developing countries) have adopted a set of economic policies that effectively reduce economic rewards to small-scale agricultural producers by lowering the prices they receive for the commodities they produce and increasing the prices they must pay for the goods they purchase, both production inputs and consumer items.

This position has found powerful reinforcement in the research of John C. de Wilde, whose book, *Agriculture, Marketing and Pricing in Sub-Saharan Africa*, was published approximately three years after the studies by Berg and Bates.[3] For all these authors, the common denominator of agricultural policy in Africa is its attempt to use the agricultural sector to provide economic resources to be dispensed elsewhere in the society, especially to urban industries and consumers. The end result of such policies has been a powerful disincentive effect, producing a pandemic pattern of agricultural stagnation. The principal symptoms of this stagnation are falling per-capita food production and a steady loss in the continent's share of world trade in exportable agricultural commodities.

The most useful point of departure for understanding the internalist perspective on the agricultural policies of contemporary African governments is the straightforward distinction made by political scientists, between strong states and weak states. Strong states are those able to resist short-term political pressures in order to implement economic policies that are in the long-term national interest. Japan offers perhaps the most frequently cited example of a strong state. Japan's tax policies have, for many years, discouraged present consumption in order to stimulate a high rate of savings for long-term capital investment. The government has been able to direct capital toward industries that exhibit a strong prospect of international competitiveness, such as the automobile and consumer electronics industries. Weak states exhibit the opposite economic tendency: They cannot suppress consumption in order to generate high rates of capital investment. Instead, they must be constantly attentive to short-term political factors and must, as a result, pursue economic policies that do not promote long-term economic growth. The United States is frequently offered as an example of a weak state, because its contemporary economic policies respond to political pressures in ways that have not only promoted harmful budget and trade deficits but have weakened the international competitiveness of the industrial sector.

The distinction between strong and weak states does not involve absolutes, but rather, a continuum along which governments can be scattered according to their relative strengths and weaknesses. On this continuum, the majority of African states can best be understood as weak: They generally lack the political consensus that stems from clear, ongoing majority support; their political institutions are not well grounded in a tradition of legitimization that transcends particular regimes and policies; financial stringencies sometimes cripple even the most rudimentary operation of the state apparatus; and political cleavages based on ethnic and class differences are so intense as to pose a constant danger of political overthrow. Thus, despite the high visibility of authoritarian rule and the widespread use of repression to maintain political power, many African governments are prone to instability and must therefore formulate economic policies that offer the best prospects of short-term political survival.

The second step in developing the internalist perspective on agricultural policies is to graft onto the notion of weak state a second explanation—urban bias. This concept finds its most powerful expression in the work of Michael Lipton (Institute of Development Studies, Sussex University). His work on the urban basis of economic policy in developing countries is of such great importance that it is only fair to note that many of the ideas that he first developed were taken up and further crystalized by Robert Bates and Elliot Berg.[4] Linked with the weak-state hypothesis, the idea of urban bias provides a powerful theory that helps illuminate the reasons why African governments have formulated and implemented a set of policies that have suppressed the growth of their most important economic sector. The weak-state notion suggests that governments that are not well institutionalized can survive only by accommodating their most powerful constituencies. The idea of urban bias suggests that, in contemporary Africa, the most potent constituencies are urban interest groups, whose economic interests have a decisive impact on economic policy. Taken together, these two ideas constitute a compelling argument, to the effect that agricultural policies in Africa are adverse to the best economic interests of the agricultural sector, having been formulated and implemented as a political response to the economic demands of urban populations.

The reasons why this can happen so consistently are readily discernible: Urban groups not only have the capacity to make their economic interests instantly known to those in political authority, but can threaten the political survival of governing elites that fail to respond to their interests. The power of urban groups is, in the main, geopolitical in nature. They are physically located at the epicenter of the political system. By organizing street demonstrations, work stoppages, silent protests, or public rallies, they can convey their discontents directly to governing elites and, indeed, threaten the very foundations of weak regimes. Lipton has generalized this notion in the following terms:

> The daily contacts of, and pressures on, central decision-takers in poor countries come overwhelmingly from small groups of articulate, organized or powerful people in regular contact with senior officials and politicians . . . . Leaders of labour, and of public and private capital and management, in construction, railways and government services; prominent academics and other intellectuals; influential editors and radio producers—these, and not just leaders of industry, are the threateners, promisers, lobbyists, dinner companions, flatterers, financiers and friends to senior administrators and politicians in all countries, rich and poor. They are almost always urban.[5]

With such enormous power at their disposal, urban groups can demand that their discontents be given an immediate policy response.

The concept of urban bias does not claim that all urban social groups are possessed of uniform political influence, even in relation to their rural counterparts. It would be absurd on the face of it to suggest that the political power of urban workers or the urban underemployed is in any way commensurate with that of high-ranking politicians, wealthy industrialists, or members of the bureaucratic elite. Nor does the concept of urban bias view rural populations as uniformly powerless. It would be equally absurd to place large-scale farmers, peasant smallholders, landless agricultural workers, and workers in rural services in a common political category. The point being suggested here, following Lipton's analysis, is substantially different: to wit, the decisionmakers who formulate and implement economic policy typically find it politically advantageous to create policy frameworks that benefit urban dwellers as a common social category, at the expense of rural dwellers.

Lipton offers cheap-food policy as the most compelling illustration of this proposition, for it is unambiguously clear that urban populations as a whole benefit from policies that lower the price of food staples, while rural dwellers, especially producers, suffer income reduction.[6] Precisely the same argument could be made, however, utilizing a variety of other policies, three of which this chapter considers. One is currency overvaluation, which artificially heightens the purchasing power of wage earners by cheapening imported goods. As Lipton notes, "the management of foreign exchange in most poor countries cheapens non-farm inputs and makes non-farm outputs more costly."[7] Another is the use of fiscal policy (deficit budgeting) to boost the level of wage employment. Overstaffing the bureaucracy, including parastatal corporations, generally benefits urban dwellers to a far greater degree than it benefits their rural counterparts. The industrial policy of import substitution also benefits urban dwellers by providing an artificial prop for the wages of both workers and management while, at the same time, increasing the costs to rural consumers of the goods these industries produce.

In Lipton's view, the reasons for urban bias are partly attitudinal. Policymakers throughout the developing world believe that the agricultural sector represents the "backward" part of their national economies, and that if they are to develop "modern" economic systems, agriculture must be made to provide the resources for industry. Often, Lipton argues, these policymakers "wrongly conclude that rapid industrialization at the expense of agriculture can produce rapid development."[8] From this perspective, it is permissible to use agriculture exploitively because farmers themselves are often socially reactionary and reluctant to innovate, because they do not respond to economic incentives, and because an emphasis on agricultural development would, therefore, project an unfavorable national image. If the ultimate source of such attitudes were to be identified, it would almost certainly be the development theories of an entire generation of scholars in the 1960s. The common denominator of such otherwise highly diverse scholars as Lucien Pye, W. W. Rostow, and W. Arthur Lewis was the belief that agriculture could be used to finance development throughout the rest of the economy.

Exploiting agriculture was feasible because of the political weakness of rural social groups. If urban interest groups are powerful because of their physical proximity to the heart of the national political process, then rural groups are relatively powerless because of their remoteness. Throughout Africa, rural producers have been vulnerable to policies that exploit them because they are least able to do anything about it. The political weakness of agricultural populations stems from a variety of factors, but the most basic of these is simply their lack of access to capital cities. Distance alone makes it all but impossible for Africa's rural populations to exercise effective influence on the national political process. In addition, these populations are almost invariably fragmented along ethnic and linguistic lines, divisions that severely complicate any effort to develop concerted political action. Indeed, African governments have often been highly successful at manipulating rural ethnic divisions in such a way as to direct political discontent away from the central state. And, since the level of formal education in the countryside is generally lower than it is among urban dwellers, the level of political consciousness and capacity for political organization is commensurately lower. The end product of these factors has been chronic political weakness relative to such highly powerful groups as trade unions, students, and the white-collar classes.

Of all the factors that have influenced agricultural policy in Africa, none is so important or powerful as the simple imperative of political survival. African governments are desperately concerned about the volatility of their urban constituencies. Keith Hart has stated this point bluntly with respect to West Africa:

> The short-term preoccupation of West Africa's rulers is with the immediate danger of an unsatisfied urban mob. Long-term planning for the countryside is entirely incompatible with the siege mentality of politicians, soldiers and bureaucrats who are literally counting the days before they lose their power (and lives) in the face of growing anger. . . . This anger means most in the major cities; it commands constant attention and the award of temporary palliatives, one after the other, all adding up to the relative impoverishment of farmers.[9]

Hart's is perhaps the strongest statement of the urban bias thesis. But in advancing this point of view, he is joined by numerous other analysts of African agriculture, including John de Wilde, whose inventory of the pressures on agricultural policy includes "a determination to keep down the cost of living, especially for urban consumers who, incidentally, include the civil servants and politicians."[10]

The most frequent objection to the concept of urban bias is that it links a set of social groups so disparate as to have no common political interests. What, after all, could urban political- and private-sector elites, members of the white-collar middle classes, industrialists, workers, and the urban unemployed possibly have in common? These groups would appear to be so various as to undermine entirely the validity of a notion based on the premise of urban solidarity. The answer is that these groups have a good many interests in common. All, for example, benefit from economic policies that cheapen foodstuffs. Since food purchases consume a very large proportion of the incomes of working- and middle-class families in Africa, urban groups benefit collectively from policies that lower the price of this necessity. Food is a wage good (one of the factors that determine the level of wages). Industrial elites favor cheap food because it enables them to maintain low wage levels. Governmental elites also favor cheap food: It permits political leaders to enlarge their patronage networks by employing large numbers of low-paid workers.

All of these urban groups favor economic policies that boost their purchasing power as wage earners. Since Africa's middle and working classes, whether in the public or private sector, have in common the fact that their income takes the form of a salary, they share an interest in economic policies that increase their purchasing power by lowering the cost of commodities they seek to consume. This interest extends not only to domestically produced foodstuffs, but to imported goods as well. The living standard of Africa's urban dwellers now depends on the availability and affordability of a wide range of imported commodities, especially consumer durables. Since the cost of imported goods can be lowered, at least in the short run, through overvaluating national currency, urban dwellers have a clear common interest in exerting upward pressures on their nations' exchange rates. In sum, otherwise highly diversified and potentially antagonistic urban interest groups find common cause in the implementation of economic policies that raise their incomes relative to those of other groups in their society, specifically rural agriculturists.

In a critique of Robert Bates' articulation of this approach, Manfred Bienefeld has suggested that it fails to provide a satisfactory answer for the question, "why should reasonable men adopt public policies that have harmful consequences for the societies they govern?"[11] The difficulty, perhaps, lies in establishing precisely what is meant by the term "reasonable" when applied to the policy frameworks adopted and implemented by political leaders. Reasonability in the behavior of public officials may well involve the need to accept political reality largely as a given. Political leaders everywhere are compelled to deal with difficult choices between the demands of powerful economic-interest groups and the broader long-range interests of society.

The form of this conflict may vary considerably from place to place. At the local level, for example, it may take the form of divergence between the demands of real-estate developers and the value of environmental preservation. In national politics, it may manifest itself as conflict between manufacturers and the public interest over such issues as consumer safety or industrial protectionism. Pluralist politics had been discovered and researched long before David B. Truman's classic work on the subject, but he articulated as well as anyone has since the most plausible response to Bienefeld's question: The sum of effective group demands on a political system does not necessarily equal generally beneficial social consequences. The public interest is often lost sight of in the welter of group pressures on a political system.[12]

Throughout much of modern Africa, the conflict between political pressures and broader social need typically presents itself as a tension between the demands of urban social groups on the one hand and rural groups on the other. The concept of urban bias, then, helps explain why such a large number of African governments have framed agricultural policies that have adverse effects on the most important sector of their national economies. Politically irresistible urban pressures have meant that African governments are driven by survival imperatives that override their concern for a sound agricultural policy. These imperatives include the need to expand public services, and to promote an industrial sector as a means of increasing urban employment opportunity. The primary imperative, however, is the provision of cheap food and inexpensive imported goods, even at the expense of policies that lower the incentives for agricultural producers. In addition to the pressure of day-to-day survival, then, independence presented African governments with a set of economic responsibilities that required vastly greater resources than had previously been available.

Newly independent African states have, for example, considered themselves under a deep obligation to deal with urgent social problems such as urban unemployment. Although rarely articulating explicitly the principle of the state as employer of last resort, many have in fact behaved as if this were a fundamental basis for ongoing political legitimacy. They have rapidly expanded their employment rolls to provide jobs in the public sector to persons who could not be absorbed elsewhere in the economic system.[13] This is clearly evident in the unbridled growth of government bureaucracies and parastatal bodies in Africa, an expansion that has been out of all proportion to the financial capacities of the countries involved. David Abernethy has calculated the extent of this growth:

> A rough estimate is that regular line agencies of central and local governments in the region (South Africa excluded) grew from 1.9 million to 6.5 million between 1960 and 1980, i.e. about 240% over two decades. If one adds nonfinancial parastatal organizations, public sector employment rose from about 3.8 million to approximately 10 million (i.e. about 160%) over this same period. By 1980 the public sector, including parastatals, probably accounted for 3% of the region's population and half the number in non-agricultural employment.[14]

One of the most pernicious aspects of this growth is that governments have also felt compelled to emulate the generous salary structures of the colonial governments that had preceded them. High salary scales together with lavish supplemental benefits, especially at the upper reaches of Africa's public bureaucracies, have been an enormous cost burden on weak and undeveloped national economies.

Agriculture was clearly the only economic sector large enough to provide revenues for this expansion. During the generation that followed the end of colonial rule, agriculture came to be treated as an object of economic extraction, an almost infinitely elastic source of tax revenue needed to implement policies whose basic intent was to provide the services and industries that would make for a more quiescent urban political environment.

There have been other political imperatives as well, among them the nationalist commitment to promote the growth of the industrial sector. Until the early 1970s, there was a strong consensus among development economists that the most expeditious means to achieve this goal was to create industries based on the principle of import substitution. This strategy of industrial development seemed to offer a number of important advantages. It was generally thought, for example, to provide a quick and efficient means not only of generating urban industrial employment but of conserving the foreign-exchange resources that were being spent to import light consumer goods. And, in cases where import-substituting industries were able to develop a high degree of productive efficiency, they might be able to develop regional export markets, thus earning a certain amount of foreign exchange.

The critical question was where to obtain the capital with which to finance the new industries. Again, the only realistic answer was the domestic agricultural sector, for though some capital investment might be forthcoming from abroad, this was unlikely to be sufficient in most countries. In any case, many African political leaders harbored deep suspicions about multinational corporations and their investment activities in the Third World. Import substitution as an industrial strategy, then, required that agriculture be treated as a source of investment capital for the establishment of an urban manufacturing sector, rather than as the object of policies designed to further its own development.

PATTERNS OF INTERVENTION

Price Regulation

African governments have intervened in their agricultural sectors in a variety of ways. Of these, by far the most common is direct governmental regulation of producer prices. In *Markets and States in Tropical Africa*, Robert Bates presents a convincing argument that, since independence, African governments have employed their ability to establish monopolistic control of agricultural pricing to suppress the farm-gate prices of agricultural commodities far below levels that would have prevailed if a free market in agricultural commodities had been allowed to operate. Surveying a range of producer prices for export crops, for example, Bates concluded that "in most instances, they [agricultural producers] received less than two-thirds of the potential sales realization, and in many cases they received less than one-half."[15] The suppression of export-crop prices was not begun by Africa's independent regimes. It was initiated by colonial governments, which also viewed the export sector as a source of tax revenue and foreign exchange. But independent governments, under pressure from populations that had been politically mobilized during the nationalist era, and therefore especially needy of revenues with which to carry forward the projects that had been promised as the benefits of political freedom, pursued this policy with intensified vigor.

Bates found a similar pattern in the food-producing sector, where newly independent African governments had also enlarged on policies of price regulation that had been initiated by colonial regimes. Here, too, it seemed that African governments, responding to the wide array of political pressures for cheap food staples, had suppressed the prices of domestically produced foodstuffs far below the world-market price levels of similar commodities. John de Wilde has argued that suppression of producer prices for domestic food crops is far more severe than that for export commodities, where there has been some tendency to pass through world-market prices. In *Agriculture, Marketing and Pricing in Sub-Saharan Africa,* he has argued:

> Government intervention in the marketing and pricing of food products has probably been marked by the most serious deficiencies. In this field, governments have been caught up in a conflict between the political necessity they have evidently felt to keep food prices low for urban consumers and the need to stimulate domestic production of food. Reconciliation of this conflict has been virtually impossible.[16]

The widely shared consensus that urban political pressures are at the root of the problem of agricultural policy in modern Africa has disturbing implications: It suggests that it may be difficult to create a social coalition that would facilitate reform of this key policy.

African governments have frequently accompanied the tendency toward price suppression for staple foodstuffs with systems of uniform or pan-territorial pricing. This has introduced further harmful distortions into the market for food staples. It has, for example, added further to the disincentive for food producers who are located adjacent to urban markets. Since food staples are relatively expensive to transport (their value per unit is low), uniform national pricing in effect compels nearby producers to absorb the transportation costs of farmers who are located at greater distances from their markets. Nearby farmers are thereby discouraged from growing food staples, while those in more remote regions, whose transportation costs are indirectly subsidized, have little or no incentive to shift to crops of higher value per unit. Moreover, since government-set prices remain constant throughout the year, farmers tend to concentrate their sales to government purchasing agencies during the period immediately following the harvest. This can easily result in severely overtaxing purchasing, processing, and storage facilities during the harvest period, while offering farmers no incentive to hold back a portion of their production for the off-season, when national supplies might be lower.

Since it is impossible to measure the cumulative impact of these distortions, it would be premature to suggest that liberalization of food-marketing systems would result in food self-sufficiency for African countries, but there is compelling reason to believe that they could move substantially closer to this goal. At the same time, the concerns of those who fear that a freer food market would inevitably lead to urban inflation can be relatively easily accommodated. Food-aid programs could play a critical role in moderating the short-term impact of price liberalization until such time as improved producer prices bring about an additional supply of locally produced staples.

In the long run, price liberalization could well result in lower real prices for basic food items than those that currently prevail. As statist systems of food distribution have become less and less efficient, greater and greater proportions of Africa's urban populations have been compelled to obtain their food supplies in informal markets, where prices are driven up by the need to operate in an extralegal fashion. It is to be expected that once informal marketing systems are fully legalized, the prevailing prices will fall.

Currency Overvaluation

A second governmental policy that has contributed to the present agricultural crisis is the widespread tendency toward currency overvaluation.[17] The practice of setting official exchange rates at levels far higher than would prevail if there were free convertibility has set in motion a number of powerful disincentives to agricultural productivity. Perhaps its greatest impact has been to tilt the internal terms of trade massively in favor of the cities and against the countryside.[18] Currency overvaluation tends to lower the cost of living of urban consumers by cheapening imported goods, including foodstuffs, while raising the prices of high-demand items in the countryside. It has thus contributed to major economic anomalies. Africa's upper- and middle-class elites have grown increasingly accustomed to a material lifestyle that includes a host of artificially cheapened imported goods, ranging from automobiles to expensive household appliances and luxury items. Since the foreign exchange utilized to finance these imports is typically generated by agricultural exports, overvaluation penalizes the rural producer by just about the same amount it rewards the urban consumer.

The impact of currency overvaluation on agricultural exports has been disastrous. The producer price of export crops is normally a direct function of the conversion rate between foreign and domestic currencies: the greater the overvaluation, the fewer units of local currency per unit sold are realized by the agricultural producer. This problem may help explain the severe cash squeeze experienced by many of Africa's export-oriented agricultural marketing boards. To the extent that their income in local currency is a function of the conversion rate, they too are penalized by a policy that overvalues the local currency in relation to the foreign exchange their crops have generated.

Agricultural parastatals in Africa have generally found ways to compensate for the overvaluation penalty by passing the tax on to the farms. The most common methods include not paying farmers or making only partial delayed payments. And African governments concerned about the political loyalties of parastatal personnel invariably make up for parastatal operating deficits through supplemental budgetary appropriations. The final result is that it is only the producers who really suffer from the artificial exchange rate. Since their prices remain low, and since governments rarely seem to feel that it would be as worthwhile to subsidize the growers as the parastatals, the net effect of overvaluation is an income transfer from rural farmers to the urban middle classes.

Overvaluation has also resulted in an indirect rise in the price levels of consumer goods and vital necessities purchased in the countryside. As one of the building blocks in the industrial policy of import substitution, the intent of overvaluation has been to encourage the growth of urban industries by lowering their costs for capital goods, raw materials, and spare parts. Despite the availability of artificially cheapened inputs, these industries have tended to be inefficient, high-cost producers. To a very large degree, however, the goods produced in these industries are of special importance to rural consumers. These goods include such basic household items as kitchen utensils, cooking stoves, and lamps; such important personal items as cotton cloth and soap; and such vital agricultural implements as hoes and ploughs. Since imported substitutes for these goods are not available or are available only at high price levels induced by protective tariffs, rural consumers are compelled to acquire the more expensive (and frequently lower quality) local items.

Although currency overvaluation theoretically lowers the cost of imported agricultural inputs such as fertilizers, equipment and pesticides, its practical effect has been entirely the opposite. The reason is not difficult to discern. When a local currency is overvalued, the most immediate effect is that foreign exchange becomes scarce because demand is high for imported products bought with local currency. As a result, foreign currency must itself be rationed. In this process, as in so many others, the tendency of African governments has been to favor urban consumers at the expense of rural producers. Thus, though imported inputs are technically inexpensive, there is an extreme shortage of supply. This generates the need for a system of rationing, and, when this occurs, the real prices paid by consumers are substantially higher, a result of intensive demand pressures. The rationing process also gives rise to serious distributional inequities, since large capital-intensive farmers are in a stronger position to bid for vital inputs than are smallholders or peasant producers.

Overvalued exchange rates have also had a serious impact as a disincentive to local food production. Since the costs of foreign foodstuffs are artificially lowered (along with those of other imported goods), it has become increasingly commonplace for Western grains such as wheat, corn, and rice to be less expensive in African markets than the same items, or equivalent staples, produced by local farmers. Sometimes the price structure of imported grains is lowered still further because they have entered the country on concessional terms as food aid, rather than as direct sales. Since it is all but impossible for donor agencies and African governments to prevent food from assistance programs entering local markets, food aid sometimes competes directly with local production. Occasionally, this competition has been actively encouraged by governments that are interested in holding urban food costs at the lowest possible levels.[19] But the resulting disincentive effect on local producers has often been so great that it completely discourages their production for urban markets and launches a cycle of ever-increasing dependency on food imports.

When this process is under way, the difficulty of rebuilding local food production systems is compounded. Once local food producers have withdrawn from markets that are dominated by artificially cheapened imports, and have become accustomed to trading their goods in informal or illegal cross-border markets, it becomes extremely difficult to recapture their involvement in the official national economy. At the same time, Africa's urban consumers frequently become acclimated, in terms of diet as well as price, to inexpensive foreign grains. Once this has occurred, governments that are more concerned about short-term political stability than with the economic recovery of the peasant sector find it all but impossible to disengage from exchange-rate practices that undermine the livelihood of their rural populations.

Parastatal Corporations

The principal means African governments have used for regulating and administering their agricultural sectors has been the creation of a system of official agricultural marketing boards. As parastatal corporations, these marketing boards are typically given a legalized monopoly over acquiring, processing, and vending stipulated agricultural commodities. If a crop has been given over to the authority of an official marketing agency, it is generally illegal for a producer to sell more than a specified amount to any other agency, or for a purchaser (individual or commercial) to obtain a supply elsewhere. In many cases, the agricultural marketing boards are also entrusted with the responsibility for carrying out a number of critically important service functions, such as credit provision, the distribution of inputs, and research on improved methods of crop husbandry. The marketing-board system was originated during the colonial era to conduct the international vending of export crops, but official marketing agencies are as common today in the field of domestic food production. Since it has become increasingly commonplace for African governments to establish an official marketing agency for any crop of economic significance, many countries have up to a dozen of these parastatal corporations operating in the rural sector.

Among contemporary observers of African agriculture, there is a close-to-unanimous consensus that the performance of the agricultural marketing boards has been abysmal, and that they are among the major reasons for the continent's agricultural decline. They seem almost universally to be characterized by waste, inefficiency, mismanagement, and corruption. The list of documented administrative shortcomings of many agricultural marketing boards is so extensive that it is sometimes surprising that they function at all. Standards of accountability are woefully inadequate or nonexistent, with the result that it is often impossible to determine how much revenue is being expended for a particular purpose over a given period of time. Bribery of parastatal personnel is commonplace. Since parastatal officials have an economic monopoly enforced by the police powers of the state, they have an almost limitless opportunity to extort illicit payments from farmers under their jurisdiction. Since parastatals are sometimes viewed by political leaders as instruments of patronage, they have been subjected to gross overstaffing. Indeed, the selection and promotion of key parastatal administrators is sometimes based on political criteria, which have little to do with administrative performance. Parastatal salary scales and fringe benefits are often extremely generous, sometimes exceeding those available in the civil service by a wide margin. There are virtually no incentives for efficient performance or penalties for maladministration.

The end result of these shortcomings is that parastatal operating margins (the percentage of income from crop sales absorbed in internal operations) are often ruinously high, leaving little income with which to make payments to the producers. Indeed, there have been some cases in which the managerial expenses of agricultural parastatals actually exceeded the return they received from market sales! As a result, they have sometimes fallen far behind in their payments to farmers, in some cases delaying payment by as much as two or three years; or they have made only partial payment or have paid in worthless scrip that farmers find they cannot use in the marketplace. Administrative inefficiency and financial corruption have generated a deeply strained relationship between the agricultural parastatals and their producer clienteles, a factor that, in itself, has led innumerable farmers to abandon official state-controlled markets for the greater freedom and flexibility of the informal marketplace. Perhaps more importantly, the compulsion to deal with inefficient and extortionary bureaucracies has operated as a fundamental disincentive to increased agricultural production.

Import Substitution

The policy of industrialization through import substitution has had disastrous effects on the agricultural sector. The ongoing capital requirements of the new industries have proved to be so great that agriculture has been virtually starved of the capital necessary for its own modernization. In retrospect, it is surprising that so little attention was paid to the amount of hard currency that would be required to launch a series of consumer-goods industries and to keep them supplied with up-to-date capital equipment, spare parts, and imported raw materials. But it may be useful to recall that agricultural commodities had enjoyed an unprecedented price boom during the mid-1950s, following the Korean War, and that, as a result, African countries came to independence with foreign-exchange reserves that appeared to be fully adequate. Of the many constraints on industrial strategy that were initially considered, the most important seemed to revolve around the lack of skilled personnel, and the absence or relative weakness of the entrepreneurial class. Very few developmental experts considered foreign-exchange constraints a major obstacle to successful industrialization, perhaps in part because import substitution was considered to be a method of conserving, not expending, foreign exchange.

The principal sources of hard currency for financing Africa's new industries were the agricultural marketing boards dealing with export crops. So, almost universally, African governments hungry for the wherewithal to launch an industrial revolution turned to marketing-board reserves as their principal source of investment capital. The operative idea was that the difference between the prices that the marketing boards paid their farmer clienteles and the prices they received on world markets would be used as venture capital for the new industrial sector. This decision converted the marketing boards from rural-oriented institutions, whose principal mandate was the economic vitality of export-oriented agriculture, to the financial launching pad for urban industrial development, a wholly new function.

Siphoning off marketing-board reserves bears a great deal of the blame for the steady deterioration of Africa's position as a leading exporter of agricultural commodities. As the capital needs of urban industries grew, producer prices for export crops had to be reduced to a lower and lower percentage of the world-market price so as to replenish the marketing-board reserves. The capital requirements of urban industries also reduced the capacity of the marketing boards to conduct their other assigned functions, such as research and the provision of services. Within a few years, the marketing boards were converted from allies of the rural producer to adversaries, exploiting the productivity of export farmers but delivering little, if anything, in return.

Africa's attempt to industrialize through import substitution has now been generally acknowledged as a costly experiment that has failed dismally in the majority of cases. Michael Roemer is expressing a fairly widespread sentiment in the following criticism:

> Economists have universally condemned this strategy as typically practiced. Yet, although it is losing favor everywhere, it is still widely in use in Africa. The fundamental problem with import-substitution strategies in Africa is that they focus development efforts on industrialization, although it is agriculture that remains the base of the economy and that employs the great majority of workers.[20]

Import-substituting industries in Africa have been a continuing burden on the earnings from agricultural exports; to this degree, they have prevented reinvestment in the agricultural sector, gradually depleting its capital base and diminishing its capacity to respond to changing conditions of demand in the world market.

Lack of flexibility to respond to short-term market niches has sometimes been cited as a significant reason why Africa has fallen so far behind other developing areas in maintaining its share of the world's agricultural trade. The roots of this problem can also be traced to import substitution. An export orientation requires that there be considerable efficiency and mobility in the internal allocation of productive resources. Import substitution by its very nature defeats this requirement. It commits vast resources for long periods of time to industries that are assumed to be uncompetitive in international markets. Import-substituting industries have, for example, absorbed capital that might more effectively have been used to finance a wide variety of activities that would have helped boost agricultural exports. Import substitution has contributed directly to capital starvation in the countryside, and therefore to the lack of resources available to develop agricultural products that would be competitive in the international marketplace.

Protected industrial development has also been an important contributing factor in shifting the internal terms of trade within African countries against the rural sector. Because of their lack of efficiency, import-substituting industries have had to be given a high level of protection from foreign competition. Thus, the goods that they produce are almost invariably much higher priced than consumer goods available from abroad; at the same time, consumer goods have now become an integral part of Africa's rural lifestyle.

As the effective incentive has fallen, so has the level of marketed production. In the most extreme cases, export farmers have turned away from export crops that are subject to government controls and have chosen to cultivate unregulated commodities. Since these are typically food items for local consumption, the impact on export volumes and hence on export earnings has been extremely serious.

CONCLUSION

The internalist position is rarely presented by its advocates as a rebuttal of the importance of external factors. But there is an implicit position on the dialogue between these two distinct analytic frameworks: that is, that until policy reform has taken place, and the economic distortions associated with inappropriate policies have been removed, it is impossible to assess the weight of external factors. The remainder of this volume can be read as an attempt to validate that particular premise. It attempts to demonstrate that Kenya's agricultural policies are sufficiently defensible on economic grounds that its agricultural sector is probably performing about as well as can be expected under current world-market conditions. The constraints on Kenya's future economic growth are primarily external, deriving either from the broad international economic environment or from the virtual economic collapse of adjacent countries. For Kenya's economic performance to improve substantially, there would need to be dramatic economic changes outside its national boundaries.

Tanzania, on the other hand, makes the case for internalist thinkers. It offers a perfect example of the ways in which inappropriate agricultural policy can produce disastrous economic results. At the present time, there is simply no way to measure the effects of adverse international influences on its economic performance. Its precipitous economic decline can be explained almost wholly on the basis of extremely questionable policy decisions in such areas as exchange-rate management, commodity pricing, parastatal management, and industrial strategy. Tanzania's economic performance can be dramatically improved through policy reforms in these areas.

NOTES

1. Robert Bates has authored numerous works that develop this position, but his single most influential study is *Markets and States in Tropical Africa: The Political Basis of Agricultural Policies* (University of California Press, Berkeley and Los Angeles, 1981). Elliot Berg was the principal author of the widely cited World Bank report entitled *Accelerated Development in Sub-Saharan Africa: An Agenda for Action* (The World Bank, Washington, D.C., 1981).

2. Michael Lipton, *Why Poor People Stay Poor: Urban Bias in World Development* (Harvard University Press, Cambridge, MA, 1976).

3. John C. de Wilde, *Agriculture, Marketing and Pricing in Sub-Saharan Africa* (Crossroads Press, Los Angeles, 1984).

4. Lipton, *Why Poor People Stay Poor.*

5. Ibid., pp. 61–62.

6. Ibid., pp. 66–67.

7. Ibid., p. 296.

8. Ibid., pp. 64-65.

9. Keith Hart, *The Political Economy of West African Agriculture* (Cambridge University Press, Cambridge, England, 1982), p. 102.

10. De Wilde, *Agriculture, Marketing and Pricing,* p. 3.

11. Manfred Bienefeld, "Analyzing the Politics of African State Policy: Some Thoughts on Robert Bates' Work," *IDS Bulletin* 17, no. 1 (January 1986), p. 6.

12. David B. Truman, *The Governmental Process: Political Interests and Public Opinion* (Alfred A. Knopf, New York, 1959).

13. For an excellent analysis of state growth as a deterrent to agricultural development, see David B. Abernethy, "Bureaucratic Growth and Economic Decline in Sub-Saharan Africa: A Drama in Twelve Acts." In *Africa's Development Challenges and the World Bank,* ed. Stephen Commins (Boulder, CO, Lynne Rienner, 1988).

14. David B. Abernethy, "Bureaucratic Growth and Economic Stagnation in Sub-Saharan Africa," (Unpublished manuscript, Stanford University, n.d.), p. 16.

15. Bates, *Markets and States in Tropical Africa,* p. 29.

16. De Wilde, *Agriculture, Marketing and Pricing,* p. 118.

17. Francophone African countries that use the CFA franc as their national currency are, of course, a major exception to this generalization. This currency is directly convertible to the French franc.

18. For one discussion of this problem, see Ravi Gulhati *et al., Exchange Rate Policies in Eastern and Southern Africa 1965–1983,* World Bank Staff Working Papers no. 720 (Washington, D.C., 1985).

19. For a full discussion of this problem, see Tony Jackson, *Against the Grain: The Dilemma of Project Food Aid* (Oxfam, Oxford, 1982). See especially Ch. 8, "Project Food Aid as Competition with Local Food Production," pp. 85–93.

20. Michael Roemer, "Economic Development in Africa: Performance Since Independence, and a Strategy for the Future," *Daedalus* (Spring 1982) p. 132.

·PART 2·

·4·
The Statistical Picture

Chapter 4 begins the second part of this volume, which examines the agricultural performance of two African countries in order to illuminate the differences between them. Kenya and Tanzania have been chosen for several reasons, but principally because they share a sufficient number of basic similarities for comparison of the effects of agricultural policy to make sense. Some of these similarities have been well stated by Joel Barkan:

> Similar in population, these two neighbors share a common and related history dating back to the precolonial era, a common culture and ethnic makeup, and a common set of geographical and natural conditions that bear on the day-to-day lives of their people. These shared experiences gave rise to two states that, at the formal end of the colonial period, were fundamentally alike in terms of the the structure of their political economies, and their capacity to become viable and independent national entities.[1]

Kenya and Tanzania are roughly equal in population, for example, each numbering just over 20 million persons. And since they are adjacent, neither can be said to possess a locational advantage vis-à-vis the world markets to which they both export.

These two countries also share similar flora, both producing essentially the same set of export crops and food staples.[2] Since both are overwhelmingly dependent on the export of coffee and tea, it can be argued that they confront an identical international environment. Since both countries are possessed of a wide and similar range of agroecological zones, they are also able to cultivate a large number of secondary export and food crops. Tanzania and Kenya have both been able to export sisal, pyrethrum, cashew nuts, and horticultural products, though in differing amounts. In each, maize is the principal food staple, though each also grows large volumes of rice, wheat, and millet to supplement maize for local consumption. Perhaps most importantly, both countries are extremely poor, dependent on agriculture to provide economic livelihood for at least 80 percent of their population. Indeed both have been classified by the UN as among the world's poorest countries, falling into the category that some observers now refer to as the "fourth world."

It would be misleading, however, to suggest that this comparison involves wholly like national entities. No two countries are identical, and there are a number of major historical and politicoeconomic differences between Kenya and Tanzania. Of these, at least four stand out: (1) the nature of the settler presence; (2) the countries' legal status during colonial rule; (3) the significance of ethnicity in the contemporary political process; and (4) their different resource endowments.

THE SETTLERS

Far and away the most visible difference between Kenya and Tanzania throughout the colonial period was that Kenya was a British settler colony, founded and developed with the intention that it remain a permanent domicile for an overseas community of migrant British nationals. The British government actively encouraged the process of settler migration by making land available on highly attractive terms to returning British servicemen after both world wars. By the end of the 1950s, there were approximately 30,000 British settlers in Kenya, nearly all of whom regarded themselves as more or less permanent residents. The settlers enjoyed strong ties with the roughly equal number of British colonial administrators, many of whom could be considered settlers, since they looked forward to settling permanently in the country once their term of administrative service ended. The sense of political kinship between the settlers and colonial administrators was extremely strong, and some observers have suggested that local administrators identified more closely with settlers on vital policy issues than with the Colonial Ministry in Great Britain.

The settler factor in Kenya has received so much attention that it sometimes obscures the fact that Tanzania was also, to some degree, a settler society. But in Tanzania, the settler factor was substantially different both in its salience and in its political meaning. Of the roughly 3,000 persons who, between the wars, considered themselves permanent settlers in Tanzania, the vast majority were not British, but German, Italian, or Greek. As a result, their ties to the British colonial administration were weak, and their abilities to influence colonial policy practically negligible. Indeed, when World War II broke out, it became the responsibility of the colonial government in Tanganyika to arrest and imprison Italian and German settlers as potential enemies of Great Britain, an action that meant there was virtually no settler community of significance in the country during the critical period between 1945 and independence in 1966. Thus, when the Tanzanian nationalist movement began to take shape in the mid-1950s, there was no settler opposition to the principle that the country should move smoothly and expeditiously toward independence.

LEGAL STATUS DURING COLONIAL RULE

Kenya and Tanzania were also distinguished by having completely different legal statuses within the British colonial system. Kenya was a British colony, except for a small coastal area that had separate status as a protectorate. During the interwar period, Tanganyika was a League of Nations Mandate and, after World War II, a UN trusteeship territory. The difference in the legal status of the two countries had considerable bearing on the nature of colonial rule.

According to B. T. G. Chidzero, Tanzania's legal status as a ward of the international community afforded it both advantages and disadvantages.[3] The principal advantage of international oversight was that it acted as a liberalizing influence on British colonial policy in the country. British colonialism in Tanganyika was far more benign than in Kenya, affording Tanzanians a much greater degree of political and civil freedoms, including freedom of the press and freedom of association. Indeed, the international presence may even have helped to stimulate the growth of African nationalism, for both the League of Nations and the UN actively encouraged the organized expression of African opinion about political conditions in the country. Chidzero also credits international supervision in Tanganyika with the fact that the settler community there never attained either the numerical size or the political leverage of the Kenyan settler community, as a result, the alienation of African land to make way for European farms was minimal. He concludes:

> the net result is that international trusteeship has generally rendered British rule less a matter of expediency and more a matter of principle and moral obligations, less a function of settler pressure and more geared to the terms of international obligations.[4]

Most importantly, international trusteeship may have accounted for the British colonial administration's resistance to the inclusion of Tanzania in an East African federation dominated by Kenya.

The international factor may also have slowed the pace of private investment in Tanganyika. Chidzero believes it is likely that foreign corporations and individuals were deterred by the fact that UN supervision made Tanzania's steady movement toward independence virtually certain to succeed. Kenya, by contrast, seemed to represent a safer investment opportunity, since the colonial presence there would be of a more long-term nature. Private corporations and individuals contemplating investment in this region of the world would, in other words, have been attacted to Kenya, not only because of its more gentle climate and superior amenities, but because the country's colonial status seemed to lessen the risk involved in investing capital there. If Kenya was more developed economically because it was the chosen residence for permanent British settlers, it was also richer by virtue of having been able to attract a much larger flow of overseas capital investment.

ETHNICITY AND POLITICS

So much has been written about the importance of ethnicity in the Kenyan political process that it would be superfluous here to do more than reiterate the obvious.[5] Suffice it to say that ethnicity has played a far greater role in Kenyan politics, both before and since independence, than it has in Tanzania. Time and time again the key variable in explaining party alignments and realignments, the formation and dissolution of political coalitions, and a variety of political subprocesses (such as administrative appointments) appears to be ethnicity. Nearly every commentary on contemporary Kenyan politics, whether journalistic or academic, calls particular attention to the changing political place and role of such large and powerful ethnic communities as Kikuyu and Luo and, under the present administration, the political rise of Kalenjin communities.

In Tanzania, on the other hand, ethnicity seems conspicuous by its absence. Here, there has never been a serious issue of ethnic domination by one or more ethnic subgroups, and both the nationalist movement and national politics as a whole appear to be remarkably uninfluenced by this factor. Unlike Nairobi, Dar es Salaam is not located in an area identified with the country's most numerous and powerful ethnic community, and, as a result, Tanzania's capital has taken on a conspicuously panethnic quality. The political unity of the country has been positively promoted by several important factors. First, Tanzania has a national language, Swahili, and even though it is not the first language for the majority of Tanzanian citizens, it is spoken and understood sufficiently well to help promote a sense of linguistic unity. Second, and perhaps more important, Tanzania's early postindependence political process was untroubled by the sharp class divisions that became quickly visible in Kenya. Some observers have suggested the reason for this is Tanzania's relatively low level of economic development during the late colonial era.[6]

RESOURCE ENDOWMENTS

From the standpoint of physical resources for agricultural development, the difference between Kenya and Tanzania is overwhelming. It is best stated bluntly: Kenya has an extremely limited land base and Tanzania does not. Although Kenya is about 225,000 square miles in size, roughly two-thirds the square mileage of Tanzania, only a small fraction of this land is suitable for agriculture. Most geographers concur that Kenya's medium- to high-potential agricultural regions amount to about one-fifth of the country's total area; that is, approximately 40,000 to 45,000 square miles. Virtually all of the northern two-thirds of Kenya is arid or semi-arid desert, and much of the rest is either mountainous and forested or within the country's national parks and game reserves. If urban and semi-urban areas are subtracted from the remainder, the land available for agriculture is extremely limited. It is no secret why land scarcity and the politics of landlessness have always been of singularly great importance in the country's political process.

The extreme scarcity of arable land in Kenya cannot be treated entirely as an economic liability. Since the vast majority of the country's high-potential area is geographically concentrated (consisting basically of an irregular, rectangular band about 300 miles wide and about 100 miles north to south), infrastructural development has been a far simpler matter for Kenya than for countries whose fertile areas are more scattered. A given unit of expenditure on infrastructure in Kenya has been able to provide market access for a far larger proportion of the country's marketed production, especially of exportable crops, than has been the case in Tanzania, where virtually separate road systems, involving far greater distances, have had to be built to reach the sisal, cotton, coffee, and tea regions. Tanzania's principal maize-producing areas are similarly scattered, located in the southern and extreme southwestern regions of the country, where population densities are relatively low. It has required still another network of roads to reach the areas of high population density on the eastern coast and along the northern border.

On the other hand, Tanzania seems blessed with an abundance of medium- and high-potential agricultural land; the availability of arable land is not itself a significant constraint on economic development. Vast portions of its 365,000-square-mile area are already under cultivation, and with only minimal adaptation (such as tsetse fly clearance), huge additional regions would become suitable for agricultural purposes. Indeed, it appears that the principal reason that additional land has not been brought under cultivation is that Tanzania does not have a problem of per-capita land availability. Since landlessness is not a social problem, land pressure does not figure prominently in national politics. Because agricultural suitability varies not only with the quality of the soil base but with rainfall amounts and predictability, disease infestation, and access to transportation routes, it would be hazardous to offer a precise comparison of Tanzania's and Kenya's arable land areas. But, at a minimum, Tanzania appears to enjoy an agricultural land base at least several times greater than that of its northern neighbor.

Tanzania's great advantage in arable land area has been offset to some degree by the fact that the most developed agricultural regions are, for the most part, near the country's borders, at some remove from both its capital city and its major ports. Its major exportable commodities are grown in the northwestern regions of the country bordering Kenya and Uganda. Coffee is grown in the Mount Kilimanjaro and Pare Mountains areas, adjacent to Kenya, and even more distantly, outside Bukoba, in the West Lake area, near the southern border of Uganda. Similarly, cotton is grown principally in the area south of Mwanza, near the border of Zaire. The principal food-growing regions seem also to be closer to neighbor countries, such as Zambia and Malawi, than to Tanzania's own important urban centers, such as Dar es Salaam, Tanga, Arusha, and Moshi. Because of the considerable physical distances involved, transportation of agricultural commodities has always been a source of greater difficulty for Tanzania than for Kenya. But the distance factor could easily be exaggerated, because Tanzania's road and railway systems have deteriorated badly since independence, whereas Kenya's have been considerably improved.

The critical question is whether these differences, important as they were and are, help account for the widely varying development policies these countries have adopted since independence. This issue could be debated at great length, since it involves nothing less than the extent to which the postindependence politicoeconomic trajectory of an African country is determined by its colonial legacy. To answer this question for Kenya and Tanzania, it is useful to return to Barkan's astute analysis. In his judgment, these two countries shared a common range of economic options when they became independent. Each was in a strong position to make its own determination of the meaning of national development, and its own choices about the strategies by which development might be pursued. Moreover, in the years immediately following independence, they adopted strikingly similar political goals and remarkably similar means of achieving them.

> Both commenced a rapid expansion and Africanization of the civil service by building on the administrative framework established during the colonial period. Both sought to accelerate the rate of economic growth via heavy infusions of foreign aid and foreign private investment, and both sought to maintain relatively smooth relations with the United Kingdom . . . while at the same time professing a foreign policy of nonalignment.[7]

Barkan's analysis makes it clear that the diverse development strategies of Kenya and Tanzania are the product of postindependence political choice. The same interpretation applies to the patterns of economic performance associated with those strategies.

Among scholars of African development, these two countries have become virtually synonymous with fundamentally different approaches to development. Since attaining independence in the early 1960s, Kenya has followed a market-oriented development strategy, emphasizing the importance of private land ownership and the development of a sizable class of independent smallholders. Since the early 1980s, Kenya has sought assiduously to bring its major economic policies into close alignment with recommendations made by the economic advisors of the World Bank and IMF. Although there is a considerable amount of state involvement in and control of the agricultural sector, as there is elsewhere in its economic system, Kenya has generally come to be considered one of Africa's leading examples of the "capitalist" strategy of economic development. This may reflect its continuing emphasis on the private ownership of agricultural land,

and on the legitimacy of the private sector as a vehicle for national economic growth.

Tanzania, by contrast, has received a lot of attention for its choice, in 1967, of a socialist approach to development. The former president, Julius Nyerere, has received international acclaim for his personal articulation of the country's socialist program. Tanzania's development strategy placed primary emphasis, until the mid-1970s, on the creation of socialist villages, in which land would be collectively held and production would be collectively organized. Its approach to development has also emphasized state ownership of major business concerns, including banks, insurance companies, large manufacturing industries, and international trading firms. Although Tanzania does have a small private sector, its growth has been strongly discouraged by the government. The general orientation of Tanzanian authorities has been that developing private enterprise is inimical to the well-being of the people.

These different development policies have produced strikingly different economic results. Kenya has emerged as one of sub-Saharan Africa's most conspicuous success stories and today features perhaps the most advanced and complex agricultural sector of any independent African country. Since its independence in December 1963, Kenya has enjoyed consistent agricultural growth and today ranks among the world's leading exporters of coffee and tea. Tanzania, by contrast, has experienced declining agricultural production and, since the early 1980s, has registered negative rates of growth in the agricultural sector. Since the country's most precipitous decline has been in the area of export-oriented agriculture, earnings of hard currency have concomitantly fallen off. By causing a reduction in the country's import capacity, including the capacity to import industrial inputs, falling export volumes have, in turn, depressed industrial productivity.

WHAT DO THE STATISTICS REVEAL?

The following tables and graphs, which display production and yield figures for some of the principal crops grown in Kenya and Tanzania, may help to illustrate the key differences in their agricultural performance. The conventional categorization of crops in Africa distinguishes between cash (or export) crops and food crops. To present a fairly comprehensive portrait of agricultural performance in Kenya and Tanzania, it would be useful to have a slightly more elaborate set of categories. The statistical and graphic materials presented below are grouped into three broad categories: (1) export crops; (2) "industrial" or import-substituting crops; (3) food crops (subdivided into preferred and nonpreferred grains). Four crops have been selected for statistical and graphic presentation under each of these categories: sisal, cashew nuts, coffee, and tea as exports; cotton, sugar, tobacco, and barley as industrials; and corn, wheat, millet, and sorghum as food grains.

Export Crops

The overwhelming difference between the agricultural performances of Kenya and Tanzania is in the area of export crops. Tanzania's agricultural performance fully merits the term "disaster," while Kenya's exhibits the country's most dramatic accomplishments. The significance of differential performance in this agricultural sector cannot be overstated. The heart of Tanzania's contemporary economic crisis is an acute scarcity of foreign exchange; this is directly attributable to the country's woeful performance in the area of agricultural exports.

Sisal

During the late colonial and early postcolonial periods, sisal was, measured in terms of foreign-exchange earnings, Tanzania's principal export crop. Throughout the 1960s, Tanzania was regularly producing approximately 200,000 tons of this commodity for export. As Table 4.1 reveals, sisal production had fallen to less than one-fourth of this amount by the mid-1980s, and the downward production trend portended even further declines. Sisal has never been a significant export commodity for Kenya, and its production of this commodity has basically remained stagnant—at or about the 50,000-metric-ton/year level since the immediate postindependence period. Because of falling world prices, neither country has had a strong incentive to emphasize sisal production. While this factor may help account for Kenya's indifferent performance, it does not fully account for the precipitous downward trend in Tanzania.

Sisal may well represent the clearest casualty of Tanzania's experiment in socialist development. Approximately 50 percent of Tanzania's sisal estates were nationalized in the late 1960s and placed under the jurisdiction of the Tanzania Sisal Authority. Most observers concur that poor management on the nationalized estates was the principal factor accounting for the precipitous decline in production. By the mid 1980s, the remaining private plantations were producing a vastly disproportionate share of the country's sisal crop, with one estate, Amboni, accounting for about 30 percent of total production.

Cashew Nuts

During the period immediately following independence, Tanzania was able to boost cashew nut production dramatically, from about 50,000 metric tons per year to more than 125,000 metric tons per year in the early to mid-1970s (see Table 4.2). Its success with this crop was so great that in 1974 cashew nuts briefly assumed a position as the country's leading foreign-exchange earner. By the mid-1980s, these achievements had been erased and the country's annual production of cashew nuts was lower than at any time since independence.

Cashew nut production in Tanzania may be counted among the conspicuous casualties of the country's efforts at socialist development. The production decline can be accounted for almost entirely by the government's program of moving small-scale peasant producers into socialist villages. In pursuing this program, the Tanzanian government moved large numbers of cashew nut producers into villages so far distant from the cashew groves that it became extremely difficult for the growers to harvest their crop or to attend to tree husbandry during the off-season. John de Wilde describes the problem:

> A survey conducted by the Ministry of Agriculture in 1980/81 in Mtwara, Lindi and the Coast regions (which accounted for 88% of output) showed that 13% of cashew plots had been abandoned, that only 25% were within a one mile radius of farm houses, 56% within a two miles radius and 17% beyond four miles.[8]

The contrast in Kenya's production of this crop is astonishing. Between 1961 and 1984, Kenya increased cashew nut production fivefold, an average yearly increase of 14 percent.

Coffee and Tea

Coffee and tea, presently the major foreign-exchange earners for both Kenya and Tanzania, present similar contrasts and may be considered together (see Tables 4.3 and 4.4). Kenya has vastly outperformed Tanzania, achieving enormous increases in annual output of these two high-value crops. Significantly, Kenya and Tanzania produced approximately equal volumes of coffee during the late 1960s, approximately 50,000 to 60,000 metric tons per year. By the mid-1980s, Kenya had increased coffee production about two and one-half times, to 120,000 metric tons per year. In addition, Kenya had gained an enviable market position because of the high quality of its coffee.

Tanzania simply failed to keep pace. Despite a vast inpouring of capital and technical assistance by foreign donors, its annual coffee production had actually dropped somewhat by the mid-1980s. Just as significantly from the standpoint of export earnings, Tanzania was experiencing great difficulty in maintaining the quality of its coffee. During the three-year period from 1977/78 to 1980/81 alone, the proportion of Tanzanian coffee production in above-average grades fell from 9 percent to less than 3 percent.[9]

Tea is the single crop that most clearly illustrates the production disparity between the two countries. From the mid-1960s to the mid-1980s, Kenya increased its annual output of tea almost sixfold, from about 25,000 metric tons per year to nearly 150,000 metric tons per year—an annual increase of almost 11 percent. Tanzania was also able to achieve a sizable production increase during this period, increasing its output from about 7,000 metric tons per year to about 18,000 metric tons. While this may appear commendable viewed in percentage terms, it is less impressive as an aggregate amount. Over a period of nearly twenty years, during which

Tanzania was receiving considerable amounts of donor assistance for tea production, and despite the fact that Tanzania has highly favorable growing conditions for tea, total annual production was increased by only slightly more than 10,000 tons.

Industrial Crops

The term "industrial crops" is used here to designate those agricultural commodities that sustain an important domestic import-substituting industry: cotton for the textile industry; sugar for the baking and confectionery industries; tobacco for the cigarette industry; and barley for the brewing industry. The role of agriculture in import substitution is not often recognized, but successful cultivation of crops in this category can contribute not only to significant foreign-exchange conservation through import reduction but also to the growth of an industrial sector that utilizes locally producible raw materials. In this category of crops, Kenya has significantly outperformed Tanzania, though the differences are slightly less striking than in the case of exportable commodities.

Cotton

Between 1966 and 1985, Kenya's cotton production more than tripled, growing from about 4,000 metric tons per year to 13,000 metric tons in 1985/86 (see Table 4.5). Despite a scarcity of suitable land—much of Kenya's cotton must be cultivated in semi-arid regions—this period saw an annual production increase of about 7.3 percent and an annual yield increase of nearly 4 percent. Tanzanian cotton production reflected an opposite trend, falling from 78,000 metric tons in 1966/67 to less than 50,000 metric tons in 1985/86, a drop of nearly 40 percent. There is an odd irony in these figures. Kenya's increase in cotton production fueled a boom in the textile industry; production capacity substantially outstripped the supply of locally produced cotton, causing a need for imports even as crop output was surging. Because of Tanzania's acute foreign-exchange crisis, occasioned in large measure by the collapse of the country's export crops, there was a sharp decline in the production capacity of the country's textile industry. As a result, Tanzania was compelled to become a cotton exporter even during an era in which local production fell by more than one-third.

Sugar

Over the same twenty-year period, Kenya increased sugar production about sixfold, from 655,000 metric tons in 1966/67 to 3,910,000 metric tons in 1984/85 (see Table 4.6). Tanzanian sugar production failed to double during the same period, increasing from about 900,000 metric tons in the mid-1960s to only about 1,400,000 metric tons in the mid-1980s.

Sugar offers an excellent example of the extent to which changes in the international marketplace can be so great that a country becomes the victim of its own success. Kenya invested heavily in expanding its sugar industry—both production and refining capacities—in the early 1970s, at a time when the world price of sugar was extremely high (approaching U.S. $0.25 per pound in 1973). The price was so high that it tempted Kenya to expend considerable foreign exchange to import capital goods for sugar production. Under these conditions, investment in sugar production appeared to be a prudent policy option. By the mid-1980s, however, global overproduction, combined with the increased use of corn fructose as an industrial substitute, had caused the world price of sugar to plummet to a fraction of its former level (about U.S. $0.06 per pound in 1985). Since Kenya's production costs are considerably above the present world price level, there has been heavy criticism by World Bank officials, who now believe that this is an uneconomic crop for the country and that Kenya should shift its resources to other commodities.

Tobacco

Kenya increased tobacco production nearly fiftyfold between 1966 and 1984, and though this increase came on top of an extremely small base, it is nevertheless useful as an indicator of the sort of production gains that can occur when smallholder farmers are encouraged to produce a high-value crop under highly favorable economic conditions (see Table 4.7). Tanzania's production trend for tobacco is a reflection of the country's overall economic malaise. Between the mid-1960s and the mid-1970s, Tanzanian smallholders were able to increase tobacco production from about 5,000 metric tons per year to more than 18,000 metric tons per year, a growth of 260 percent. This increase came about partially because farmers were able to trade tobacco relatively freely in parallel markets, which operated openly despite the government's efforts to assert pricing and marketing controls. By the late 1970s, however, acute shortages of inputs needed for curing the tobacco leaf had taken a severe toll, and production dropped to 10,000 tons per year, about 53 percent of its level only eight years earlier.

Barley

Kenya's success in bringing about rapid increases in barley production to support the growth of its brewing industry has been so great that this crop could, with only slight exaggeration, be considered under the export category (see Table 4.8). During the mid-1980s, Kenya became a significant exporter of beer, its popular Tusker brand reaching the European and U.S. markets in early 1987. Between 1961 and 1984, Kenya's barley production increased more than sixfold, to well over 80,000 metric tons per year. Because Tanzanian barley production began from a much smaller base, its increase was substantially greater in percentage terms. But the most significant figure for this crop is average yearly change. Over the twenty-three-year period covered by FAO statistics, Kenya's average yearly increase was well over 3,000 metric tons. Tanzania's average increase, despite a large unfilled demand for beer, was only about 200 metric tons per year.

Food Crops: Preferred and Nonpreferred Grains

Most analyses of food production in African countries treat grains as a homogenous category and do not distinguish between preferred and nonpreferred varieties. While this approach can be defended from a caloric and nutritional standpoint, it has a serious shortcoming from the standpoint of an effort to assess agrarian performance. An important qualitative dimension of a country's agricultural success or failure has to do with the degree to which it can provide its citizens with the food items they enjoy and prefer, as opposed to those that are utilized because the preferred items are in short supply. In Kenya and Tanzania, corn is the basic preferred food staple, though wheat has become increasingly popular, especially among urban consumers. Millet and sorghum, on the other hand, are not preferred by either rural or urban consumers; their consumption tends to reflect the fact that, as drought-resistant crops, they tend to be more easily available during periods of climatic or economic difficulty.

A major word of warning is in order with respect to the accuracy of the available statistics on food-grain production in these countries. The figures presented are susceptible to considerable inaccuracy and thus must be treated with great caution. Whereas a country's total production of export and industrial crops can be crosschecked in several ways, the total volume of its food crops cannot be easily estimated or verified. A certain percentage of a country's grain production is consumed at home, by peasant households; since this percentage is subject to widely varying estimates, the aggregate amount of household production cannot be accurately measured. Indeed, where official pricing and marketing systems are in place, as in Kenya and Tanzania, peasant households frequently develop a vested interest in concealing their production figures from both national and international agencies. Much domestically produced grain in these countries is sold in parallel markets, in order to avoid official marketing and price controls; a substantial proportion is sold across national borders. Although the figures presented below have been checked insofar as possible for accuracy and internal consistency, they should be treated as broad indicators of performance rather than as precise measurements.[10]

Corn and Wheat

The difference in agricultural performance between Kenya and Tanzania appears to narrow considerably when domestic food-grains are taken into account (see Tables 4.9 and 4.10). Although Kenya's production figures have remained consistently higher than Tanzania's for both corn and wheat, Tanzania seems clearly to have enjoyed a higher rate of increase for both these commodities than has Kenya, especially since the mid-1970s, when the government shifted producer prices to encourage higher output of food items. Tanzania's success in encouraging rapid increases in corn production was especially dramatic after 1975. By the mid-1980s, there were strong indications that it would soon overtake Kenya with respect to this commodity.

The picture for wheat is slightly different. Tanzania succeeded in increasing total wheat production by a slightly higher percentage than did Kenya but, as in the case of barley, it had begun from a very low base. Thus, though its percentage figures appear commendable, its total production of wheat remained low. The more significant and revealing figure is average increase per year. Here, the difference is both striking and in Kenya's favor. Throughout the twenty-one-year period from 1966 to 1987, Kenya was able to achieve an average annual increase of well over 5,000 metric tons of wheat per year. Tanzania's average annual increase, despite very heavy assistance from the government of Canada, was only about 1,700 tons per year.

Wheat production and consumption have important theoretical significance in analyses of the relationship between agriculture and development in Third World nations, because wheat is increasingly not only the most preferred of the preferred grains but an indicator of rising social affluence. Urban consumers with disposable incomes tend to prefer wheat products, not only because they taste better but because wheat is purchased in final form, as bread or rolls, and thus does not involve additional preparation time in the household. For this reason, it may be instructive briefly to compare total wheat consumption in the two countries. During the three-year period 1984–1986, wheat production in Kenya totaled 723,000 metric tons. Wheat imports during this period amounted to approximately 545,000 metric tons. Combining these figures, we find that total national wheat consumption was approximately 410,000 tons per year. During the same period, Tanzanian wheat production totaled 230,000 metric tons, and wheat imports about 180,000 metric tons. Combining these figures, we find that annual wheat consumption in Tanzania was about 136,000 metric tons, only about one-third that for Kenya.

Millet and Sorghum

If Tanzania has decisively outperformed Kenya in any category, it is with respect to the drought-resistant, nonpreferred grains, millet and sorghum (see Tables 4.11 and 4.12). During the period 1966–1987, Tanzanian production of these two commodities soared dramatically. Its production of millet more than doubled, from about 130,000 metric tons to nearly 300,000 metric tons, and its sorghum production increased more than fourfold, from 165,000 metric tons to 670,000 metric tons. Significantly, Kenya's production of these two crops dropped almost as dramatically. Its millet production halved during this period, from 136,000 metric tons to only about 60,000; its sorghum production in 1987 was only slightly more than one-third of the 1966 level.

Production Trends for Food Grains

The critical question is what conclusion can be drawn from the production trends in food grains. The most easily apparent conclusion is that, during the period 1966–1987, Kenya was less interested in reducing food imports than in shifting its production emphasis from nonpreferred to preferred grains, especially wheat, as an agricultural policy response to rising urban affluence. Tanzania's agricultural emphasis during this same period was to minimize food imports and to reduce the country's foreign-exchange costs for the grains it did have to import, by shifting to drought-resistant crops that required low levels of imported inputs.

Because Kenya's and Tanzania's national priorities were so different, it is difficult to judge which was the more successful. But the figures on which a partial judgment can be made are shown in Table 4.13. During the five-year period 1976–1980, Tanzania's grain imports were higher than Kenya's by an average of slightly more than 50,000 metric tons per year. Stated somewhat differently, Kenya's grain imports during that period were about 72 percent of Tanzania's. This relationship was reversed during the five-year period 1981–1985. During this latter period, Tanzania's grain imports, though increasing by more than 110,000 metric tons per year over the earlier period, were only about 70 percent of Kenya's imports, which had leapt to more than three times their former level.

Tanzania had clearly enjoyed marginal success in pursuing a strategy of food self-sufficiency. But if the figures on food production and imports are viewed in the broader context of those for agricultural exports and commodities for industrial production, the costs of this strategy were unbearably high. For, in order to attain a marginally greater degree of food self-sufficiency than had Kenya, Tanzania had had to endure abysmal performance in the areas of exportable and industrial crops.

NOTES

1. Joel D. Barkan, "Comparing Politics and Public Policy in Kenya and Tanzania," in *Politics and Public Policy in Kenya and Tanzania,* ed. Joel D. Barkan (Praeger, New York, 1984), p. 3.

2. These observations draw heavily on David K. Leonard, "Class Formation and Agricultural Development," in *Politics and Public Policy,* ed. Joel D. Barkan.

3. B. T. G. Chidzero, *Tanganyika and International Trusteeship* (Oxford University Press, London, New York, Toronto, 1961).

4. Chidzero, *Tanganyika,* p. 255.

5. See, for example, the classic volume by Donald Rothchild, *Racial Bargaining in Independent Kenya: A Study of Minorities and Decolonization* (Oxford University Press, London, New York, and Toronto, 1973).

6. For a fuller exposition of these points, see Lionel Cliffe, "The Political System" in *One Party Democracy,* ed. Lionel Cliffe (East African Publishing House,

Nairobi, 1967), pp. 1–20.

7. Barkan, *Politics and Public Policy*, p. 4.

8. John de Wilde, *Agriculture, Marketing and Pricing in Sub-Saharan Africa* (Crossroads Press for African Studies Association and African Studies Center, Los Angeles, 1984), p. 38.

9. Ibid., p. 35.

10. For this reason, the author has chosen not to include figures on rice production in this chapter. The official FAO and USDA/ERS figures on rice production in Tanzania are so inconsistent with that country's official figures for marketed production, rice imports, and total domestic consumption as to lack credibility. The FAO estimate for Tanzanian rice production in 1982 and 1983 is 400,000 metric tons per year. But the Tanzanian National Milling Corporation (NMC) reported total purchase of only about 20,000 metric tons/year for those years; the Tanzanian government estimates total rice consumption at only about 110,000 metric tons per year. In addition, rice imports during these two years were more than 90,000 metric tons per year.

TABLE 4.1 Sisal Production and Yield, 1961-1984

| | PRODUCTION (Thousand Metric Tons) | | | | CALCULATED YIELD (Metric Tons/Hectare) | | | |
| | Kenya | | Tanzania | | Kenya | | Tanzania | |
Year	Amount	Change	Amount	Change	Amount	Change	Amount	Change
1961	63	N/A	201	N/A	0.84	N/A	0.96	N/A
1962	60	-5.5%	218	8.2%	0.85	1.2%	0.99	3.2%
1963	71	19.6%	218	0.1%	0.89	4.7%	0.99	0.1%
1964	67	-5.5%	234	7.3%	0.86	-3.0%	1.03	4.1%
1965	64	-5.0%	218	-6.8%	0.83	-3.8%	1.01	-2.4%
1966	57	-10.5%	225	3.4%	0.87	4.3%	0.87	-14.0%
1967	52	4.0%	220	-2.2%	0.77	-10.9%	0.91	4.9%
1968	50	-2.7%	194	-12.0%	0.90	16.5%	0.78	-14.4%
1969	50	-1.0%	209	8.0%	0.96	6.4%	0.81	4.8%
1970	44	-11.8%	202	-3.4%	0.84	-11.8%	0.81	-0.8%
1971	45	2.0%	181	-10.4%	0.86	2.0%	0.86	6.0%
1972	41	-8.1%	157	-13.4%	0.79	-8.1%	0.76	-11.1%
1973	58	40.9%	155	-0.9%	1.12	40.9%	0.81	6.0%
1974	87	32.9%	143	-8.3%	1.63	31.3%	0.74	-9.2%
1975	44	-49.6%	128	-10.9%	0.91	-44.2%	0.78	6.1%
1976	34	-23.1%	119	-6.9%	0.83	-8.2%	0.95	20.8%
1977	33	-0.4%	105	-11.8%	0.82	-1.7%	0.95	-0.3%
1978	31	-5.9%	92	-12.5%	0.71	-12.6%	0.79	-16.7%
1979	36	13.7%	81	-12.9%	0.84	14.7%	0.82	4.3%
1980	47	28.7%	86	5.6%	0.99	17.8%	0.65	-21.4%
1981	41	-11.9%	74	-14.2%	1.03	4.6%	0.74	14.0%
1982	50	21.1%	61	-17.8%	1.25	21.1%	0.80	8.2%
1983	50	-0.7%	47	-22.5%	1.24	-0.7%	0.78	-1.8%
1984	50	0.6%	45	-4.4%	1.25	0.6%	0.71	-9.7%
Averages	51	1.0%	151	-6.0%	0.95	2.7%	0.84	-0.8%

SOURCE: U.N., Food and Agricultural Organization, Statistical Tape.
NOTE: Minor discrepancies may appear due to rounding.

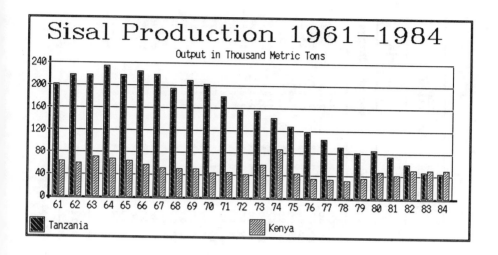

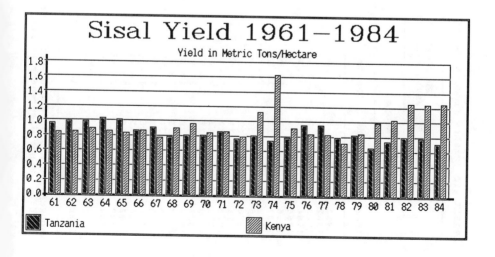

TABLE 4.2 Cashew Production and Yield, 1961-1984

| | PRODUCTION (Thousand Metric Tons) | | | | CALCULATED YIELD (Metric Tons/Hectare) | | | |
| | Kenya | | Tanzania | | Kenya | | Tanzania | |
Year	Amount	Change	Amount	Change	Amount	Change	Amount	Change
1961	3	N/A	50	N/A	10.00	N/A	0.60	N/A
1962	7	133.3%	70	40.0%	10.00	0.0%	0.65	7.6%
1963	7	0.0%	50	-28.6%	10.00	0.0%	0.63	-3.6%
1964	9	34.3%	71	42.0%	10.00	0.0%	0.71	13.6%
1965	9	-4.3%	76	7.0%	10.00	0.0%	0.67	-5.3%
1966	10	10.0%	83	9.5%	9.90	-1.0%	0.69	3.1%
1967	12	19.2%	84	0.7%	9.83	-0.7%	0.60	-13.7%
1968	9	-28.0%	93	10.4%	10.00	1.7%	0.57	-5.2%
1969	7	-15.3%	96	3.5%	9.60	-4.0%	0.52	-7.8%
1970	22	208.3%	107	12.3%	9.87	2.8%	0.58	10.5%
1971	19	-13.5%	126	17.6%	9.85	-0.2%	0.60	4.2%
1972	12	-37.6%	126	-0.7%	9.98	1.4%	0.63	4.3%
1973	15	26.8%	145	15.5%	10.12	1.4%	0.60	-3.7%
1974	16	4.9%	122	-19.2%	9.98	-1.4%	0.61	0.7%
1975	22	35.3%	116	-4.8%	9.82	-1.6%	0.61	0.2%
1976	28	29.6%	84	-27.8%	10.00	1.9%	0.62	1.6%
1977	35	25.0%	93	11.5%	10.00	0.0%	0.58	-7.1%
1978	36	2.9%	68	-26.6%	10.00	0.0%	0.62	8.1%
1979	18	-96.8%	57	-19.9%	7.32	-26.8%	0.60	-4.4%
1980	15	-18.0%	41	-27.5%	7.50	2.5%	0.59	-0.6%
1981	15	0.0%	34	-17.6%	7.50	0.0%	0.60	1.2%
1982	18	20.0%	44	29.9%	7.20	-4.0%	0.61	1.4%
1983	12	-33.3%	32	-27.8%	4.80	-33.3%	0.55	-9.1%
1984	15	20.0%	44	27.3%	6.00	25.0%	0.66	19.0%
Averages	15	14.0%	80	1.2%	9.14	-1.6%	0.61	0.7%

SOURCE: U.N., Food and Agricultural Organization, Statistical Tape.
NOTE: Minor discrepancies may appear due to rounding.

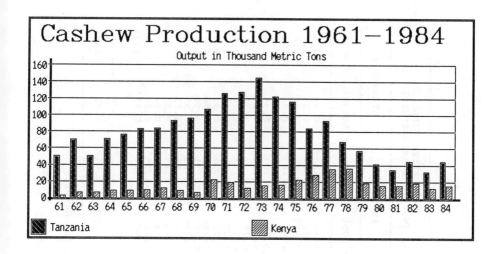

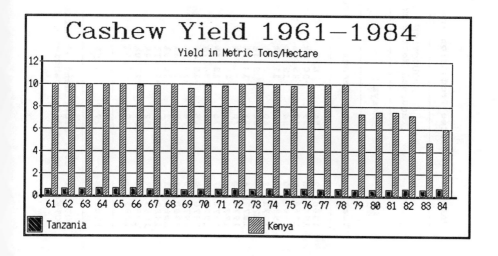

TABLE 4.3 Coffee Production and Yield, 1966–1985

| | PRODUCTION (Thousand Metric Tons) | | | | CALCULATED YIELD (Metric Tons/Hectare) | | | |
| | Kenya | | Tanzania | | Kenya | | Tanzania | |
Year	Amount	Change	Amount	Change	Amount	Change	Amount	Change
1966/67	56	N/A	60	N/A	0.66	N/A	0.44	N/A
1967/68	39	-30.4%	44	-26.7%	0.46	-30.4%	0.36	-18.9%
1968/69	48	23.1%	57	29.5%	0.56	23.7%	0.62	71.8%
1969/70	54	12.5%	46	-19.3%	0.64	12.5%	0.43	-31.3%
1970/71	60	11.1%	57	23.9%	0.71	11.1%	0.52	22.8%
1971/72	60	0.0%	51	-10.5%	0.71	0.0%	0.49	-6.2%
1972/73	62	3.3%	48	-5.9%	0.70	-0.8%	0.51	4.1%
1973/74	71	14.5%	55	14.6%	0.70	-0.3%	0.50	-2.1%
1974/75	70	-1.4%	45	-22.2%	0.70	-0.4%	0.38	-32.2%
1975/76	66	-5.7%	58	28.9%	0.59	-15.1%	0.47	23.7%
1976/77	75	13.6%	48	-17.2%	0.71	19.3%	0.55	18.0%
1977/78	101	34.7%	50	4.2%	0.78	10.0%	0.50	-10.3%
1978/79	85	-15.8%	51	2.0%	0.70	-10.7%	0.50	1.0%
1979/80	74	-14.9%	48	-6.3%	0.62	-12.2%	0.55	8.3%
1980/81	92	24.3%	58	20.8%	0.74	18.5%	0.51	-6.7%
1981/82	102	10.9%	64	10.3%	0.80	9.1%	0.52	1.4%
1982/83	89	-12.7%	58	-9.4%	0.74	-7.7%	0.53	3.1%
1983/84	92	3.4%	62	6.9%	0.72	-3.1%	0.57	7.9%
1984/85	126	27.0%	51	-21.6%	0.90	20.1%	0.45	-28.3%
1985/86	120	-4.8%	49	-3.9%				
Averages	77	4.9%	53	-0.1%	0.69	2.5%	0.49	1.5%

SOURCE: U.S. Department of Agriculture, Economic Research Service.
NOTE: Minor discrepancies may appear due to rounding.

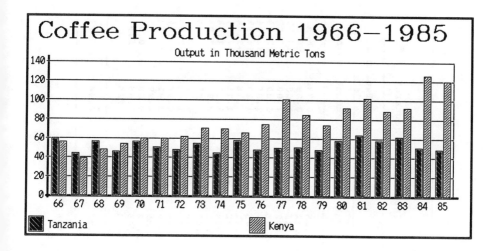

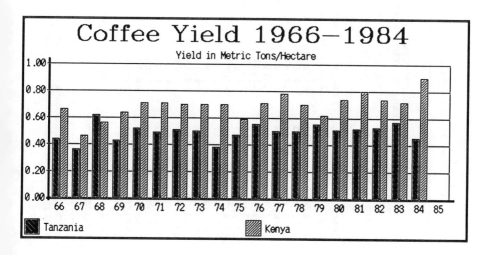

TABLE 4.4 Tea Production and Yield, 1966-1985

| | PRODUCTION (Thousand Metric Tons) | | | | CALCULATED YIELD (Metric Tons/Hectare) | | | |
| | Kenya | | Tanzania | | Kenya | | Tanzania | |
Year	Amount	Change	Amount	Change	Amount	Change	Amount	Change
1966/67	25	N/A	7	N/A	1.25	N/A	0.93	N/A
1967/68	23	-8.0%	7	0.0%	1.12	-10.7%	0.88	-6.3%
1968/69	30	30.4%	8	14.3%	1.46	30.4%	1.00	14.3%
1969/70	36	20.0%	9	12.5%	1.32	-9.5%	1.00	0.0%
1970/71	41	13.9%	8	-11.1%	1.36	3.3%	0.80	-20.0%
1971/72	36	-12.2%	11	37.5%	1.07	-21.3%	1.05	31.0%
1972/73	53	47.2%	13	18.2%	1.45	35.5%	1.20	14.9%
1973/74	57	7.5%	13	0.0%	1.41	-2.6%	1.16	-3.6%
1974/75	53	-7.5%	13	0.0%	1.22	-15.8%	1.11	-4.5%
1975/76	57	7.5%	14	7.7%	1.14	-6.3%	1.13	1.6%
1976/77	62	8.8%	14	0.0%	1.13	-1.2%	0.93	-17.9%
1977/78	86	38.7%	17	21.4%	1.47	29.5%	0.99	7.2%
1978/79	93	8.1%	17	0.0%	1.70	15.8%	0.97	-2.3%
1979/80	99	6.1%	18	5.6%	1.69	-0.7%	1.00	2.9%
1980/81	90	-9.1%	17	-5.6%	1.46	-13.2%	0.94	-5.6%
1981/82	91	1.1%	16	-5.9%	1.22	-16.3%	0.91	-3.2%
1982/83	96	5.5%	16	0.0%	1.25	2.4%	0.89	-2.8%
1983/84	120	25.0%	16	0.0%	1.52	21.3%	0.89	0.0%
1984/85	116	-3.4%	17	5.9%	1.45	-5.0%	0.94	5.9%
1985/86	147	26.7%	15	-11.8%	1.60	10.3%	N/A	N/A
Averages	70.6	10.9%	13.3	4.7%	1.36	2.0%	0.94	0.7%

SOURCE: U.S. Department of Agriculture, Economic Research Service.
NOTE: Minor discrepancies may appear due to rounding.

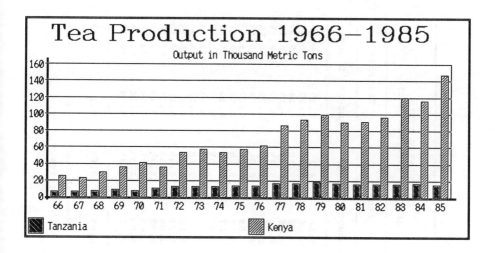

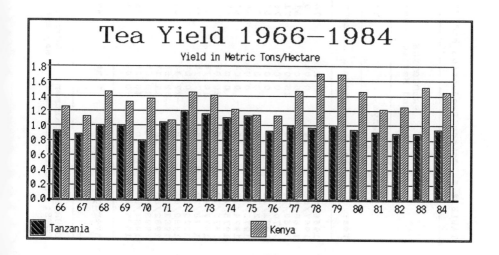

TABLE 4.5 Cotton Production and Yield, 1966–1985

	PRODUCTION (Thousand Metric Tons)				CALCULATED YIELD (Metric Tons/Hectare)			
	Kenya		Tanzania		Kenya		Tanzania	
Year	Amount	Change	Amount	Change	Amount	Change	Amount	Change
1966/67	4	N/A	78	N/A	0.06	N/A	0.17	N/A
1967/68	4	0.0%	70	-10.3%	0.06	0.0%	0.17	0.9%
1968/69	4	0.0%	51	-27.1%	0.06	9.2%	0.14	-19.5%
1969/70	5	25.0%	71	39.2%	0.06	0.3%	0.16	16.1%
1970/71	5	0.0%	76	7.0%	0.06	5.2%	0.17	6.1%
1971/72	5	0.0%	65	-14.5%	0.09	45.3%	0.16	-5.9%
1972/73	5	0.0%	77	18.5%	0.09	0.0%	0.19	18.5%
1973/74	5	0.0%	65	-15.6%	0.09	0.0%	0.17	-11.1%
1974/75	5	0.0%	66	1.5%	0.07	-30.2%	0.17	-2.4%
1975/76	5	0.0%	45	-31.8%	0.07	0.0%	0.19	16.6%
1976/77	6	20.0%	69	53.3%	0.05	-31.0%	0.19	-2.7%
1977/78	7	16.7%	50	-27.5%	0.06	11.1%	0.13	-32.2%
1978/79	11	57.1%	56	12.0%	0.09	65.0%	0.12	-4.2%
1979/80	11	0.0%	60	6.7%	0.08	-11.7%	0.13	6.7%
1980/81	8	-27.3%	54	-10.0%	0.06	-30.4%	0.12	-6.9%
1981/82	9	12.5%	45	-16.7%	0.08	48.6%	0.11	-7.2%
1982/83	8	-11.1%	43	-4.4%	0.07	-15.9%	0.12	4.8%
1983/84	6	-25.0%	47	9.3%	0.03	-53.8%	0.14	14.4%
1984/85	10	40.0%	46	-2.2%	0.06	41.3%	0.14	-1.0%
1985/86	13	30.0%	48	4.3%	0.07	15.7%	0.14	-0.1%
Averages	7	7.3%	59	-0.4%	0.07	3.6%	0.15	-0.5%

SOURCE: U.S. Department of Agriculture, Economic Research Service.
NOTE: Minor discrepancies may appear due to rounding.

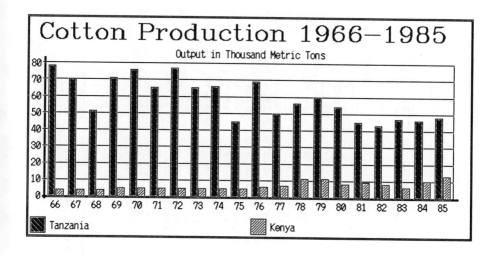

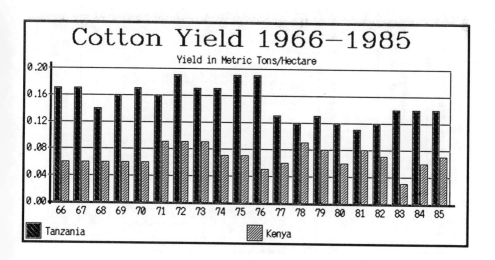

Table 4.6 Sugar Production and Yield, 1966-1985

| | PRODUCTION (Thousand Metric Tons) | | | | CALCULATED YIELD (Metric Tons/Hectare) | | | |
| | Kenya | | Tanzania | | Kenya | | Tanzania | |
Year	Amount	Change	Amount	Change	Amount	Change	Amount	Change
1966/67	655	N/A	891	N/A	38.24	N/A	28.05	N/A
1967/68	896	36.9%	934	4.8%	40.87	6.9%	28.29	0.9%
1968/69	1,137	26.9%	1,030	10.3%	42.84	4.8%	29.59	4.6%
1969/70	1,541	35.5%	1,141	10.8%	58.43	36.4%	30.35	2.6%
1970/71	1,731	12.4%	1,090	-4.5%	54.96	-5.9%	28.67	-5.5%
1971/72	1,663	-3.9%	1,091	0.1%	80.67	46.8%	27.27	-4.9%
1972/73	1,352	-18.7%	1,107	1.4%	76.39	-5.3%	26.99	-1.0%
1973/74	1,910	41.2%	1,155	4.4%	70.48	-7.7%	28.18	4.4%
1974/75	2,124	10.1%	1,157	0.1%	72.49	2.8%	29.67	5.0%
1975/76	2,080	-2.1%	1,177	1.7%	66.02	-8.9%	30.18	1.7%
1976/77	2,088	0.4%	1,280	8.8%	69.36	5.1%	30.48	1.0%
1977/78	2,327	11.5%	1,340	4.7%	72.27	4.2%	29.78	-2.3%
1978/79	2,819	21.1%	1,347	0.5%	79.19	9.6%	29.93	0.5%
1979/80	3,678	23.2%	1,765	23.7%	99.93	20.8%	30.43	1.6%
1980/81	4,532	23.2%	1,535	-13.0%	121.18	21.3%	30.10	-1.1%
1981/82	4,422	-2.4%	1,459	-5.0%	113.67	-6.2%	30.40	1.0%
1982/83	3,628	-18.0%	1,415	-3.0%	92.78	-18.4%	30.11	-1.0%
1983/84	3,846	6.0%	1,337	-5.5%	118.33	27.5%	30.39	0.9%
1984/85	3,910	1.6%	1,477	9.5%	111.71	-5.9%	30.14	-0.8%
Averages	2,439	11.4%	1,249	2.8%	77.88	6.7%	29.42	0.4%

SOURCE: U.S. Department of Agriculture, Economic Research Service.
NOTE: Minor discrepancies may appear due to rounding.

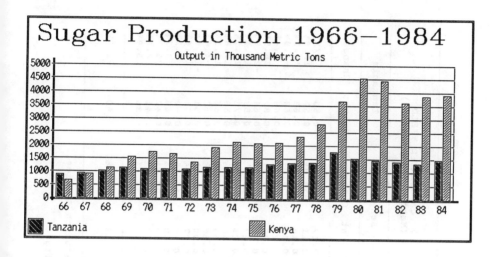

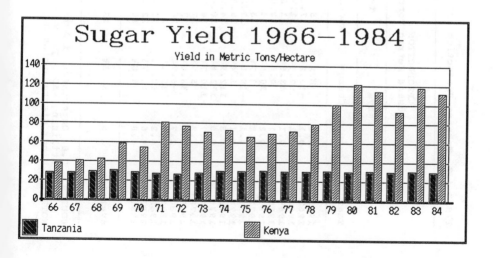

TABLE 4.7 Tobacco Production and Yield, 1966-1984

| | PRODUCTION (Thousand Metric Tons) | | | | CALCULATED YIELD (Metric Tons/Hectare) | | | |
| | Kenya | | Tanzania | | Kenya | | Tanzania | |
Year	Amount	Change	Amount	Change	Amount	Change	Amount	Change
1966	0.1	N/A	5.1	N/A	0.12	N/A	0.50	N/A
1967	0.1	-23.2%	7.8	51.9%	0.11	-10.9%	0.57	13.9%
1968	0.1	50.9%	11.7	50.4%	0.16	50.9%	0.68	18.1%
1969	0.1	53.8%	11.1	-5.3%	0.25	53.8%	0.63	-6.9%
1970	0.1	0.0%	12.0	8.4%	0.25	0.0%	0.68	8.4%
1971	0.2	30.9%	14.2	18.2%	0.32	30.9%	0.87	26.9%
1972	0.2	3.7%	13.1	-7.7%	0.33	3.7%	0.64	-25.9%
1973	0.1	-18.0%	13.0	-0.3%	0.27	-18.0%	0.53	-17.1%
1974	0.1	1.4%	18.2	28.2%	0.26	-5.3%	0.73	26.5%
1975	0.3	112.9%	14.2	-22.0%	0.40	54.1%	0.58	-19.8%
1976	0.8	172.6%	18.8	33.1%	0.59	46.0%	0.66	13.1%
1977	1.7	110.7%	18.3	-2.8%	0.86	46.8%	0.63	-4.4%
1978	1.8	5.9%	17.1	-6.9%	0.90	4.7%	0.51	-18.6%
1979	2.9	38.0%	17.2	0.8%	0.97	6.8%	0.61	16.6%
1980	2.7	-5.7%	16.8	-2.5%	0.79	-18.6%	0.62	1.2%
1981	3.7	35.1%	16.1	-4.0%	0.98	25.3%	0.64	3.7%
1982	5.2	40.8%	13.6	-15.6%	1.18	20.0%	0.47	-26.3%
1983	4.6	-11.7%	12.0	-11.7%	0.69	-41.3%	0.41	-12.8%
1984	4.8	4.8%	10.0	-20.0%	0.69	-0.6%	0.36	-15.9%
Averages	1.6	33.5%	13.7	5.1%	0.53	13.8%	0.60	-1.1%

SOURCE: U.S. Department of Agriculture, Economic Research Service, utilizing FAO figures.
NOTE: Minor discrepancies may occur due to rounding.

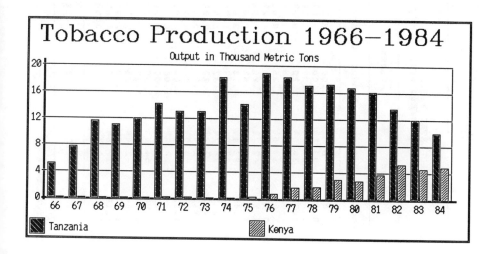

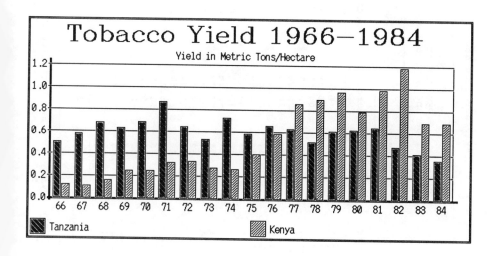

TABLE 4.8 Barley Production and Yield, 1961-1984

Year	PRODUCTION (Thousand Metric Tons)				CALCULATED YIELD (Metric Tons/Hectare)			
	Kenya		Tanzania		Kenya		Tanzania	
	Amount	Change	Amount	Change	Amount	Change	Amount	Change
1961	14	N/A	0.1	N/A	1.07	N/A	1.00	N/A
1962	10	-26.0%	0.1	0.0%	0.71	-33.1%	1.00	0.0%
1963	20	100.0%	0.2	100.0%	1.61	124.7%	1.33	33.3%
1964	20	-2.5%	0.3	50.0%	1.77	10.5%	1.20	-10.0%
1965	13	-32.8%	0.2	-33.3%	1.41	-20.6%	1.25	4.2%
1966	14	-10.1%	0.2	0.0%	1.61	14.6%	1.25	0.0%
1967	6	-55.7%	0.5	128.0%	0.67	-58.7%	1.30	4.2%
1968	12	85.0%	0.4	-7.9%	1.12	67.7%	1.20	-7.9%
1969	11	-4.5%	0.1	-78.3%	1.19	6.4%	0.61	-49.4%
1970	16	44.4%	0.4	53.8%	1.48	24.4%	0.93	53.8%
1971	18	13.0%	0.4	171.4%	0.92	-37.8%	1.27	35.7%
1972	17	-9.9%	0.4	15.8%	1.18	28.7%	1.47	15.8%
1973	31	89.7%	1.5	234.1%	1.21	2.2%	1.13	-22.9%
1974	31	-1.4%	0.9	-63.3%	1.19	-1.4%	0.90	-20.4%
1975	32	4.5%	2.0	122.2%	1.16	-3.0%	1.00	11.1%
1976	36	11.9%	2.0	0.0%	1.17	1.1%	1.00	0.0%
1977	46	27.4%	2.0	0.0%	0.84	-28.2%	1.00	0.0%
1978	35	-25.2%	2.0	0.0%	0.61	-27.8%	1.00	0.0%
1979	75	53.9%	3.1	34.4%	0.94	54.6%	1.09	8.9%
1980	82	9.3%	3.5	14.8%	0.96	2.9%	1.17	7.1%
1981	80	-2.4%	4.0	14.3%	0.94	-2.4%	1.25	7.1%
1982	85	6.3%	4.5	12.5%	1.00	6.3%	1.29	2.9%
1983	100	17.6%	4.6	2.2%	1.18	17.6%	1.28	-0.6%
1984	85	-17.6%	4.7	2.1%	1.06	-9.7%	1.27	-0.6%
Averages	37	12.8%	1.6	33.6%	1.12	6.0%	1.13	3.1%

SOURCE: U.N., Food and Agricultural Organization, Statistical Tape.
NOTE: Minor discrepancies may appear due to rounding.

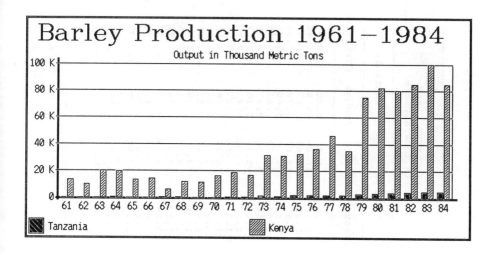

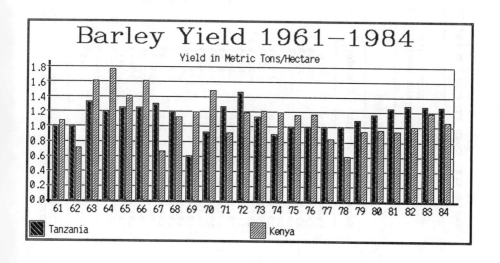

TABLE 4.9 Corn Production and Yield

| | PRODUCTION (Thousand Metric Tons) | | | | CALCULATED YIELD (Metric Tons/Hectare) | | | |
| | Kenya | | Tanzania | | Kenya | | Tanzania | |
Year	Amount	Change	Amount	Change	Amount	Change	Amount	Change
1966	1,451	N/A	880	N/A	1.20	N/A	0.80	N/A
1967	1,633	12.5%	549	-37.6%	1.40	16.8%	0.55	-31.4%
1968	1,600	-2.0%	664	20.9%	1.32	-5.6%	0.65	19.3%
1969	1,400	-12.5%	730	9.9%	1.12	-15.0%	0.72	9.9%
1970	1,500	7.1%	870	19.2%	1.20	6.7%	0.86	19.1%
1971	1,300	-13.3%	850	-2.3%	1.04	-13.3%	0.86	0.7%
1972	1,700	30.8%	900	5.9%	1.36	31.3%	0.90	4.3%
1973	1,600	-5.9%	781	-13.2%	1.28	-5.9%	0.78	-13.2%
1974	1,600	0.0%	784	0.4%	1.28	0.0%	0.71	-9.6%
1975	1,900	18.8%	1,332	69.9%	1.52	18.8%	1.21	69.9%
1976	2,195	15.5%	1,513	13.6%	1.76	15.5%	1.16	-3.9%
1977	2,205	0.5%	1,648	8.9%	1.76	0.5%	1.27	8.9%
1978	1,895	-14.1%	1,465	-11.1%	1.65	-6.6%	1.13	-11.1%
1979	1,450	-30.7%	1,726	15.1%	1.07	-53.4%	1.28	11.9%
1980	1,750	20.7%	1,500	-13.1%	1.18	9.5%	1.11	-13.1%
1981	2,200	25.7%	1,430	-4.7%	1.30	10.7%	1.06	-4.7%
1982	2,340	6.4%	1,200	-16.1%	1.36	4.5%	0.89	-16.1%
1983	2,070	-11.5%	1,525	27.1%	1.36	0.1%	1.13	27.1%
1984	1,700	-21.8%	2,013	24.2%	1.06	-28.2%	1.83	38.3%
1985	2,700	58.8%	2,127	5.7%	1.64	54.0%	1.52	-17.0%
1986	2,730	1.1%	2,210	3.9%	1.61	-1.9%	1.47	-3.0%
1987	2,450	-10.3%	2,100	-5.0%	1.44	-10.3%	1.56	5.6%
Averages	1,880	3.6%	1,309	5.8%	1.36	1.3%	1.07	4.4%

SOURCE: U.S. Department of Agriculture, Economic Research Service.
NOTE: Minor discrepancies may appear due to rounding.

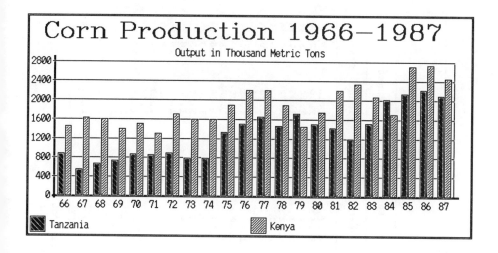

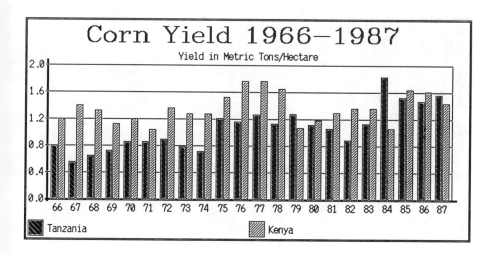

TABLE 4.10 Wheat Production and Yield, 1966-1987

| | PRODUCTION (Thousand Metric Tons) | | | | CALCULATED YIELD (Metric Tons/Hectare) | | | |
| | Kenya | | Tanzania | | Kenya | | Tanzania | |
Year	Amount	Change	Amount	Change	Amount	Change	Amount	Change
1966	128	N/A	39	N/A	1.17	N/A	1.15	N/A
1967	162	26.6%	31	-20.5%	1.34	14.0%	1.00	-12.8%
1968	216	33.3%	44	41.9%	1.62	21.3%	1.16	15.8%
1969	242	12.0%	39	-11.4%	1.73	6.4%	1.03	-11.4%
1970	222	-8.3%	61	56.4%	1.62	-6.3%	1.02	-0.9%
1971	206	-7.2%	84	37.7%	1.70	5.1%	1.08	5.9%
1972	164	-20.4%	98	16.7%	1.76	3.6%	1.08	0.0%
1973	150	-8.5%	78	-20.4%	1.69	-4.4%	1.42	31.7%
1974	149	-0.7%	46	-69.6%	1.49	-13.1%	1.00	-41.8%
1975	158	6.0%	56	21.7%	1.50	1.0%	1.00	0.0%
1976	176	11.4%	58	3.6%	1.50	0.0%	1.18	18.4%
1977	178	1.1%	62	6.9%	1.58	4.7%	1.38	16.4%
1978	166	-6.7%	55	-11.3%	1.39	-11.4%	1.06	-23.2%
1979	201	17.4%	60	8.3%	1.72	18.8%	1.09	3.0%
1980	205	2.0%	50	-16.7%	1.64	-4.5%	1.00	-8.3%
1981	213	3.9%	90	80.0%	1.58	-3.8%	1.29	28.6%
1982	225	5.6%	86	-4.4%	1.55	-1.7%	1.32	2.9%
1983	205	-8.9%	74	-14.0%	1.71	10.1%	1.23	-6.8%
1984	95	-115.8%	93	20.4%	0.86	-97.8%	1.33	7.2%
1985	240	152.6%	72	-22.6%	1.69	95.7%	1.14	-14.0%
1986	245	2.1%	70	-2.8%	2.23	31.8%	1.17	2.1%
1987	225	-8.2%	65	-7.1%	2.16	-2.9%	1.30	11.4%
Averages	189.6	4.3%	64.1	4.4%	1.60	3.2%	1.16	1.1%

SOURCE: U.S. Department of Agriculture, Economic Research Service.
NOTE: Minor discrepancies may appear due to rounding.

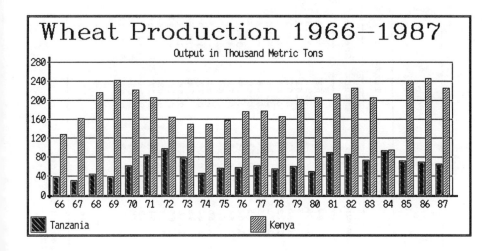

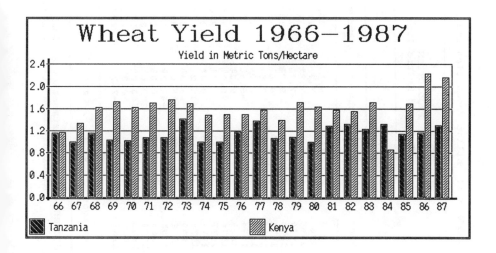

TABLE 4.11 Millet Production and Yield, 1966–1987

Year	PRODUCTION (Thousand Metric Tons)				CALCULATED YIELD (Metric Tons/Hectare)			
	Kenya		Tanzania		Kenya		Tanzania	
	Amount	Change	Amount	Change	Amount	Change	Amount	Change
1966	136	N/A	131	N/A	1.84	N/A	0.62	N/A
1967	141	3.7%	165	26.0%	1.88	2.3%	0.83	32.3%
1968	130	-7.8%	122	-26.1%	1.73	-7.8%	0.61	-26.1%
1969	120	-7.7%	110	-9.8%	1.60	-7.7%	0.52	-14.1%
1970	130	8.3%	138	25.5%	1.73	8.3%	0.65	24.3%
1971	130	0.0%	138	0.0%	1.71	-1.3%	0.66	1.0%
1972	135	3.8%	128	-7.2%	1.75	2.5%	0.64	-2.6%
1973	135	0.0%	136	6.3%	1.75	0.0%	0.68	6.3%
1974	128	-5.5%	88	-54.5%	1.64	-6.8%	0.49	-39.1%
1975	128	0.0%	160	81.8%	1.64	0.0%	0.73	48.8%
1976	128	0.0%	130	-18.8%	1.60	-2.5%	0.65	-10.6%
1977	130	1.6%	220	69.2%	1.60	0.3%	0.63	-3.3%
1978	130	0.0%	319	45.0%	1.60	0.0%	0.73	15.3%
1979	110	-18.2%	335	4.8%	1.36	-18.2%	0.74	2.6%
1980	80	-27.3%	380	13.4%	1.00	-26.4%	0.84	13.4%
1981	52	-35.0%	350	-7.9%	0.65	-35.0%	0.78	-7.9%
1982	30	-42.3%	373	6.6%	0.64	-1.8%	0.83	6.6%
1983	30	0.0%	206	-44.8%	0.64	0.0%	0.87	4.9%
1984	10	-200.0%	267	22.8%	0.10	-531.9%	0.81	-7.4%
1985	60	500.0%	300	12.4%	0.75	642.5%	0.83	3.0%
1986	65	8.3%	273	-9.0%	0.87	15.6%	0.83	-0.7%
1987	60	-7.7%	290	6.2%				
Averages	99.9	8.3%	216.3	6.8%	1.34	1.6%	0.71	2.3%

SOURCE: U.S. Department of Agriculture, Economic Research Service.
NOTE: Minor discrepancies may appear due to rounding.

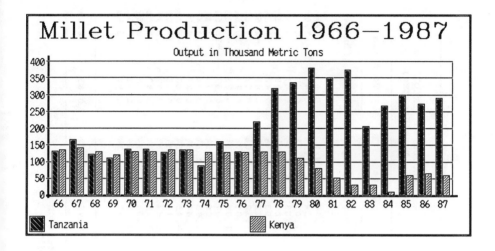

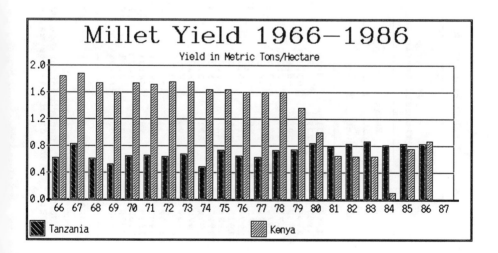

TABLE 4.12 Sorghum Production and Yield, 1966-1987

| | PRODUCTION (Thousand Metric Tons) | | | | CALCULATED YIELD (Metric Tons/Hectare) | | | |
| | Kenya | | Tanzania | | Kenya | | Tanzania | |
Year	Amount	Change	Amount	Change	Amount	Change	Amount	Change
1966	231	N/A	165	N/A	1.10	N/A	0.53	N/A
1967	239	3.5%	127	-23.0%	1.14	3.5%	0.41	-23.0%
1968	220	-7.9%	153	20.5%	1.07	-5.7%	0.49	18.6%
1969	205	-6.8%	126	-17.6%	1.03	-4.5%	0.41	-16.3%
1970	220	7.3%	107	-15.1%	1.09	6.8%	0.35	-15.1%
1971	220	0.0%	149	39.3%	1.09	-0.5%	0.48	39.3%
1972	230	4.5%	164	10.1%	1.12	3.0%	0.47	-2.5%
1973	230	0.0%	130	-20.7%	1.12	0.0%	0.37	-21.6%
1974	219	-5.0%	230	43.5%	1.06	-5.7%	0.74	50.5%
1975	219	0.0%	330	43.5%	1.06	0.2%	0.73	-1.2%
1976	223	1.8%	260	-21.2%	1.07	0.4%	0.47	-35.5%
1977	220	-1.3%	521	100.4%	1.06	-0.9%	0.74	57.4%
1978	221	0.5%	451	-13.4%	1.05	-0.5%	0.64	-13.4%
1979	186	-18.8%	500	9.8%	0.89	-18.8%	0.71	9.8%
1980	200	7.5%	500	0.0%	0.95	7.5%	0.68	-5.4%
1981	94	-53.0%	525	5.0%	1.12	17.5%	0.75	11.0%
1982	56	-40.4%	554	5.5%	0.64	-42.5%	0.92	23.1%
1983	35	-37.5%	793	43.1%	0.29	-54.7%	0.90	-2.5%
1984	98	64.3%	492	-61.2%	0.63	53.9%	0.98	8.5%
1985	100	2.0%	724	47.2%	0.65	2.0%	0.91	-8.0%
1986	100	0.0%	670	-7.5%	0.67	3.3%	0.96	5.8%
1987	85	-15.0%	670	0.0%				
Averages	175.0	-4.5%	379.1	9.0%	0.95	-1.8%	0.65	4.0%

SOURCE: U.S. Department of Agriculture, Economic Research Service.
NOTE: Minor discrepancies may appear due to rounding.

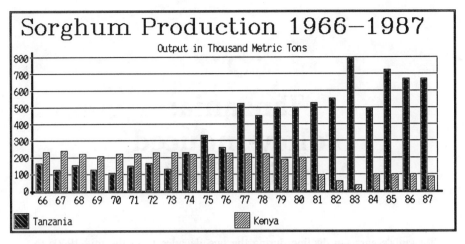

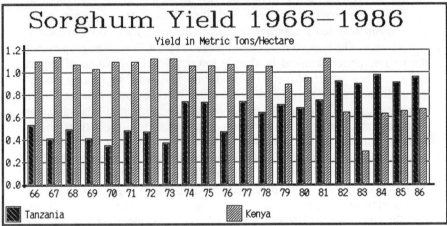

TABLE 4.13   Total Grain Imports, 1976-1985
(in metric tons)

	Kenya	Tanzania
1976-1980 5 Yr. Avg.	649,000 129,700	906,100 181,200
1981-1985 5 Yr. Avg.	2,081,200 416,400	1,466,700 293,300

SOURCE: U.S. Department of Agriculture,
Economic Research Service.

·5·
Tanzania: Policy-Induced Agrarian Decline

Tanzania's agrarian decline during the two decades from the mid-1960s to the mid-1980s provides a near-perfect illustration of the cause-and-effect relationship between inappropriate agricultural policy and poor economic performance. The agricultural policies pursued by the Tanzanian government during this period resulted in sharply lowered levels of output of export crops, and in a pattern of food-crop production that, while registering modest gains, did not enable the country to avert high levels of grain imports. Under extreme pressure from the IMF, the World Bank, and a host of bilateral donor organizations, Tanzania has now committed itself to a process of policy reform. But nearly two years after an agreement with the IMF had initiated—in the summer of 1986—a process of policy reform called the Economic Recovery Program, it remained unclear whether the policy changes required would be implemented with sufficient rigor to bring about an economic turnaround.

Tanzania may well have become Africa's most important test case for structural adjustment. If so, this would involve a major historical irony. Approximately twenty years ago, Tanzania established a leading position on the continent as one of Africa's most serious experiments in the implementation of a socialist strategy of development. Indeed, the widespread attention currently given to Tanzania's economic plight reflects the country's long-standing role as the embodiment of the deepest hopes and aspirations of the international Africanist community. It may also reflect Tanzania's position as a leading example of independent Africa's worst economic performance. Between 1966 and 1985, Tanzania became one of the sick countries of Africa. Even the country's most ardent sympathizers felt compelled to acknowledge an economic deterioration of calamitous proportions. There was widespread speculation that meaningful economic recovery might be all but out of reach. Critics of the country's experiment in socialist development forecast an even bleaker future: continuing economic decline characterized by worsening balance-of-payments difficulties; high rates of inflation; a further disintegration of the country's physical infrastructure; the continuing deterioration of basic social services, especially in rural areas; and a growing atmosphere of cynicism and corruption on the part of the country's political leadership.

THE SYNDROME OF ECONOMIC DECLINE

The symptoms of Tanzania's economic decline formed an interlocking syndrome, in which the various components reinforced one another as cause and effect. As a result, the country's downward spiral took on the quality of a vicious circle: Worsening performance in one sphere of the economic system resulted from and contributed to worsening trends in other sectors. It is this quality of interrelatedness that has made the search for solutions so difficult, for it has meant that there was no single aspect of the overall economic situation that could productively be identified for special remedial attention. Because Tanzania's economic malaise was so advanced, it provided an especially dramatic illustration of this problem. But the symptoms of its current economic state could also be found in a number of other African countries. The symptoms of malaise include the following:

1. *Declining export volumes:* as the statistical materials in the previous chapter reveal, the core of Tanzania's economic collapse is the near-catastrophic drop in the production of exportable and industrial crops.[1] Tanzania's export volumes have declined steadily since the end of the 1960s and, by 1980, were less than half those of 1970.[2] For certain of the country's major exports, the fall was precipitous. Recall that between the early 1970s and mid-1980s, for example, cashew nut exports fell from more than 125,000 tons per annum to about 40,000 tons, and sisal exports from more than 200,000 tons per annum to less than 50,000 tons. Coffee production had remained stagnant at its mid-1960s level, and tea production, though showing a modest increase, was only about 15 percent of Kenya's. Recall, as well, that Tanzania's production of industrial crops such as sugar, tobacco, cotton, and barley was extremely poor compared to Kenya's, and that production of such vitally important industrials as tobacco and cotton had fallen substantially since the mid-1970s.

An integral aspect of Tanzania's export problem is the declining quality of certain of its key crops. Even while volumes were increasing as a result of heavy capital inputs during the late 1970s, there was a marked deterioration in the quality of Tanzania's coffee exports. Between 1977/78 and 1980/81, the proportion of Tanzania's coffee production graded above the "basic" or average grade fell from nearly 10 percent to only about 2.5 percent, while production in grades below basic increased from about 56 percent to more than 90 percent.[3] Declines in the quality of important exports also occurred in the cases of tobacco and cotton. The precise reasons for this problem are unclear but may have had to do with the deterioration of processing facilities, shortages of imported inputs, and chronic breakdowns in the transportation infrastructure. Whatever the reasons, falling quality levels made it necessary for Tanzania to accept lower prices for these commodities in international markets, further exacerbating the country's extreme scarcity of foreign exchange.

2. *Balance-of-payments deficits:* as a direct outgrowth of falling export volumes and the price penalties that result from lowered quality levels, Tanzania has been experiencing severe balance-of-payments deficits since the late 1970s. These deficits have been the principal source of a foreign-exchange crisis of unprecedented severity. The extreme scarcity of hard currency has, in turn, had an adverse impact upon virtually every aspect of the country's economic life. Tanzania's balance-of-payments difficulties have stemmed, in the main, from intractable deficits in the balance of trade. In 1980, Tanzania's trade deficit was more than $700 million, and since that time its annual trade deficits have varied between $425 million and $600 million.

Although infusions of external capital, such as foreign aid and private loans, somewhat ameliorated the net effect of these deficits on the country's foreign-exchange reserves, Tanzanian authorities were nevertheless compelled to impose sharp limitations on imports, which have led to serious scarcities of a wide variety of goods (including petroleum products, consumer items, and vital industrial and agricultural inputs). Chronic shortages of such economic necessities as spare parts, raw materials, and replacement equipment have, in turn, led to lower and lower rates of capacity utilization in the industrial sector and have exacerbated the agricultural crisis by reducing the country's usable infrastructure. By the early 1980s, Tanzania's physical capacity to cultivate, transport, and store agricultural products was so seriously reduced that it had become a heavy importer of food grains even during years of favorable climatic conditions.

3. *Food imports:* during the extreme drought during 1973 and 1974, Tanzania's food imports averaged approximately 350,000 tons per year. With the cessation of drought and the implementation of reforms in the food-pricing system, the need for these imports dropped abruptly and, by 1976/77, amounted to only about 80,000 tons. Because of the overall economic deterioration, however, food imports on a large scale had to be resumed in the late 1970s and, as Chapter 4 indicates, have averaged almost 300,000 tons per year since the early 1980s, an amount equal to the peak import needs of the drought period. Tanzania's food needs now seem independent of climatic conditions. Despite the fact that much of this food has been obtained on concessional terms from the donor community, food imports impose an additional burden on the country's foreign-exchange reserves. The persistent need for food imports, taken together with the problem of falling volumes of export crops, indicates that Tanzania's agricultural problem today is one of inadequate volume of total production, and that efforts at policy reform must simultaneously address the performance of both the food- and cash-crop sectors.

4. *Low industrial-capacity utilization:* extreme scarcities of foreign-exchange have had a profound effect in lowering Tanzania's rate of industrial-capacity utilization, much of its industrial sector having been developed on the principle of import substitution. Since industries that are designed to produce consumer goods for domestic consumption do not generate foreign-exchange reserves, they are dependent on the hard-currency earnings of other sectors, especially agriculture. As the value of Tanzania's agricultural exports has declined, so has its capacity to import the raw materials, spare parts, replacement equipment, and energy necessary to sustain its consumer-goods industries. The International Labour Office (ILO) has estimated that, by the early 1980s, Tanzania's industries were operating at a rate of only about 20 to 30 percent of installed capacity.[4] Since economic conditions have continued to deteriorate, that figure may now be even lower. Because of input shortages, a number of industrial plants have been shut down altogether, adding the problem of growing urban unemployment to the country's other economic difficulties. And because of the scarcity of consumer goods, especially in the rural areas, it has become increasingly difficult to induce market-responsive behavior on the part of the country's smallholders, who find little value in the acquisition of cash income.

5. *High rate of inflation:* another symptom of Tanzania's economic malaise is a high inflation rate. According to official estimates, the Tanzanian cost-of-living index increased more than tenfold during the fifteen-year period 1969–1984.[5] Even these official figures probably underestimate the true rate of inflation by a considerable amount, because the Tanzanian government's consumer-price index is constructed partially on the basis of retail food prices as set by official marketing agencies.[6] Since most Tanzanians acquire their food in informal or unofficial markets where prices are much higher, the real rate of inflation is substantially greater than that acknowledged by government officials. Most unofficial estimates place the rate of inflation in Tanzania at approximately 30 percent per year, and there is reason to believe that this figure is increasing as other aspects of the country's economic crisis worsen.[7]

Some of Tanzania's inflation is undoubtedly imported. This occurs, for example, when petroleum prices increase on the world market, thereby increasing the internal price levels of such necessities as gasoline, diesel fuel, and kerosene. But the principal causes of inflation emanate from internal aspects of the country's economic performance. Thus, for example, inflation is closely related to the chronic scarcity of consumer goods, itself a product of the country's now long-standing shortage of foreign-exchange and the low rate of industrial-capacity utilization thus induced. It is also directly attributable to the rapid growth of the money supply, the largest component of which are Tanzania's increasing budget deficits, which now regularly exceed 15 percent of GDP.

6. *Deterioration of physical infrastructure:* one of the most visible symptoms of Tanzania's economic plight is infrastructural decay. The

deterioration of the country's road and railway systems is so severe that transportation problems alone now constitute a serious constraint on the prospect of economic recovery. Some of Tanzania's most important highways have become virtually unusable. The road from Arusha to Dar es Salaam, for example, is vitally necessary for its role in carrying both coffee exports and food supplies to the nation's principal port and capital city. Once well-surfaced and easily traversable, stretches of this road at one time became so badly potholed as to require four-wheel-drive vehicles.

There have been unconfirmed reports that the country's few independent truckers have occasionally refused to allow their vehicles to use this or other highways, thus bottling up vital exports and food supplies hundreds of miles from the country's major urban centers. Similar deterioration characterizes Tanzania's once-reliable railroad system. The breakdown of roadbed and rolling stock is so severe that economically critical shipments of freight have been subjected to delays of weeks or, in some cases, months. A large proportion of the country's truck fleet has been similarly disabled for lack of spare parts or replacement vehicles. One result of the country's extreme shortage of transportation is that transportation costs have become highly inflated, thereby contributing to the country's overall high rate of inflation. Today, transportation bottlenecks pose an almost insuperable obstacle to economic recovery, since they represent a fundamental constraint on the country's export capacity.[8]

7. *Rise of the informal economy:* the emergence of a flourishing informal economy in Tanzania has been so well established that several government agencies have conducted studies in the parallel sector in order to determine the differentials between official and free-market prices. The absolute extent of the informal marketplace cannot be precisely determined, since the level of transactions occurring there is impossibly difficult to measure. Before the Economic Recovery Program began, Tanzanian government officials readily acknowledged that for such key items as food staples, the parallel market provided a far larger percentage of the country's needs than did the official marketing system. It had become increasingly commonplace to suggest that Tanzania had developed two food-delivery systems. The first was an informal marketing network, composed of small-scale private traders and utilizing locally produced foodstuffs to provide grain and other staples to the country's entire population outside Dar es Salaam. The second was the country's official grain-marketing mechanism, based on the National Milling Corporation (NMC), utilizing imported grains (including large volumes of food aid) to provide for the capital city. It reveals a great deal about the extent of Tanzania's informal market that some observers offered an even more circumscribed description of the role of the official marketing system, suggesting that it could not even provide for the entire population of Dar es Salaam, but only for the country's major institutional consumers (e.g., the army, police, schools, and hospitals).

Whichever of these descriptions is correct, it seems clear that the informal market had come to account for more than 90 percent of the country's grain trade. For the entire range of consumer durables such as bicycles, radios, and wearing apparel, which are no longer legally imported except in infinitesimal volumes, the role of the informal market may be even larger, providing nearly all of the country's supply. Since informal trade is, by definition, outside the official jurisdiction of the Tanzanian state, it is carried on tax free. This may help account for Tanzania's declining tax revenues and for its growing budget deficits. Since Tanzania's informal marketing systems seem highly profitable and have begun to sustain a growing class of private traders, serious questions arise as to what policies, if any, would enable the government to reestablish its jurisdiction over the country's internal markets.

8. *A severe debt crisis:* Tanzania finds itself in the midst of one of the developing world's most severe debt crises. According to World Bank economists, its debt-service ratio in the mid-1980s had climbed to more than 70 percent on a total outstanding debt of approximately $3.3 billion. Between 1970 and 1984, Tanzania's total external debt increased from about 21 percent to almost 70 percent of GDP.[9] To service a debt of this magnitude would impose intolerable strains on its social and economic system, requiring the cessation of entire categories of essential imports, including those required to provide even minimal inputs for its crumbling industrial sector and physical infrastructure. Since it is impossible to continue payments on a debt of this magnitude, Tanzania's only option has been to enter a state of unofficial but *de facto* default. By the mid-1980s, Tanzania was making debt payments on slightly over one-half of the amount owed, but its effective debt servicing nevertheless equalled about 35 percent of export earnings. The country's debt burden, and the constraint it imposed on securing a flow of necessary imports, was a major source of pressure to come to terms with the IMF in the summer of 1986.

The results of these trends are not difficult to discern. They include falling real GDP growth rates, and hence a commensurately larger annual drop in GDP per capita. The production of material goods has been particularly badly affected. Ndulu estimates that between 1978 and 1983, for example, total agricultural production fell by about 10 percent and manufacturing by a staggering 58 percent.[10] Services alone made it appear that Tanzania was able to sustain a somewhat stable level of per-capita income. But since the quality of services had plummeted disastrously, the unavoidable fact is that the lifestyle of the average Tanzanian was becoming considerably worse in all visible respects from one year to the next.

CAUSES OF ECONOMIC DECLINE

The pathology of economic decline in Tanzania has been subjected to far-reaching analysis. Broadly speaking, three strands of causality can be identified: (1) external factors, including the severe economic shocks to which Tanzania has been subjected in the last dozen years; (2) the country's policy of socialist development and the consequent tendency to discourage economic activity by private entrepreneurs; and (3) economic policies that have generated extreme disincentives for agricultural production. The intellectual debate among the proponents of these causal factors has generated an enormous literature on Tanzanian development.[11] And though the predominant weight of evidence suggests that internal economic policies are primarily responsible for Tanzania's current state, it seems clear that each of the three interpretations helps shed some light on the process of long-term economic decline.

External Factors

Tanzania has much in common with other countries that depend on the export of primary agricultural commodities. These countries have been severely buffeted by international economic forces since the early 1970s. Among the factors most commonly cited by those who stress external considerations are the oil-price increases of 1973 and 1979, generally depressed international price levels for agricultural products, and, especially in recent years, the sharp decline in the terms of trade for agricultural exporters. During this period, Tanzania has suffered two episodes of severe drought, first in 1973–1974 and, most recently, the disastrous East African drought of 1983–1984. Some observers also count Tanzania's costly war against Uganda in the fall of 1979 as an external factor, since it was largely necessitated by Uganda's persistent military intrusions into the West Lake region. That war not only exerted a burdensome financial toll, most frequently estimated at $500 million, but caused severe disruptions in the country's transportation system since the supply line to the front was well over 1,000 miles long.

The economic effects of successive oil-price increases have been especially harmful. It is useful to recall that as recently as early 1973, oil could be imported as cheaply as U.S. $4 per barrel. The Fall 1973 price increase tripled this figure, to approximately $12 per barrel, and the 1979 increase involved still another tripling of the price, to about $35 per barrel. By early 1980, oil was nearly ten times as costly as it had been only seven years earlier. There is a very real sense in which the entire international economic system continues to reverberate from the shocks of these price increases. They figure prominently in any analysis of the debt crisis in Latin America, and, more prominently, as a primary explanatory factor accounting for the global economic recession of the late 1970s and early 1980s. Changing oil prices are a basic component in practically every economic equation that describes the adverse changes in the international terms of trade during the past decade.

Inasmuch as Tanzania is heavily dependent on oil (some 90 percent of its energy needs being met by petroleum derivatives), oil-price increases have been especially harmful. Because of the low level of development of alternative energy sources, such as hydroelectric power or coal, Tanzania has been compelled to remain dependent on petroleum and to allocate huge sums of money for petroleum imports. By the early 1980s, Tanzania was expending more than 60 percent of its foreign-exchange earnings on petroleum products. This cost had profoundly negative implications for other economic sectors. Petroleum imports compete directly with other imports, so the allocation of foreign exchange for this commodity meant that there was less available to acquire other necessary economic inputs (such as industrial machinery and raw materials) or vital agricultural inputs (such as fertilizers, pesticides, and tractors). Oil-price increases, then, have had a direct effect in lowering the economic performance of every productive sector in the Tanzanian economy. By diminishing the available supply of consumer goods, increased petroleum costs have also indirectly affected the economy, reducing the incentives for smallholders to produce marketable surpluses.

Although adverse changes in the international terms of trade have been cited more frequently than almost any other factor in discussions of external impacts on Tanzania, its precise effects are almost impossible to calculate. There is no consensus on how to construct a terms-of-trade equation that will accurately reflect the country's actual economic experience during the past fifteen years. Economists disagree fundamentally over such basic issues as what time period to select, which commodity prices should be included in the market basket of imports, and over how to take into account what might have happened had certain factors, such as export volumes, remained constant.

The reasons for economists' disagreements are often political. Observers sympathetic to Tanzania, and to the strategy of development its leaders have chosen, generally seek to maximize the economic effects of external considerations in order to exonerate avowedly socialist policies of primary responsibility for economic failure. Their figures can be expected to demonstrate severe negative effects, often within short periods of time. Those more critical of Tanzania's avowedly socialist strategy of development are more apt to show that changes in the terms of trade, while important, are not so great over long periods of time as to constitute the primary reason for Tanzania's economic collapse.

The ILO has provided dramatic evidence of how widely terms-of-trade surveys can vary, depending on the base period chosen. In its report on Tanzania titled *Basic Needs in Danger*, it makes the following observation:

> The result of this exercize [terms of trade analysis] would look different if different base years had been chosen: from a 1975 base year, the 1980 terms of trade would still represent an improvement. In the previous

Chapter, we emphasized the swift deterioration of the terms of trade with
1977, the all-time-high as the base point.[12]

By beginning its survey during a year in which commodities prices boomed
and extending the duration of its analysis through the collapse of these prices
and the oil-price increase of 1979, the ILO was able to dramatize the
abruptness with which international economic trends shifted against
Tanzania in the late 1970s and early 1980s. For example, between 1977 and
1980, the price level of Tanzania's imports rose by nearly 50 percent, while
the prices it received for its exports were relatively stable. But the ILO report
explicitly acknowledges that a more comprehensive long-term portrait of
Tanzania's international trade position could have been presented by
beginning with 1973, a relatively normal year, and continuing through the
remainder of the decade.

A terms-of-trade survey using a periodization beginning 1973 yields
substantially different results. During the eight-year period 1973–1980,
Tanzania's terms of trade declined a total of 11 percent, or approximately 1.7
percent per year.[13] This figure, while consequential, does not demonstrate the
sort of calamitous economic shock that would explain the country's
precipitous economic decline during this period. Tanzania's foreign-exchange
crisis was not primarily the result of growing price differentials between its
exports and its imports. It resulted from declining export volumes. During
the period 1973–1980, Tanzania's export volume dropped by about 50
percent. Downward trends have been so severe as to cast doubt on arguments
stressing the external determinants of Tanzania's economic crisis, for if
Tanzania had been able to maintain the export levels of the 1970s, its current
economic crisis would be far less severe. Indeed, if it had been able to
achieve production increases comparable to those of other African nations,
crisis might have been substantially averted.

The most revealing figure for Tanzania, then, is not that for terms of
trade, but that for the level of imports that can be sustained by a country's
exports. The ILO's study reveals clearly that between 1973 and 1980, the
volume of imports commanded by Tanzania's exports fell by more than 50
percent, and that the fall in the terms of trade accounted for only a small
fraction of this loss.[14] Since the majority of low-income, oil-importing
countries, including Kenya, performed measurably better than did Tanzania
throughout the 1970s, it is impossible to avoid the conclusion that Tanzania's
economic travails were primarily the outcome of other factors, most notably
the attempt to impose a socialist framework on the country's rural areas, and
the persistent implementation of policies that discouraged agricultural
production.

Socialism and Agricultural Decline

Tanzania's attempt to implement a nationwide system of collectivized
agriculture has been extensively documented and does not call for detailed

description here.[15] Between 1969 and 1975, the Tanzanian government devoted prodigious energy and resources to a program intended to transform the socioeconomic basis of its rural economy. Its purpose was nothing less than to replace existing patterns of individualized household production with a network of village communities, in which land would be collectively held and production collectively organized. During these seven years, more than 5,000 new villages were created, or existing villages designated as "socialist," and intensive efforts were undertaken to lay the basis for collective agricultural practices. Before the collectivization program began, less than 5 percent of Tanzania's rural population lived in villages. By the end of 1975, more than 60 percent of the rural population lived in settled village communities that had embarked, to various degrees, on the implementation of collective farming. The basic goal of these villages was to develop a level of socialized production sufficiently high that the majority of each person's income would be derived from the village's collective activities.

It is now generally acknowledged that Tanzania's effort to introduce rural socialism was a disastrous failure. Although efforts to promote villagization continued after 1975, the commitment to collectivizing production was all but abandoned. The causes and economic effects of rural socialism have been vigorously debated, but it is generally acknowledged that the *ujamaa* village program contributed significantly to Tanzania's contemporary economic difficulties.[16] Against the background of Tanzania's long-standing traditions of scattered residences and individualized production, state-induced villagization promoted an atmosphere of confusion and uncertainty throughout the countryside. Since Tanzanians were unaccustomed to collective forms of production, there was widespread economic insecurity. Apprehension about the program was so prevalent that peasant morale was lowered even in regions where the government was not attempting to bring about collective patterns of land use. By the early 1970s, peasant opposition to the collective village program was so strong that, in several regions of the country, the government was compelled to use coercive means to implement it, a policy that only further heightened an already pervasive atmosphere of political and economic discontent.

The socialist village program also contributed directly to Tanzania's extreme agricultural crisis of 1974 to 1975. Collectivization sometimes interfered directly with agricultural production, as in cases where peasants were forcibly moved during the interval between planting and harvesting, or during one or the other of these seasons, when labor needs are greatest. There were also cases of peasants being moved to districts and regions that were so environmentally different from their traditional areas of residence as to be unsuitable for crops they were accustomed to grow. Since one of the key purposes of collective villagization was to promote social equality, it was sometimes accompanied by the outright confiscation of the farmlands of the country's larger-scale farmers. Inasmuch as this stratum of farmers had accounted for a very large proportion of the country's marketed agricultural surplus, the land seizures caused a severe reduction in the available food supply. Larger farmers who were somehow able to retain their lands were treated with political disparagement, publicly reviled as "kulaks" or exploiters, and openly intimidated from engaging in market-oriented production, thereby further reducing the food reserve.

The socialist strategy of development was accompanied by implacable governmental opposition to any substantial admixture of capitalist practices in the nation's development, precluding the use of open-market incentives to stimulate production. The tendency to treat capitalism as an imperialist practice, adverse to the best interests of the Tanzanian people, not only prevented the Tanzanian government from harnessing the considerable entrepreneurial talents inherent in its population, but led to a major flight of capital from the country during the late 1960s and early 1970s. It also discouraged major business corporations from making large investments in the country, thereby eliminating the foreign-capital inflows that might have stimulated economic growth. As articulated and implemented by the country's political leaders, the Tanzanian version of socialist development was an unbridled program of state regulation and control. As such, it is vulnerable to the charge that it was partly responsible for the expansion of state bureaucracy and for the rapid enlargement of public services, both of which grew out of all proportion to the country's financial or economic capacity. Socialist development bears some culpability for the large budget deficits of the late 1970s, and for the high rate of inflation these produced.

The commitment to socialism may also have contributed to Tanzanian leaders' willingness to tolerate a high degree of inefficiency and growing corruption throughout the state bureaucracy and parastatal organizations. There was a profound conviction that state-administered development, however inefficient, would produce more equitable results than the operations of private traders and entrepreneurs. President Nyerere stated repeatedly that under open-market conditions, large farmers eventually gain possession of larger and larger units of land, dispossessing small-scale peasant producers and converting them into an impoverished rural labor force. And members of his administration were convinced that if private traders were allowed to operate in the countryside, they would engage in gross economic victimization of the peasantry. As a result of these views, there was an unstated premise that socialism, with all its ills, was greatly preferable to the alternative. As a result, Tanzania's earlier efforts at policy reform have consisted largely of attempts to improve the operation of socialist institutions, rather than to introduce corrective, market-oriented practices.

Socialism, however, does not provide a full explanation of Tanzania's economic crisis, for many of the economic policies pursued by the Tanzanian government since independence are found in a large number of African nations that have little or no identification with socialist development. Indeed, the social and political objectives that motivate economic policy in Tanzania are virtually universal throughout Africa; for this reason, it would be inaccurate to view Tanzania as a unique case. Tanzanian political leaders, like others throughout the African continent, have felt impelled to implement the vision of a better society that was articulated during the nationalist period. That vision included a commitment to make public services, especially in the fields of education and health, more universally available. It also included the belief that development, in the full sense of the term, meant diversified economic growth, and must therefore encompass the industrial as well as agricultural sphere. And, like virtually every other postcolonial society in Africa, Tanzania has been driven to frame economic policies that would make for greater political stability by accommodating the demands and economic interests of its urban constituencies.

POLICY ROOTS OF ECONOMIC DECLINE

To achieve the creation of a better society, the government of Tanzania has implemented a set of economic policies designed to draw economic resources from the countryside for the purposes of enlarging the country's public services and expanding its industrial base. Four policies merit special attention because of their ruinous impact on the country's once-thriving agricultural system: (1) overvaluation of currency; (2) suppression of agricultural producer prices; (3) implementation of agricultural policy through a system of monopolistic parastatal corporations; and (4) pursuit of an industrial strategy based on the principle of import substitution. As Chapter 3 of this book indicates, this set of policies can be found in a host of African countries, including Kenya. The difference in Tanzania's case lies in the degree to which these policies have been pursued, and in the government's unwillingness to modify them—even in the face of overpowering evidence of their negative economic effects. Tanzania represents one of Africa's clearest and most dramatic examples of a policy pattern highly deleterious to the performance of the agricultural sector.

Currency Overvaluation

The effects of currency overvaluation on the agricultural sector can be devastating because, as Chapter 3 notes, overvaluation is a hidden form of taxation on the agricultural producer. It directly affects the producers of export crops because the farm-gate price levels for these commodities are, to a large extent, a function of the ratio at which the international price is converted into units of local currency. Tanzania's export farmers, like others throughout Africa, are paid for their crops in their national currency; the prices they receive are calculated on the basis of the official exchange rate between that currency and some hard currency, typically the U.S. dollar. The fewer units of local currency yielded per U.S. dollar, the lower the level of reimbursement to the farmer. Overvaluation has indirect but equivalent effects on the producers of domestically consumed food staples, for the relationship between the price level of food crops and that for exportable crops is not allowed to vary randomly. In order to prevent farmers from substituting one category of crops for the other, the producer-price levels of non-cash crops are generally set in a specific ratio to those for exportable commodities. As a result, overvaluation lowers the producer-price levels of food staples by approximately the same amount it lowers those for cash crops.

Currency overvaluation has been a major factor in reducing the prices received by Tanzanian farmers. It is difficult to measure the extent of overvaluation in Tanzania because there is no legal free market in its currency; figures for unofficial conversions are therefore somewhat unsystematic. Some indication may be derived from the fact that during the fifteen-year period 1966–1981, while Tanzania's consumer price index was increasing by nearly 500 percent, the Tanzanian shilling was devalued by only about 15 percent. This alone would indicate extreme governmental reluctance to maintain a realistic exchange rate. Even the most cautious estimates indicate that, by the end of the 1970s, Tanzania's currency was overvalued by at least 100 percent; that is, while the official rate of exchange was approximately Shs.(T) 8 per U.S. $1, street traders and merchants were regularly offering between Shs.(T) 16 and 20 per U.S. $1. Visitors to Tanzania during this period reported spot-market exchanges as high as Shs.(T) 30 or 40 per U.S. $1, a figure which, if correct, would indicate an overvaluation on the order of several hundred percent.

Tables 5.1 and 6.9 depict the extent of currency overvaluation in Tanzania and Kenya. The figures presented in Table 5.1 make it clear that, by the early 1980s, as Tanzania's economic decline worsened and inflation increased, the gap between official and unofficial exchange rates became wider and wider. Despite successive devaluations that had lowered the official exchange rate to Shs.(T) 17 per U.S. $1 in June 1984, overvaluation in the mid-1980s approached 1,000 percent and remained at that level for at least two years, until the drastic devaluation of mid-1986. This last devaluation helped to narrow somewhat the gap between official and informal exchange rates for the shilling, but as late as Summer 1987, the Tanzanian shilling was still trading on the parallel market at three to four times its official rate.

It would be a gross oversimplification to suggest that devaluation alone would stimulate recovery of Tanzania's agricultural productivity.[17] The real price levels received by Tanzanian farmers are affected by a variety of factors, including direct governmental controls, level of taxation, operating margins of the agricultural parastatals, and amount of subsidy provided for agricultural inputs. Exchange-rate policy is thus only one of a number of policies that determine whether there is sufficient incentive for farmers to produce a marketable agricultural surplus. When overvaluation approaches 500 percent, however, its effects are necessarily considerable. By reducing the prices of all traded goods, both imports and exports, it suppresses domestic production levels in at least two ways. It lowers the real return to the Tanzanian producer and encourages the importation of foreign agricultural products, the prices of which are artificially cheapened, and which can therefore outcompete domestic goods in the local market.

If overvaluation lowers the prices of tradable goods, it increases, at least relatively, the costs of nontradables, such as construction and services. Although the increased cost of services may be less readily discernible than are the lowered prices of tradable commodities, it has been important as an added disincentive to the production of marketable agricultural surpluses. It means that Tanzania's farmers confront a dismal situation: low prices for the commodities they produce and high charges for the transportation, storage, and marketing of those goods. By discouraging exports and encouraging imports, and by increasing the costs that farmers must bear for services they require, overvaluation has contributed directly to the country's agricultural stagnation, especially in the area of export crops. It is thus directly accountable for the acute scarcity of foreign exchange, and thus for the necessity of introducing a governmentally administered system of foreign-exchange rationing.

In Tanzania, as in so many other countries in independent Africa today, the process of foreign-exchange allocation is heavily influenced by political factors. It therefore provides an excellent illustration of the importance of urban bias in political decisionmaking. Since farmers are politically weak in comparison to urban pressure groups, their needs do not normally receive the highest priority. The result is a scarcity of agricultural inputs, not only because of the country's overall shortage of hard currency but because the rural sector has great difficulty in exerting claims on those foreign-exchange reserves that are available. And, contrary to the claims of those who assert that overvaluation helps farmers by lowering the cost of imported agricultural inputs, it has, in fact, had exactly the opposite effect. By insuring that imported inputs are almost always in short supply, it has resulted in their being generally obtainable only at highly inflated prices.

Suppression of Producer Prices

The government of Tanzania strictly regulates the producer prices of all of the country's major crops. Its tendency in both cases (export and food crops) has been to set prices at levels that have, over time, sharply reduced the purchasing power of farmers' incomes. As in the case of exchange-rate policy, Tanzania's tendency to implement policies marked by a strong anti-agricultural bias is clear. According to Frank Ellis, the net barter terms of trade of Tanzania's smallholder producers dropped more than 35% between 1970 and 1980, and their income terms of trade dropped more than 33% during this same period.[18] Ellis's analysis also demonstrates that Tanzanian pricing policy during this critical period was particularly biased against the producers of exportable commodities. Their net barter terms of trade dropped more than 42%, whereas those of domestic grain producers fell by only half as much, about 21%. This finding has been corroborated by Frances Stewart, who found that the 1981/82 price index of Tanzania's principal export crops had fallen to 76% of its 1969/70 level, whereas that for'food crops stood at 97%.[19]

The Tanzanian government's tendency to engage in particularly harsh suppression of export-crop prices accounts for the dramatic drop in export volumes of key commodities. Between 1969/70 and 1980/81, the real producer price of cashew nuts, for example, fell by 27%; even this represented a substantial recovery from the period 1976–1978, during which time the producer price of this commodity in real terms was only about one-half that in the earlier period. Tables 5.2 and 5.3 show current and adjusted producer prices for coffee and tea for the period 1966/67 through 1980/81. The contrasts are striking and dramatically depict the impact of currency overvaluation on the real value of the prices received by producers. During this period, the nominal price for coffee in Tanzania increased steadily, to nearly three times its 1966/67 level, but the real value of the shilling prices being paid to coffee producers tended to vary abruptly from one year to the next—though spiraling ever downward, especially during the late 1970s, as overvaluation became greater and greater. This trend was even more marked in the case of tea. The nominal price of tea increased by about 25% during the fifteen-year period under consideration, but the real purchasing power of the prices paid to tea producers fell by almost 85%. By 1980, the Tanzanian producer price for tea, adjusted for inflation, was less than one-sixth of its 1967 level.

The impact of these price trends on Tanzanian agricultural exports was considerable. De Wilde has stated it in the following terms:

> A comparison of average annual exports in 1969-1970 and 1978-1980 reveals a drop of 35% in the aggregate volume of the six principal agricultural export products, with coffee exports remaining static, sisal declining slightly, and cotton and cashew nuts experiencing a decline of 74% and 52% respectively. Only exports of tea and tobacco, which accounted for only 11% of the value of exports of all six commodities, showed increases.[20]

Stewart's figures show that during the decade 1970/71–1980/81, cotton production fell 25%; sisal production 44%; and cashew nut production almost 60%.[21] De Wilde's figures somewhat overstate the quality of Tanzania's export performance. Stable or improved export levels for coffee, tea, and tobacco lasted only until the early 1980s and were accounted for less by the appropriateness of Tanzanian policy than by the willingness of the international donor community to allot large sums of capital for projects devoted to the production of these commodities.

Tanzania's annual production of food crops has also been adversely affected by pricing policies that have lowered the return to the agricultural producer. Tables 5.4, 5.5, 5.6, 5.7, and 5.8 show nominal and real producer-price levels for five of Tanzania's major food crops—wheat, rice, corn, sorghum, and millet—for the twenty-one-year period from the mid-1960s to the mid-1980s. Despite Tanzania's avowed commitment to an agricultural policy of food self-sufficiency, the downward trends are no less striking than those for the country's principal exports. By 1986, the real producer price for wheat was less than one-fourth its 1966 level; for corn less than half; for rice about 40%; and for sorghum and millet slightly over 30% and 20% respectively.

The results directly parallel those for exportable commodities. Although levels of marketed production of food crops were subject to wide variation during this period, reflecting transient factors such as climatic instability, Tanzania had failed by a wide margin to attain food self-sufficiency. Since the early 1970s, Tanzania has been heavily dependent on imported grains. This trend marked a complete reversal of its position during much of the 1960s, when Tanzania had been able on a fairly regular basis to export to nearby countries. As Table 4.13 reveals, Tanzania's food-grain imports were approaching 200,000 tons per year during the late 1970s and had increased to approximately 300,000 tons per year during the early 1980s.

Despite increasing imports, many observers in the international donor community believe that Tanzania may, in fact, produce sufficient grain to feed its entire population—a suggestion that, if true, only reinforces an analytical emphasis on the inappropriateness of the country's exchange-rate, pricing, and marketing policies. There is a strong suspicion on the part of several of Tanzania's donor agencies that imports are necessitated by the fact that much of Tanzania's annual grain production finds its way across the country's borders, to such neighboring countries as Malawi, Zambia, Zaire, and, occasionally, Kenya. Tanzania's principal grain-growing areas, such as Arusha-Moshi and the Pare Mountains in the north-central part of the country, and vast plains area of the southern highlands along Lake Tanganyika, are located in border regions, directly adjacent to countries that have harder currencies, better supplies of consumer goods, and higher real producer prices. Because of infrastructural deterioration, southwestern Tanzania is effectively cut off from the country's principal maize markets in Dar es Salaam and Tanga. There is virtually no way to estimate the amount of Tanzanian grain traded informally across its borders. But since its grain-producing regions have the capacity to produce vast surpluses, the notion of annual production being equal to annual consumption is not unrealistic.

Tanzania's continued dependence on grain imports is all the more striking in view of the fact that the Tanzanian government took dramatic steps to increase nominal producer prices for food staples following the severe grain deficits of 1973 to 1975. Tables 5.4–5.8, on food prices, confirm Frank Ellis's analysis, which shows that, between 1973/74 and 1978/79, the government of Tanzania increased the producer prices for food staples between 200% and 250%.[22] During this period, the official producer price for maize was increased more than two and one-half times, and the prices for rice and wheat more than doubled. The effect of these price increases on marketed production was considerable. The marketed volume of staple grains increased by slightly more than 80% during this period, an improvement that alleviated but did not remove the dependence on food imports. The government's strong emphasis on the use of pricing policy as a vehicle for food self-sufficiency may, paradoxically, have contributed to the stagnation of export volumes during the same period. Export-crop prices declined by more than 30% relative to food-crop prices, as increases in the price levels for exportable commodities failed by a wide margin to keep pace with those for food items. Thus, the effect of the increased prices for food staples was to create a strong incentive, for those agricultural producers who were able to do so, to move out of the production of export crops and to concentrate on the production of food grains.

Tables 5.4–5.8, on current and adjusted food prices in Tanzania, demonstrate that the major explanation for the ongoing dependency on food imports lies in the distinction between nominal and real prices. Studies by Tanzania's Marketing Development Bureau and by the U.S. Agency for International Development (USAID) suggest that because this gap has grown larger in recent years, Tanzania may require larger volumes of food imports in the future.[23] Evidence of such a trend is indirectly provided by recurrent reports in Dar es Salaam that Tanzanian farmers have begun to shift out of controlled commodities entirely, in order to produce crops that are not covered by the government's system of regulated prices. If so, this would suggest that there are now important unanswered questions about food availability in Tanzania: specifically, what proportion of the country's food needs is being provided by the informal market in unregulated crops; and, to what extent is officially marketed production any longer even an approximate indication of the country's overall food situation?

The inappropriateness of Tanzania's agricultural pricing policies was further reinforced in the mid-1970s by the introduction of pan-territorial pricing. This system was justified by the government as a means of distributing the cost burden of agricultural services more equitably among the nation's farmers and, in this way, of achieving more equitable income distribution throughout the countryside. Before the introduction of pan-territorial pricing, the costs of transporting and marketing the country's major food staples were borne by local producer cooperatives. Inevitably, these costs were far greater for farmers in regions distant from the country's major urban markets, and the net return from sales to producers in those areas was less. As a result, there were substantial income inequalities, based on differential transportation costs, between farming communities. In 1976, the Tanzanian government dissolved the producer cooperatives and assigned their most important functions, such as purchasing, transportation, and storage, to parastatal crop authorities. The operative idea was that these crop authorities would absorb the costs of transporting and marketing—which would now be evenly distributed among farming communities irrespective of region—thereby assuring improved incomes for farmers in distant areas.

Most agronomists believe that pan-territorial pricing is questionable on economic grounds because it leads to an inefficient use of a country's resources. This can be seen most clearly by comparing the results of a territory-wide pricing system with an optimally efficient pattern of agricultural production. In an efficient system, patterns of land suitability being roughly equal, bulky commodities that have high transportation costs relative to volume would be produced as close as possible to major market centers. This would enable the country to minimize its internal transportation costs. The same logic dictates that high-value commodities with low transportation costs relative to volume be produced in distant regions.

Pan-territorial pricing produces precisely the opposite pattern: By distributing the costs of transporting and marketing evenly, it compels efficient agricultural producers with low transportation costs to subsidize marginal farmers in more distant regions. Distant farmers no longer have any disincentive to produce bulky, high-cost goods, since transportation and marketing costs no longer have a direct bearing on the farm-gate price. And since nearby farmers lose the possibility of a price advantage in producing and delivering bulky commodities such as food grains, they have an incentive to devote their production to higher-value commodities. The overall result is a food system that tends to produce food-grains with high transportation costs in distant regions and high-value crops that have low transportation costs relative to volume in districts close to major urban centers. Since the costs of transporting and marketing must ultimately be borne by the producers, pan-territorial pricing tends to penalize all farmers by increasing the cost of services as a proportion of total crop revenues.

In sum, Tanzania's system of governmentally administered producer pricing bears a heavy responsibility for the country's agrarian crisis. The effects of price suppression—lower and lower real returns to rural producers—have been compounded by the system of pan-territorial pricing, which increases the costs of rural services as a proportion of total crop value. Indeed, the pricing system has represented such a strong economic disincentive to producers that this factor alone could well account for the drastic fall in the levels of marketed production of food-grains and export crops. Its effects, however, have been seriously compounded by the maladministration of the country's agricultural parastatal corporations.

Parastatal Maladministration

Tanzania implements its price-control system through a network of parastatal crop authorities. Typically, these authorities are given a complete legal monopoly over the purchasing, storage, processing, and marketing, whether domestic or international, of a given crop. The agricultural parastatals are also generally given sole jurisdiction over other critically important activities—such as crop research, fertilizer distribution, and agricultural extension—and the import and allocation of equipment and supplies, including motor vehicles, tractors, and trucks. Their monopolistic status is entrenched by a complex set of laws and administrative regulations forbidding farmers to trade their crops on the private market or obtain agricultural services and inputs from any other source. The system of enforcement also prevents private traders from purchasing and marketing any crop that has been assigned to a parastatal authority. There are approximately a dozen major agricultural parastatals in Tanzania, including the NMC, which has sole authority over the purchasing and marketing of all food-grains.

Supporters of the Tanzanian system have defended the parastatals as economically functional. They argue that no country has been able to achieve a high level of agricultural development by relying on the operation of free-market forces, and that strict governmental regulation of commodity production and pricing is common throughout regions of the world that are seeking to maintain a high level of agricultural exports. Defenders of the system also believe that certain vital economic functions, such as price stabilization and crop research, would never be provided by the private sector, whose orientation is inevitably toward short-term profit maximization. The driving force behind the parastatal system, however, is a deep conviction that if private traders were allowed to operate in the rural areas, they would engage in unbridled economic exploitation of helpless and vulnerable peasants. The depth of this conviction may be partly a result of racial feelings, since many government officials seem convinced that if private trade were reestablished, the majority of the traders would be Asian. Tanzania's deep commitment to the parastatal system may also derive from the fact that key political leaders have tended until very recently to view governmental regulation of the agricultural sector in all-or-nothing terms and, therefore, have been unwilling to entertain proposals that call for more mixed forms of economic management.

Today, there seems little doubt that the operation of Tanzania's agricultural parastatals was one of the major factors contributing to the country's economic crisis. These organizations have exhibited pervasive patterns of inefficiency, mismanagement, and corruption. Studies by the Tanzanian government show that the administrative and operating costs of the parastatal corporations have tended to absorb a higher and higher percentage of their sales revenues; as a result, parastatal overheads have themselves contributed significantly to the downward pressure on agricultural producer prices.[24] Sometimes, the parastatals' overhead costs have been so high that there has been no cash remainder for the farmers. There are innumerable reports of producers' payments being delayed for months, or even, in certain instances, for several years. The final result of inefficient administration has been a vicious cycle of rising administrative costs (measured as a percentage of sales) and falling levels of marketed production, for, as the net return to agricultural producers has been lowered due to maladministration, the level of marketed production has dropped commensurately. Because the administrative overheads of the parastatals are fixed, per-unit costs have risen, necessarily resulting in a further lowering of the return to the producer.

This cycle is so well established and so pervasive among Tanzanian parastatals that Ellis has posited a law of rising parastatal marketing costs, noting that:

> it is possible to discern the makings of a distinctive law of motion of the export crop parastatals in Tanzania. . . . The basic mechanism of the tendency rests on the impact on *unit* marketing costs of fluctuations in the volume of produce handled when the marketing system is characterized by fixed high overheads. The effect of a reduction in output is to increase the unit costs of marketing in approximate proportion to the share of overheads in total costs. These higher unit costs are then discounted from the export price for the following crop season, resulting in a lower producer price than would be warranted by the external market situation and resulting in a further fall in output.[25]

Ellis's law reflects the dismal economic performance of Tanzania's parastatal crop authorities and the disastrous impact this has had on the country's agricultural economy. Parastatal operations have resulted in a massive transfer of income from rural producers to the Tanzanian state and, more specifically, to its urban civil servants. Although Tanzania is so poor that even its most highly placed officials live rather modestly by international standards, their lifestyle compared to that of the country's poorer farmers starkly rebuts the commonly heard claim that Tanzania has achieved social equality, albeit at the expense of economic growth.

The ills of Tanzania's agricultural parastatals have been well summarized by a Tanzanian scholar:

> –their geographically extended and uncoordinated activities necessitated the employment of a large administrative staff . . . and the establishment of parallel transport capacities that were underutilized throughout the year except during peak periods of harvests;
> –transportation of goods was hindered by poor maintenance;
> –crop collection was frequently delayed;

–yields were inappropriately graded;
–purchases were inadequately stored;
–payments for crops suffered considerable delays due to liquidity problems;
–there was uncertain and untimely distribution of chemicals and seeds.[26]

In addition, the financial losses of the parastatals were so great that their need for governmental subsidies was, in itself, a major source of the government's chronic inability to control the money supply.

The Tanzanian government has publicly acknowledged the need to improve parastatal performance and taken some steps toward this objective. In 1982, for example, the government published a lengthy statement on structural adjustment, in which an entire section was given over to specific proposals for improvements in the administration of the crop parastatals.[27] This was followed, in early 1983, by the appointment of a Presidential Commission on Cost Reduction in Nonfinancial Public Enterprises, which presented its recommendations to the government in early 1984. Many of these recommendations were incorporated into the 1984/85 budget proposals. In the budget address, the minister of finance committed the government to the goal of transforming the parastatals into financially self-sufficient institutions. The principal move toward attaining this objective was the official commitment to restoration of the country's producer cooperatives, a step that, if fully implemented, can be expected to relieve the crop parastatals of significant portions of their crop-purchasing role. It is at least implicit in the restoration of producer cooperatives that there may come to be some measure of competition in crop purchasing at the local level, and that producer prices may once again be allowed to vary by district and region. As of late 1987, however, few concrete steps had been taken to stimulate the revival of the producer cooperatives, a protracted inaction that, as clearly as any overt policy, demonstrates the deep conflicts over policy reform within the present Tanzanian government.

Industrialization by Import Substitution

In the early 1960s, Tanzania, together with many other newly independent African countries, adopted an industrial strategy based on the principle of import substitution. The basic idea was simple and compelling: to initiate the growth of an industrial sector by domestically producing simple consumer goods that were being imported in large volumes. The advantages seemed overwhelming: to promote industrial employment in the cities; to promote the training of a managerial class; to begin accumulating a background of industrial experience, which might later be applied to larger-scale enterprises; and, perhaps most importantly from an economic standpoint, to conserve foreign-exchange reserves by reducing nonessential imports. Although there would necessarily be some foreign-exchange costs involved during the start-up phase (principally to finance the import of capital goods and to pay the costs of expatriate management during an initial training period), these seemed entirely justifiable on the basis of long-range foreign-exchange conservation. Industrialization by import substitution was widely acclaimed by leading economists and other authorities on the development process, and their enthusiasm helped reinforce the inclinations of national political leaders to move in this direction.

Throughout the 1960s, there seemed little reason to doubt the viability of import substitution. New industries devoted to the production of textiles, soft drinks, beer, concrete, household utensils, soap, shoes, cigarettes, and other consumer goods seemed to be thriving. And though the foreign-exchange burden of these industries was a continuing concern, this had been fully anticipated. Since other claims on foreign-exchange earnings were relatively small, the claim exerted by the new industrial sector seemed to be manageable. Moreover, there was considerable optimism that the problems of creating regional trading communities could be resolved, and that some of the new industries might well be able to earn foreign currency by developing export markets. Import substitution was also strongly supported by the donor community, which was prepared to make financial, technical, and managerial resources available in abundance.

It is impossible to assign a precise date to the moment at which the import-substituting strategy began to appear doubtful. By the end of the 1960s, food imports had become a long-term need rather than transient necessity, and both the unit costs and volume of food imports were rising steadily. The early notion that some of the new industries could reduce foreign-exchange costs by developing local sources of raw materials seemed a distant goal (linked to the long-term development of intermediate industries) rather than an imminent possibility. It had also become clear that the East African Common Market, far from providing growing opportunity for consumer-goods exports, was early on subject to the deepening political strains that would eventually break it apart altogether. In any case, Tanzania had become a consumer-goods market for Kenyan industries to a far greater degree than it had been able to develop outside markets of its own. Even before the energy and food crises of 1973 to 1975, Tanzania found it increasingly difficult to finance the recurrent needs of the still embryonic industrial sector for capital goods, spare parts, and raw materials. After that period, skyrocketing energy costs, compounded by a food emergency that thoroughly depleted the country's remaining foreign-exchange reserves, fully exposed the intrinsic weaknesses of import substitution.

The import-substituting strategy had depended on the premise that the agricultural sector, especially agricultural exports, would be able, almost indefinitely, to provide the wherewithal to capitalize emergent industries and to finance their continuing needs. So long as agricultural exports were buoyant, and so long as the country's terms of trade were relatively stable, it did not appear necessary to question this premise. But even before the cracks in the import-substituting approach became readily apparent, its operational success depended on a long-term transfer of capital from agriculture to industry. Very few African countries have found it possible to sustain this strategy since the early 1970s; Tanzania is no exception. Like so many other African countries, Tanzania is experiencing severe industrial difficulties stemming from critical scarcities of essential imported inputs.

The critical question is whether Tanzania may have acted in ways that accentuated the internal effects of a continentwide economic crisis. This is probably the case. If the implementation of an industrial strategy of import substitution is defensible on economic grounds through the mid-1970s, its continuation beyond that point is virtually inexplicable, given the rise of other demands on foreign-exchange and the fact that other economic weaknesses in the strategy had become apparent. Despite these constraints, Tanzania reaffirmed its commitment to import substitution in 1975, introducing a new program called the Basic Industry Strategy. The key idea of the Basic Industry Strategy was to extend import substitution beyond the consumer-goods sector and to begin the domestic production of more essential products, such as agricultural implements and construction materials. Its underlying assumption was that Tanzania's foreign-exchange shortage had become so severe, owing to the high volume of food imports between 1973 and 1975, as to rule out the importation of even these economically vital inputs. Tanzanian planners had come to believe that the very survival of such key sectors as agriculture, construction, and transportation depended on the development of an internal capacity to provide for their equipment and other needs. The difficulty confronting the Basic Industry Strategy, however, was precisely the same as that confronting the consumer-goods industries based on import substitution: the launching of new industries, however conserving of foreign exchange their products might be in the long run, requires heavy initial inputs of foreign-exchange and investment capital.

To be successful, then, the Basic Industry Strategy would have had to be accompanied by an agricultural strategy that somehow boosted agricultural exports and generated sufficient foreign-exchange earnings to finance the capital requirements of the new industries. And, indeed, the Basic Industry Stategy's approach was given a momentary economic boost by the commodities boom of 1976 and 1977. This boom enabled the Tanzanian authorities to ease import restrictions temporarily and to expand the import of transportation equipment and machinery.[28] The commodities boom, however, proved to be brief and only concealed the fact that Tanzania's agricultural policy during this period was not designed to provide for long-term increases in export earnings. Rather, as its principal reaction to the food crisis of 1973 to 1975, the Tanzanian government had committed itself to the goal of food self-sufficiency, a decision that manifested itself in increased producer-price levels for food staples. The goal of food self-sufficiency, like the goal of the Basic Industry Strategy, was to conserve foreign exchange by boosting domestic production of essential goods, which were being imported in very large volumes. But, by raising the prices of food staples out of proportion to those for export crops, the government of Tanzania was setting the stage for a widespread tendency to substitute food crops for exports, and thus for a sharp reduction in export earnings.

Tanzania at the end of the 1970s gave every indication of a nation pursuing contradictory economic policies. On the one hand, it had redoubled its commitment to an industrial strategy that, for at least a few years, would require a major enhancement of the country's foreign-exchange earning capacity because it called for the import of large volumes of capital goods. On the other, it had initiated an agricultural policy that diminished the economic incentives for export-crop production in order to achieve self-sufficiency in domestic food staples. To sustain a continuing policy of import substitution, Tanzania should have adopted an agricultural policy based on the principle of comparative advantage, not food self-sufficiency. An economic analysis by the Marketing Development Bureau of the Ministry of Agriculture showed that the country could have earned, by concentrating its productive resources on key exports, far more foreign exchange than it was able to save by allotting the same resources to food production. A dollar of hard currency spent on the production of coffee or cashew nuts, for example, would have brought the country more than four times the foreign-exchange earnings that dollar could save when allotted to maize production.[29]

Even the country's food strategy seems, in retrospect, to have been poorly thought through. For, as Jennifer Sharpley has pointed out, food self-sufficiency and foreign-exchange conservation are very different matters:

> The identification of food production with economic self-sufficiency was based on the false assumption that domestic food production requires relatively few imported inputs, saves on food imports, and benefits the balance-of-payments. On the contrary, food production in Tanzania remains heavily dependent on imported inputs and foreign-exchange earnings and the supply of food is intimately linked with the performance of the agricultural export sector.[30]

Food production in Tanzania is nearly twice as import intensive as export-crop production. To be food self-sufficient, therefore, Tanzania would have to boost its hard-currency earnings considerably. Since both the industrial and the agricultural strategies required increased earnings of foreign-exchange, it is entirely unclear how Tanzania intended to generate the financial resources necessary to achieve its principal economic goals.

The real result of the industrial strategy of import substitution, however, was the tendency to starve the agricultural sector of vital capital inputs. During the second half of the 1970s, there was a major shift in the country's investment emphasis, from agriculture to industry. In 1975/76, agriculture and livestock received more than 35 percent of the country's total capital investments, and industry less than 9 percent. By 1981/82, this had been almost completely reversed: Agriculture and livestock received only about 11.5 percent of capital resource allocations, and industry nearly 30 percent.[31] Expressed in real terms, this meant that while capital allocations to all sectors, including industry, increased by 33 percent, those to agriculture dropped by about 50 percent. Under these conditions, it is not surprising that Tanzania's agricultural economy became locked in a downward spiral of seemingly irreversible production declines. Indeed, given the impact of capital starvation in addition to other adverse policies, the only surprise is that the agricultural sector performed as well as it did, a testimony perhaps to the willingness of peasant smallholders to continue their efforts even under the most difficult circumstances.

NOTES

1. Statistical figures on Tanzania should be treated with utmost caution. As the ILO has pointed out in its report entitled *Basic Needs in Danger: A Basic Needs Oriented Development Strategy for Tanzania,* "all is not well with Tanzania's statistics." (International Labour Office, Jobs and Skills Programme for Africa, Addis Ababa, 1982), p. 251. The best approach, therefore, is to treat the statistical materials on Tanzania as general approximations of economic performance.

2. Uma Lele, "Tanzania: Phoenix or Icarus?" in *World Economic Growth: Case Studies of Developed and Developing Nations,* ed. Arnold C. Harberger (Institute for Contemporary Studies, San Francisco, 1984), p. 166.

3. John C. de Wilde, *Agriculture, Marketing and Pricing in Sub-Saharan Africa* (Crossroads Press for African Studies Association and African Studies Center, Los Angeles, 1984), p. 35.

4. ILO, *Basic Needs in Danger,* p. 17.

5. This figure is taken from the 1985/86 Tanzanian budget proposal speech by Minister of Finance Cleopa Msuya, as reported in the *Daily News* (Dar es Salaam, Tanzania), June 19, 1985.

6. For a discussion of various price and cost-of-living indices in Tanzania and the inflation rate figures these generate, see "Technical Paper 15: Price Indices in Tanzania," in ILO, *Basic Needs in Danger,* pp. 391–397.

7. See, for example, Benno Ndulu, "The Current Economic Stagnation in Tanzania: Causes and Effects" (African Studies Center, Boston University, n.d.), p. 2.

8. An excellent example of transport difficulties is the case of cotton. Between 1986 and 1987, cotton production increased by about 50%, from 320,000 200-kilo

bales to 450,000. But transportation from the Sukuma region to Dar es Salaam is so poor that the government was forced to announce that it might take as long as five years to clear the backlog. See *African Economic Digest* (February 12, 1988), p. 3.

9. The World Bank, *World Development Report 1986* (Oxford University Press, New York and Oxford, 1986), Table 17, p. 212.

10. Ndulu, "Economic Stagnation," p. 4.

11. See, for example, Dean E. McHenry, Jr., *Ujamaa Villages in Tanzania: A Bibliography* (Scandinavian Institute of African Studies, Uppsala, 1981).

12. ILO, *Basic Needs in Danger*, p. 44.

13. Jennifer Sharpley, "External Versus Internal Factors in Tanzania's Macro-Economic Crisis." (Unpublished ms., 1984), Table 2, p. 8.

14. ILO, *Basic Needs in Danger*, Table 4.1, p. 36.

15. For a thorough treatment of this program, see Dean E. McHenry, Jr., *Tanzania's Ujamaa Villages: The Implementation of a Rural Development Strategy* (Institute of International Studies, University of California, Berkeley, 1979).

16. The best discussion of the contending viewpoints about the failure of the *ujamaa* village program is found in Jonathan Barker, "The Debate on Rural Socialism in Tanzania," in *Towards Socialism in Tanzania*, ed. Bismarck U. Mwansasu and Cranford Pratt (University of Toronto Press, Toronto, 1979), pp. 95–124.

17. For a cautionary statement on the benefits of devaluation, see Delphin G. Rwegasira, "Exchange Rates and the External Sector," *Journal of Modern African Studies* 22, no. 3 (September 1984), pp. 451–457.

18. Frank Ellis, "Agricultural Price Policy in Tanzania," *World Development* 10, no. 4 (1982), p. 273.

19. Frances Stewart, *Planning to Meet Basic Needs* (The Macmillan Press, London and Basingstoke, 1985), Table 9.5, p. 193.

20. De Wilde, *Agriculture, Marketing and Pricing*, p. 32.

21. Stewart, *Planning*, Table 9.6, p. 194.

22. Ellis, "Agricultural Price Policy," p. 268.

23. Andrew G. Keeler, *et al.*, *The Consumption Effects of Agricultural Policies in Tanzania,* Study prepared for USAID by Sigma One Corporation (n.p.,1982).

24. Tanzania, Ministry of Agriculture, *Crop Authorities: Financial Position and Financial Performance*, Part 1, "Summary and Conclusions" (Project Planning and Marketing Bureau, Dar es Salaam, 1983).

25. Frank Ellis, "Agricultural Pricing Policy in Tanzania 1970–1979: Implications for Agricultural Output, Rural Incomes, and Crop Marketing Costs" (University of Dar es Salaam, Economic Research Bureau, 1980), p. 38.

26. Emil Katona, "Planning and Policy Making: Factors Affecting the Recovery of the Agricultural Sector in Tanzania." (Unpublished ms., n.d.), p. 33.

27. Tanzania, Ministry of Planning and Economic Affairs, *Structural Adjustment Programme for Tanzania* (Dar es Salaam, 1982), pp. 41–45.

28. Imports of transportation equipment and machinery increased from $275 million in 1977 to $506 million in 1979.

29. Tanzania, Ministry of Agriculture, *Estimates of 1981/82 Import Requirements for the Production, Processing and Marketing of Major Crops in Mainland Tanzania* (Marketing Development Bureau, Dar es Salaam, 1982), pp. 9–10.

30. See Sharpley, "Macro-Economic Crisis," pp. 16–17, and *Estimates of 1981/82 Import Requirements for the Production, Processing and Marketing of*

Major Crops in Mainland Tanzania (Marketing Development Bureau, Ministry of Agriculture, Dar es Salaam, 1981.)

31. Alberto Ruiz de Gamboa, "Resource Allocation and the Agricultural Sector" (Unpublished ms., n.d., Dar es Salaam).

TABLE 5.1 Official and Parallel Market Exchange Rates: Tanzania Shilling (TSh)

YEAR	Official Rate	Parallel Rate	Ratio: Parallel to Official
1965	7.14	8.52	1.19
1966	7.14	8.64	1.21
1967	7.14	8.68	1.22
1968	7.14	8.25	1.16
1969	7.14	9.10	1.27
1970	7.14	10.45	1.46
1971	7.14	15.00	2.10
1972	7.14	15.40	2.16
1973	6.90	13.45	1.95
1974	7.14	14.00	1.96
1975	8.26	25.00	3.03
1976	8.32	20.40	2.45
1977	7.96	15.15	1.90
1978	7.41	11.75	1.59
1979	8.22	13.50	1.64
1980	8.18	26.50	3.24
1981	8.32	24.35	2.93
1982	9.57	29.15	3.05
1983	12.35	50.00	4.05
1984	17.80	180.00	10.11
1985	17.80	180.00	10.11
1986	40.00	160.00	4.00

SOURCES: Official and parallel exchange rates 1965-1984: Philip P. Cowitt (ed.), World Currency Yearbook (International Currency Analysis, Brooklyn, N.Y., 1985) p. 738; Franz Pick, Pick's Currency Yearbook 1976-1977 (Pick Publishing Corp, New York, 1978) p. 571; and Pick's Currency Yearbook 1970, p. 485. Official exchange rates 1985 and 1986: annual budget addresses of the minister of finance, the Honorable Cleopa Msuya. Parallel rates, 1985-1988: by interview in Dar es Salaam.

TABLE 5.2   Coffee Prices in Tanzania, 1966/67-1980/81

	CURRENT PRODUCER PRICES Official Rates in TSh/Ton		ADJUSTED PRODUCER PRICES Prices in Constant (1967) U.S.\$ Adjusted to Parallel Market Exchange Rates	
Year	Amount	Index	Amount	Index
1966/67	4528	100	539	100
1967/68	4221	93	486	90
1968/69	4414	97	514	95
1969/70	3674	81	367	68
1970/71	6177	136	508	94
1971/72	6552	145	360	67
1972/73	7744	171	401	74
1973/74	9468	209	529	98
1974/75	7284	161	352	65
1975/76	17288	382	429	80
1976/77	17300	382	497	92
1977/78	17300	382	628	116
1978/79	11700	258	510	95
1979/80	12700	280	433	80
1980/81	12550	277	192	36

SOURCE: U.S. Department of Agriculture, Economic Research Service.

TABLE 5.3 Tea Prices in Tanzania, 1966/67-1980/81

	CURRENT PRODUCER PRICES Official Rates in TSh/Ton		ADJUSTED PRODUCER PRICES Prices in Constant (1967) U.S.$ Adjusted to Parallel Market Exchange Rates	
Year	Amount	Index	Amount	Index
1966/67	7121	100	848	100
1967/68	7121	100	820	97
1968/69	6702	94	780	92
1969/70	6370	89	637	75
1970/71	6067	85	499	59
1971/72	5058	71	278	33
1972/73	4311	61	223	26
1973/74	4390	62	245	29
1974/75	6800	95	328	39
1975/76	6990	98	173	20
1976/77	8680	122	249	29
1977/78	12030	169	437	51
1978/79	8130	114	354	42
1979/80	8880	125	303	36
1980/81	8730	123	134	16

SOURCE: U.S. Department of Agriculture, Economic Research Service.

TABLE 5.4   Wheat Prices in Tanzania, 1966-1986

CURRENT PRODUCER PRICES Official Rates in TSh/Ton			ADJUSTED PRODUCER PRICES Prices in Constant (1967) U.S.\$ Adjusted to Parallel Market Exchange Rates		
Year	Amount	Index		Amount	Index
1966	595	100		70.86	100
1967	571	96		65.78	93
1968	580	97		67.51	95
1969	542	91		54.20	76
1970	513	86		42.22	60
1971	556	93		30.52	43
1972	570	96		29.53	42
1973	570	96		31.86	45
1974	770	129		37.19	52
1975	1000	168		24.00	35
1976	1200	202		34.44	49
1977	1250	210		45.38	64
1978	1250	210		54.40	77
1979	1348	227		45.97	65
1980	1650	277		25.25	36
1981	2200	370		33.22	47
1982	2500	420		29.50	42
1983	3300	555		23.43	33
1984	4500	756		9.45	13
1985	7200	1210		15.12	21
1986	9000	1513		22.50	32

SOURCE: U.S. Department of Agriculture, Economic Research Service.

TABLE 5.5   Rice Prices in Tanzania, 1968-1986

CURRENT PRODUCER PRICES Official Rates in TSh/Ton			ADJUSTED PRODUCER PRICES Prices in Constant (1967) U.S.$ Adjusted to Parallel Market Exchange Rates	
Year	Amount	Index	Amount	Index
1968	472	100	54.94	100
1969	531	113	53.10	97
1970	607	129	49.96	91
1971	549	116	30.14	55
1972	589	125	30.51	56
1973	574	122	32.09	58
1974	619	131	29.90	54
1975	1000	212	24.80	45
1976	1000	212	28.70	52
1977	1200	254	43.56	79
1978	1200	254	52.32	95
1979	1500	318	51.15	93
1980	1750	371	26.78	49
1981	2300	487	34.73	63
1982	3000	636	35.40	64
1983	4000	847	28.40	52
1984	6000	1271	12.60	23
1985	8000	1695	16.80	31
1986	8800	1864	22.00	40

SOURCE: U.S. Department of Agriculture, Economic Research Service.

TABLE 5.6   Corn Prices in Tanzania, 1968–1986

	CURRENT PRODUCER PRICES in TSh/Ton		ADJUSTED PRODUCER PRICES Prices in Constant (1967) U.S.$ Adjusted to Parallel Market Exchange Rates	
Year	Amount	Index	Amount	Index
1968	265	100	30.85	100
1969	250	94	25.00	81
1970	249	94	20.49	66
1971	253	95	13.89	45
1972	274	103	14.19	46
1973	309	117	17.27	56
1974	500	189	24.15	78
1975	750	283	18.60	60
1976	800	302	22.96	74
1977	850	321	30.86	100
1978	849	320	37.02	120
1979	1000	377	34.10	111
1980	1000	377	15.30	50
1981	1500	566	22.65	73
1982	1750	660	20.65	67
1983	2200	830	15.62	51
1984	4000	1509	8.40	27
1985	5200	1962	10.92	35
1986	5800	2189	14.50	47

SOURCE: U.S. Department of Agriculture, Economic Research Service.

TABLE 5.7   Sorghum Prices in Tanzania, 1968-1986

	CURRENT PRODUCER PRICES Official Rates in TSh/Ton		ADJUSTED PRODUCER PRICES Prices in Constant (1967) U.S.$ Adjusted to Parallel Market Exchange Rates	
Year	Amount	Index	Amount	Index
1968	294	100	34.22	100
1969	300	102	30.00	88
1970	374	127	30.78	90
1971	334	114	18.34	54
1972	397	135	20.56	60
1973	371	126	20.74	61
1974	555	189	26.81	78
1975	750	255	18.60	54
1976	900	306	25.83	75
1977	1000	340	36.30	106
1978	1000	340	43.60	127
1979	1000	340	34.10	100
1980	1000	340	15.30	45
1981	1000	340	15.10	44
1982	1600	544	18.88	55
1983	2000	680	14.20	41
1984	3000	1020	6.30	18
1985	4000	1361	8.40	25
1986	4400	1497	$11.00	32

SOURCE: U.S. Department of Agriculture, Economic
Research Service.

TABLE 5.8   Millet Prices in Tanzania, 1968-1986

	CURRENT PRODUCER PRICES Official Rates in TSh/Ton		ADJUSTED PRODUCER PRICES Prices in Constant (1967) U.S.$ Adjusted to Parallel Market Exchange Rates	
Year	Amount	Index	Amount	Index
1968	439	100	51.10	100
1969	383	87	38.30	75
1970	521	119	42.88	84
1971	519	118	28.49	56
1972	517	118	26.78	52
1973	516	118	28.84	56
1974	609	139	29.41	58
1975	850	194	21.08	41
1976	950	216	27.27	53
1977	2000	456	72.60	142
1978	2000	456	87.20	171
1979	2000	456	68.20	133
1980	1500	342	22.95	45
1981	1500	342	22.65	44
1982	1500	342	17.70	35
1983	2000	456	14.20	28
1984	3000	683	6.30	12
1985	4000	911	8.40	16
1986	4400	1002	11.00	22

SOURCE: U.S. Department of Agriculture, Economic Research Service.

·6·
Kenya: Policy-Induced Agrarian Success

Kenya is an agricultural success story, and in this respect it demonstrates the opposite side of the Tanzanian case: the extent to which policies favorable to the agricultural sector can help stimulate its rapid development. Kenya today features perhaps the most advanced and complex agricultural sector of any independent sub-Saharan country. During the decade following independence, its agricultural GDP grew at the strikingly buoyant rate of more than 4.5 percent per annum. Since the early 1970s, this growth rate has slowed somewhat, averaging only about 3 percent per year during the decade from 1975 to 1985.[1] But the most remarkable feature of Kenya's contemporary agricultural performance is that it has been able to sustain positive growth despite a number of serious economic constraints, including a limited area of arable land, and an international environment that, as Chapter 2 of this volume shows, is adverse to the economic prospects of countries dependent on the export of primary agricultural products.

Like its neighbors, Kenya has had to cope with the effects of serious droughts, including the extraordinarily severe drought of 1984. But unlike other African countries, Kenya has proved able to manage the impact of that drought without significant incidents of famine and while continuing its economic growth. Kenya has also been compelled to cope with extreme price fluctuations for its principal agricultural exports, coffee and tea. The world price of tea, for example, escalated dramatically during 1984, then fell by more than 50 percent in 1985. A similar fluctuation occurred in the world price of coffee when the Brazilian drought of 1985–1986 created a momentary scarcity. When Brazil reentered the world market in late 1986, the price of coffee also fell by more than 50 percent. Kenya is inevitably vulnerable to this kind of shock.

Despite its accomplishment, there is reason for concern about Kenya's economic future. As many observers have pointed out, the rate of agricultural growth in recent years has barely kept pace with population increase, variously estimated at between 3.5 percent and 4 percent per annum. Some observers believe that Kenya's strategy for achieving economic development has distributed the benefits of growth unevenly among the country's social classes.[2] As a result, Kenya has begun to exhibit some destabilizing socio-economic problems, including rural landlessness, high unemployment, and a heightened incidence of urban crime. These problems have led to the reemergence of political opposition to the government's agricultural policies, and to demands for programs to distribute the country's wealth more equitably.

There is also serious concern over Kenya's ability to maintain an average rate of agricultural growth approaching 3 percent per year. As population increases have pressed against the limits of the country's high- and medium-potential arable land, it has been necessary to create new agricultural settlements in semi-arid regions. Since these regions are both costly to develop and intrinsically less productive than the high- and medium-potential regions, the development of semi-arid lands, however necessary, could seriously lower the country's average rate of agricultural growth. If this rate drops below the rate of population increase, a sharp decrease in rural per-capita income would inevitably follow, adding further momentum to radical political dissent.

THE "SOFT-OPTION" THESIS

Developmentally oriented aid organizations, such as the World Bank, have expressed serious doubts that Kenya will be able to achieve an adequate rate of agricultural growth in the future.[3] This judgment is based partially on the view that Kenya's high rate of agricultural growth during the first decade of independence was attained largely by implementing a set of agricultural policies that development experts sometimes refer to euphemistically as the "soft options." The first of these was to expand the land area under cultivation in the country's high- and medium-potential regions. After independence, the government undertook a substantial program to purchase large-scale settler farms and distribute the lands to African smallholders. Inasmuch as the settler farms often tended to have a certain proportion of unutilized or underutilized land, the redistribution program quickly resulted in a measurable enlargement of the acreage under cultivation in the country's major region of high-potential land.

A second source of Kenya's rapid agricultural growth immediately following independence was the elimination of restrictions on African cash-cropping. Until the late colonial period, Africans had been forbidden by law to cultivate coffee or tea, a restriction that, while justified on grounds of quality control, was in fact intended to protect the economic position of White-settler farmers. Once this regulation was removed, coffee and tea production grew rapidly. Between 1955 and 1977, tea production increased almost 11 percent *per year*, while coffee production increased by very nearly the same amount—about 9.8 percent per year. As a result of the massive influx of African farmers into cash-crop cultivation, the output of these two crops increased eightfold and accounted for very nearly half of the total increase in agricultural production during this period.[4]

A third major source of agricultural growth following independence was the introduction of scientifically advanced methods of production, dramatically increasing yields. During the twenty-year period from 1955 to 1975, tea and coffee yields approximately doubled. Coffee production, for example, increased from slightly less than half a ton to more than one ton per hectare, while the tea yield increased from approximately 0.9 tons to about 1.6 tons per hectare. Wheat output also doubled from 1955 to 1975, and substantial yield increases were recorded for industrial crops such as wattle and sisal.[5] The most dramatic success, however, came about as a result of the introduction of a new high-yielding variety of maize, which increased production per hectare between 50 and 300 percent, depending on region.[6] Experts in Kenya's Ministry of Agriculture have suggested that the introduction of hybrid maize enabled Kenya's food production to keep pace with population increases for more than a decade.

Soft-option advocates believe that the production gains from these sources had been more or less exhausted by the mid-1970s. They feel that though there is a certain amount of unused high-quality land still available, its supply does not begin to compare with that which existed at the end of the colonial era. In addition, the production gains that could be brought about by allowing Africans to engage in the cultivation of the country's principal cash crops have for the most part been realized. Although the number of African smallholders producing coffee and tea will undoubtedly continue to increase, the pace of this growth is unlikely to compare with that of the 1960s. A similar situation is frequently said to exist with respect to the possibility of increased yields. A continuing process of agricultural research, and the continued application of scientific methods to agricultural production, will undoubtedly result in ongoing improvements in future yields. But there is little prospect of a momentous innovation such as hybrid maize, which, by improving yields dramatically, released high-potential lands for other agricultural purposes.

Since the mid-1970s, Kenya has been in a peculiar kind of economic steady state. When compared to most other African societies, the performance of Kenya's agricultural sector, which continues to register an annual rate of growth of between 2 and 3 percent per year, is a remarkable achievement, one that ought to command the profound admiration of development analysts. But because of the combination of high rate of population increase and limited supply of arable land, the most common reaction has been deep concern about Kenya's economic future, and, in particular, its capacity to provide meaningful economic opportunity for future generations. The figures, as stated by the World Bank, are indeed ominous:

If nonagricultural employment were to grow at 4.6% per annum . . .

agricultural employment would have to grow to 9.9 million by the turn of the century (2.6 times the 1976 level) to prevent unemployment from growing. If population and labor force growth continued at 3.5% while non-agricultural employment grew at only 4% it would be over 200 years before the agricultural labor force stopped growing. Since this would imply a total labor force of over 6 billion people, it is obvious that mortality rates would rise and economic stagnation set in long before such a point was reached.[7]

The bank's report goes on to point out that even if nonagricultural employment were to expand at the presently unimaginable rate of 6 percent per year, the agricultural sector would be compelled to continue absorbing workers for an additional fifty years, growing to a work force of nearly 12 million (three times its size in 1976) merely to prevent an increase in unemployment. It does, indeed, appear that unless Kenya's present high rate of population increase is reduced to more manageable levels, or unless there is an unanticipated burst of growth in the industrial sector, the country is destined to suffer from higher levels of unemployment and stagnating per-capita income.

It is regrettable, however, that this issue is so often linked to critical judgments about the performance of the agricultural sector, for the tendency to link population and agricultural growth makes it appear that avoiding large-scale unemployment is the principal or even sole objective of agricultural policy. As the quotation from the World Bank's report indicates, it has become almost axiomatic among development economists that the agricultural sector must bear the major responsibility for absorbing Kenya's future labor surplus, and that agricultural performance is critically reflected on unless it does so. This point of view could be debated at great length. Suffice it to say here that rising levels of unemployment are better understood as the outcome of dynamic or stagnant performance in a variety of economic spheres, including the state and its subsidiary organs, industry and manufacturing in the modern sector, and the growth or shrinkage of opportunity in the informal or parallel economy.

The tendency to freight agriculture with responsibility for ameliorating Kenya's widely anticipated crisis of unemployment obscures the fact that the agricultural sector has performed commendably during recent decades, generating increased economic opportunity for a rapidly growing population. Kenya's total population in 1948 was only about 5.4 million persons. As recently as 1969, the total population was less than 11 million, indicating that it has very nearly doubled in the past sixteen years, and nearly quadrupled in less than forty years. The overwhelming proportion of this increase has been successfully absorbed into the agricultural sector, either into traditional agriculture or into smallholder cash-cropping. That the country has been able to achieve this absorption despite its extremely limited arable land, during a period of increased technological adaptation in agricultural production, and while maintaining economic growth in the agricultural sector, is a stunning accomplishment.

Kenya's achievement is all the more impressive when it is realized that employment generation is only one of the goals of its agricultural policy. Three other critically important objectives of agricultural policy are: (1) to provide a high degree of food self-sufficiency; (2) to generate rapid increases in foreign-exchange earnings, and (3) to help stimulate a positive rate of economic growth per capita. It is well worth recalling that these goals are not basically compatible. Pricing policies designed to increase the country's aggregate level of food production, for example, could bite into the production of exportable agricultural commodities by encouraging the substitution of food staples for export crops. Perhaps most important, programs designed to make the agricultural sector Kenya's employer of last resort, such as radical land redistribution, could badly undermine the productivity of this sector as a whole. At the very least, it seems, such a policy would drastically undermine efforts to produce a marketable food surplus adequate to provision the country's rapidly growing urban-industrial population, thereby fundamentally diminishing the prospects of attaining the other goals of agricultural policy.

Several conclusions can be drawn from this conundrum. The first and most obvious is that agriculture alone, however positive its long-term economic performance, cannot solve Kenya's serious development problems. It will be virtually impossible for Kenya to avoid high rates of unemployment in the near future unless the country's present rate of population increase is substantially reduced. Second, even if population growth does abate, it will be essential for Kenya to generate a relatively high rate of employment increase in the nonagricultural sectors, lest there be mounting and ultimately irresistible pressures to implement politically compelling but economically questionable land-redistribution programs. Third, even under the best of circumstances (lower population growth and a high rate of industrial growth), the agricultural sector will have to provide a livelihood for about twice as many persons in the year 2000 as it did in the mid-1980s: about 10 million as opposed to about 5 million persons. The most important conclusion, however, may have to do with the essential complementarity of agricultural and nonagricultural growth. The agricultural and nonagricultural sectors support and stimulate one another in myriad ways, so that stagnating performance in one area is bound to have profound repercussions on the other.

The ultimate measure of Kenya's economic achievement is that its agricultural sector has performed exceptionally well, not only in providing employment opportunity in the countryside but in satisfying the country's other developmental goals as well. Food self-sufficiency is an excellent example. In general, Kenya is a heavy importer of foodstuffs only during severe drought years (such as 1984), when climatic failure causes a severe and largely unpredictable drop in the supply of maize. Agriculture has also proved itself a durable and reliable earner of foreign-exchange, accounting consistently over the past three decades for between two-thirds and three-fourths of the country's foreign-exchange earnings. The foreign-exchange earnings generated by the agricultural sector are directly related to Kenya's outstanding record in attaining food self-reliance. According to UN figures, the 1984 drought was so severe that it required Kenya to import nearly 1 million tons of grain during 1984 and 1985. But of this amount, nearly 60 percent was acquired at strictly commercial rates rather than as food aid.[8]

The foreign-exchange earnings generated by agricultural exports have been absolutely critical for the health of Kenya's industrial sector. Modern-sector industry in Kenya, as in so many other African countries, has been built principally on the basis of import substitution and, therefore, depends almost entirely on the foreign-exchange earnings from agriculture to finance its imports of capital goods, spare parts, and raw materials. Thus, though population growth may well present the possibility of a socially troubled future, Kenya's agricultural record since independence is best viewed as one of considerable achievement in the face of daunting physical, political, and economic difficulties.

THE "HARD-OPTION" THESIS

Kenya's ongoing achievements in the agricultural sector suggest that there is an alternative to the point of view presented in the World Bank study: that is, the basis for Kenya's agricultural success lies equally in the fact that, since independence, the government has pursued a series of hard-option policies favorable to the growth of the agricultural sector. These hard options include: (1) land policy; (2) pricing policy; (3) exchange-rate policy; and (4) administration of agricultural parastatals. The hard-option thesis presents a compelling explanation of how the government of Kenya has been able to foster the ongoing development of a dynamic and highly productive agricultural sector since the mid-1970s. It also suggests that Kenya may be in a strong position to continue its record of agricultural achievement in the foreseeable future.

Kenya's agricultural system today is the envy of both its immediate neighbors and other countries in independent sub-Saharan Africa. Its success in achieving that status is largely attributable to the government's willingness to resist political pressure to introduce an agricultural policy based on the demands of its urban constituencies. The notion of urban bias does not provide a fully satisfactory explanation of agricultural policies and programs. It makes at least as much sense to think of Kenya's agricultural policy as driven by a fundamental concern for the economic well-being of smallholder and large-scale farmers.

POLICY ROOTS OF AGRICULTURAL GROWTH

Land Policy

As Chapter 2 points out, Kenya inherited one of Africa's most dualistic agricultural systems. Between one-fourth and one-fifth of its high- and medium-potential land, nearly 12,000 square miles, was held by a European settler community consisting of about 3,000 families, principally of British descent. Known as the White Highlands, the settler region in fact comprised three different agroeconomic zones, including about 3 million acres of mixed farms, about 2 million acres of large-scale plantations, and about 2.4 million acres devoted to commercial ranching. About 300,000 more acres had been set aside for European occupancy but not settled at the time of independence, making a total of more than 7.5 million acres.

The end product of agrarian dualism during the colonial era was vast socioeconomic inequality. A tiny European minority, less than one-half of 1 percent of the total population of the country, possessed nearly one-quarter of the country's best arable land and lived in great affluence.[9] European farmers owned lavish homes and enjoyed a lifestyle that could be compared with that of the most well-to-do landowning classes in England. The African majority, by contrast, was deeply impoverished. Overcrowding in the African areas was so severe that the vast majority of people lived in extreme poverty; a large proportion of African families had to supplement their farm income by having one or more members engage in migratory agricultural labor or move permanently to the city. Landlessness had become a critical social problem within African society, and though the absolute extent of this phenomenon is difficult to gauge, it has been estimated that, by the end of the colonial period, about 250,000 Africans were employed as permanent resident laborers on European farms. Several times that number had become a more or less permanent urban work force.[10]

The government of Kenya came under enormous political pressure to engage in wholesale redistribution of European land to African farmers, producing bitter political division within the governing party. One faction of the Kenya African National Union (KANU) gained considerable popularity by arguing for outright appropriation of the White Highlands, so that the large farms and plantations could be immediately parcelled out among African smallholders. For those who hold that Kenya's early postindependence agricultural growth was achieved principally by implementing a soft-option strategy, it is well worth remembering that resistance to this sort of pressure probably constituted one of the most difficult acts in African political history.

The KANU government was fundamentally committed to a thorough Africanization of the White Highlands, but it was just as committed to the principle that the transfer of land from Europeans to Africans should not undermine the highly productive agricultural economy the European settlers had created. Thus, though the socioeconomic deprivation endured by Africans during the colonial period made it critically important to have some sort of program for transferring land, it did not lead to a policy of redistribution to the landless. Leading members of the Kenyan elite were more committed to the principle that Africans should aspire to the same degree of agricultural prosperity that Europeans had enjoyed during the era of British rule. Although this principle has frequently been criticized as legitimizing large-scale land acquisition by members of the political elite, it has also resulted in a strong commitment to developing an African smallholder farming community, and to implementing policies designed to insure their economic stability.

The Kenyan government's commitment to continuing economic growth in the agricultural sector has been so strong that the basic operating premises of its land policy have remained constant since independence: First, there should be minimum changes in the structure of the highly productive agricultural economy developed by the European settler community; second, insofar as possible the basic configuration of this sector should be maintained while pursuing land transfers; third, transfers should create individually owned farms, not collective holdings, large enough to produce marketable surpluses of export and food crops. Finally, and perhaps most importantly, the government was committed to the continuation of a free market in land, so that efficient and productive farmers would be able to replace inefficient and unproductive ones. Government lending institutions, such as the Agricultural Finance Corporation encourage this process by foreclosing on loans that are in arrears, so that farms can be resold.

Resettlement

When Kenya became independent in December 1963, widespread landlessness represented a pressing social problem. There was a continuing and bitter resentment that Europeans owned such a large percentage of the country's arable land, a feeling of such political force that it had fueled the Mau Mau land freedom movement of 1952 to 1956. There were some politicians who believed that the Kenyan government ought simply to expropriate the European farms and redistribute them to African families. The predominant feeling in governmental circles, however, was skepticism about the economic value of resettlement, which was viewed purely as a political necessity, to be pursued as a limited and temporary expedient, only until more economically productive policies could be implemented.

The government's skepticism toward land resettlement resulted in an extremely limited program that had surprisingly little long-term impact. The sole program of any significance for redistributing European farms to African ownership was the "million-acre scheme," which was implemented between independence and the mid 1960s.[11] This scheme, which was financed principally by the British government, was fairly simple in conception. The government of Great Britain advanced to the Kenyan government about £12.5 million (U.S. $37 million at the then-prevailing exchange rate). Of this amount, one-third was considered as an outright gift and two-thirds as a long-term (30-year), low-interest loan. The funds were to be used to purchase British-owned farms at fair market value in hard currency for redistribution to African settlers. The cost of each farm would then be prorated among the new settlers, who were assigned mortgages by the Kenyan government, so that it could repay the two-thirds of the original grant that was a loan; the one-third gift, in effect, was passed on to the African settler family.

Between 1961 and 1965, the government purchased about 1,100 settler farms, totalling about 1.4 million acres. As the million-acre scheme progressed, it divided into two separate projects, a high-density scheme and a low-density scheme, the latter receiving additional financial support from the International Bank for Reconstruction and Development (later the World Bank) and the Canadian Development Corporation. High-density farms varied in size between 11 and 54 acres, depending on the quality of the soils and type of crop to be cultivated, but averaged approximately 32 acres. The basic intention was to provide a farm income, after expenses, of between U.S. $100 and $200 per year. The low-density farms varied between 12 and 56 acres, averaging approximately 36 acres. The intention here was to provide a farm income, after expenses, of approximately U.S. $300 per year. The high-density scheme, which continued to constitute the main portion of the project, ultimately settled approximately 30,000 African families; the low-density scheme settled about 4,500 families.

The key point is that Kenya's only resettlement project of any magnitude resulted in the redistribution of the European highlands to only about 35,000 African families, fewer than 200,000 persons. Because the central portions of the European farms, including farm buildings and principal access road, were sometimes retained for direct sale to prospective African purchasers, the total land area involved in resettlement was less than the 1.4 million acres originally purchased—amounting to only about 1.25 million acres. Almost all of this land was in the mixed-farm areas, and, since this segment of the highlands had swelled to about 3.4 million acres by the eve of independence, the land redistribution program involved only about 35 percent of the mixed-farm agroeconomic zone. The ranch and plantation areas were little affected, remaining practically intact. Although the Kenyan government did undertake a number of other resettlement projects, these were of even less economic significance. Almost all involved either marginal agricultural areas or sections of the European highlands that, while intended for settler occupation, had never been cleared for agricultural purposes.

It is of utmost significance that even the resettled areas of the highlands have since been subjected to market forces. The policy of the Kenyan government has been to foreclose on the mortgages of resettled families who default. When this occurs, the farm in question is sold at auction to a new purchaser, whose claim to the land is not based on landlessness and need, but rather on capacity to make repayments on the new mortgage that is created. As a result of this policy, substantial numbers of the originally settled African families no longer reside on the farms they were awarded under the million-acre scheme. No precise figures on the rate of default on the original mortgages are available. As a result, estimates of the default rate vary widely but are generally considered as being between 40 and 80 percent, depending on the precise area, the particular settlement scheme involved (high or low density), and the size of the original farm. As a result of the auction system, many of the mixed farms that were purchased for redistribution have undergone a partial process of reconsolidation, as the more successful farmers have been able to acquire the farms of their less successful neighbors.

By 1965, subsidized resettlement of the former European areas had all but ceased to be an official policy of the Kenyan government. There was a growing attitude that the settlement schemes were intolerably expensive, and, indeed, that the high mortage costs that the new settlers were forced to absorb would inevitably result in a high rate of default. This attitude was conspicuously reflected in the Kenyan government's official statement about the country's future economic development, *African Socialism and Its Application to Planning in Kenya,* which read, in part:

> We have to consider what emphasis should be given in future to settlement as against development in African areas. The same money spent on land consolidation, survey, registration and development in the African areas would increase productivity and output on four to six times as many acres and benefit four to six times as many Africans.[12]

Although the transfer of European lands to Africans would continue, there was a growing conviction that it should involve the sale of intact farms on the basis of willing buyer–willing seller transactions.

Registration
The Kenyan government's principal land policy to date has been to encourage private ownership of land in the roughly four-fifths of the arable areas that had always remained under African occupation. This policy had its origins in the colonial period, during the State of Emergency, when a portion of the European settler community came to believe that its interests could be preserved through the creation of a sizable African landowning class. It was hoped that this would blunt the sharpness of racial conflict between Europeans and Africans by creating a socioeconomic milieu in which conflict was based more on class considerations. If this could be brought about, African landowners with a stake in the existing system of land distribution might side with European landowners against political movements seeking radical change in Kenya's agricultural economy.[13] In the early 1950s, the principal assistant to the minister of agriculture, Mr. R. J.

M. Swynnerton, devised a plan to change the existing basis of land ownership in the African regions by introducing privately held land titles. The idea underlying his Land Consolidation and Registration program was to consolidate fragmented, tiny parcels of land into economically viable parcels and then register individual freehold titles.

The Swynnerton Plan, as this program came to be called, has had a far greater impact on Kenyan society than has the program of land transfer. As intended, the Swynnerton Plan launched an African landowning class that, by the mid-1980s, amounted to nearly 2 million households. During the final decade of colonial rule, the program proceeded somewhat slowly, and by December 1963, only about 600,000 hectares had been fully consolidated and registered. The government of independent Kenya has been able to improve appreciably on this record. Believing that the slow pace of the program was brought about by the costly and cumbersome administrative and judicial processes involved in the consolidation of land units into viable parcels, it abandoned this aspect of the program and concentrated instead solely on accelerating the award of individual title deeds to existing land units. By 1984, approximately 6.7 million hectares, an area almost double that reserved for European settlement during colonial times and representing a major proportion of the best quality land in the African regions, had been registered under individual title.[14]

Kenya's deep commitment to land registration has evoked a certain amount of debate. Some development analysts have criticized the program as a major contributor to the growing inequality of land ownership, and as a contributing factor to growing landlessness. Others assert that Kenya's ability to sustain a positive rate of agricultural growth has resulted more from the removal of restrictions on African cultivation of cash crops, and from such factors as technological innovation and the cultivation of previously unutilized areas, than from particular forms of land tenure. Whatever the empirical force of these arguments, it seems clear that they have not diminished the Kenyan government's commitment to land registration; in the most recent development plan, Kenya announced its intention to accelerate the program.[15]

The government's continuing commitment to this policy reflects its conviction that a free market in land is an essential basis for the economic growth of the agricultural sector. There is an unshakable assumption, for example, that the free market can bring about the most efficient pattern of land allocation and use. Government leaders defend this belief on the basis that individual ownership of land encourages landowners to invest in the development of their farms, and that it facilitates private lending for agricultural development, since land titles can be used as collateral for loans. Defenders of the program also point out that it helps break down the cultural and physical boundaries between ethnic communities by promoting land occupancy on an individual rather than group basis, and that, in the Kenyan context, private ownership has positive ecological ramifications, since individual landholders have a personal stake in protecting the long-term value of their investment.

Pricing Policy

The most useful point of departure for understanding agricultural producer pricing in Kenya is to recollect that independent African countries as a group have been criticized for a tendency to suppress agricultural producer prices below levels that provide farmers with adequate production incentives. In such analyses, the key explanatory hypothesis is generally urban bias, the notion that producer prices are fixed on the basis of political pressures exerted by urban interest groups. This analytical viewpoint has been well documented by the World Bank and by independent academic observers.[16] Kenya, however, may well represent Africa's major exception to this generalization. According to Cathy Jabara, an agricultural economist with the USDA, Kenya's pattern of producer pricing does not conform to the World Bank model. Her analysis of Kenya's pricing policies from 1972 to 1983 suggests an opposite conclusion:

> Within the period covered by this analysis, Kenya has used agricultural pricing policy to create incentives for increased agricultural production and to meet its development goals of promoting smallholder production. This finding runs counter to the widely held notion that pricing policy in African countries is uniformly inimical to producer interests. . . . Significantly, this conclusion was reached by taking into account real income received from agricultural production, as well as real prices received by producers.[17]

To understand Kenya's producer pricing policies, it is useful to divide its crops into three categories: (1) export crops; (2) domestic food staples, especially maize; and (3) crops that substitute for agricultural imports.

Export Crops

The second cornerstone of Kenya's agrarian success has been the government's ability to maintain an overall pattern of commmodity pricing that provides adequate incentives for producers of a wide variety of agricultural commodities to market an increasing volume of crops. This is most conspicuous in the case of Kenya's principal agricultural exports, coffee and tea. Export volumes of these two crops have continued to grow in a steady upward trajectory since the mid-1970s. Kenya's pricing policy on coffee and tea differs fundamentally from that of virtually every other independent African country, in that the government does not set producer prices for these commodities. Rather, it allows the prices to be determined by and vary with the world market price. The export-pricing policy adopted by Kenya has been commonly referred to as a "throughput" system; that is, the world market prices of coffee and tea are simply passed on to the growers, after a modest percentage has been deducted to cover the operating costs of the parastatal corporations that handle the purchasing, transporting, and marketing of these commodities.[18]

As a result, Kenya's situation is markedly different than that of the vast majority of African countries, whose export producers have suffered from a steadily declining share of their crops' world-market value. Kenya's coffee and tea farmers have enjoyed a high percentage of the international price. Although generalizations about this factor are extremely hazardous, because of the abrupt year to year fluctuations in the world prices of agricultural commodities, members of the planning staff in Kenya's Ministry of Agriculture and Livestock Development calculate that Kenya's tea producers, on average, receive more than 90 percent of the world-market price, and that coffee producers generally receive about 70 percent.[19]

Kenya's system of "throughput" pricing has immense theoretical significance. It contradicts the most common generalization about independent Africa's stagnating volume of export crops and its attendant loss of world-market share in exportable agricultural commodities: state suppression of producer prices. Kenyan agricultural authorities maintain that it is critically important, in the case of their country, to make a fundamental distinction between low producer prices as set by state agencies, and the adverse impact of generally low commodity prices in the world marketplace. From their standpoint, Kenyan export-crop producers suffer far more from low and very unpredictable international commodity prices than from the tendency of the government to lower prices far below world-market levels. (See Tables 6.1 and 6.2.)

Kenya's willingness to base producer prices for coffee and tea on prevailing international marketplace prices has resulted in a steady growth in exported volumes. As the statistical material in Chapter 4 reveals, growth in production of export crops during the past decade has been nearly comparable to that during the decade following independence, an achievement that is especially remarkable given the fact that Kenya's early growth occurred on top of a very small base. Between 1965 and 1975, Kenya's marketed coffee production had roughly doubled, increasing from between 35,000 and 40,000 metric tons to between 70,000 and 80,000 metric tons per year. Tea production nearly tripled during the same period, growing from about 20,000 metric tons to about 55,000 tons per year during the period 1973–1976. Kenya has enjoyed an almost equivalent increase in the pace of production of these crops during the past decade. By the mid-1980s, exports of each crop had begun to approach a consistent level of 120,000 tons per year. In 1984, for example, exports of coffee and tea reached 118,000 tons and 116,000 tons respectively, despite the fact that this was a year of extreme drought.

Contrary to the views of those who felt that Kenya had exhausted the potential for expanding the land area under cultivation, it has also been able to achieve substantial increases in the acreage devoted to these two crops.

Between 1979/80 and 1983/84, for example, the total land area devoted to coffee increased by very nearly 50 percent, from 102,000 to 150,000 hectares. The land area devoted to tea has grown more slowly, increasing by only about 5 percent during the same period. But this may be less a result of exhausted potential to expand the land area devoted to tea than of the fact that, in order to protect the quality of its tea exports, the Kenyan government has imposed rigid restrictions on the spread of tea plantations and has allowed only gradual expansion of smallholder cultivation. There is also reason to doubt the suggestion that Kenya has exhausted the potential for further production increases based on improved methods of husbandry. In the case of both crops, yields per hectare are approximately twice as high on the large-scale plantations, where the most up-to-date methods of cultivation are employed, than in the smallholder areas. This would appear to indicate that there is considerable opportunity for increased production based on better husbandry on smallholder farms.

Maize

Maize is by far the most important food crop grown in Kenya. It is generally estimated to provide between 50 and 70 percent of the caloric intake of the population. It probably accounts for between 35 and 40 percent of the total land under cultivation. And if the value of maize grown for home consumption is added to that purchased in the marketplace, it is also the country's single most valuable crop. Maize is also by far the country's least-understood agricultural good. Very little is known, for example, about what proportion of the country's total maize crop is consumed directly by peasant households, or about what percentage is marketed informally rather than through the country's official grain parastatal, the National Cereals and Produce Board (NCPB). As John de Wilde has pointed out, these uncertainties continue to generate debates about such basic matters as whether smallholder maize growers respond to price incentives, the total amount of land devoted to maize, total annual maize production, and the country's average maize yield per hectare.[20]

No other single aspect of Kenya's agricultural policy has been as controversial as maize pricing. The government has adopted a policy of strictly regulating the price of maize at all levels, not only the price paid to the producer, but those that can be legally charged at the processing and retail levels as well. Because maize prices are a matter of such great importance to both producers and consumers, the final decisions about prices are made at the highest levels of government. It is generally understood that the country's producer prices reflect the political inputs of the president, key members of the cabinet, and the highest-ranking administrative officials of certain ministries, including Agriculture and Livestock Development, and Finance and Planning.

It may be useful to recapitulate briefly the manner in which the government arrives at its official prices: Each fall, following the

September–October harvest, the Planning Section of the agricultural ministry begins research, the purpose being to forecast the country's maize requirements for the following year and the price level that will be necessary to elicit the appropriate amount of marketed surplus. The minister, acting on this research, makes price recommendations to the cabinet early in the calendar year, normally well before the end of January. After approximately one month's deliberation at the cabinet and presidential levels, maize prices are announced in early to mid-February.

The idea underlying the pricing cycle is that since approximately three-fourths of the country's maize crop is planted in early spring (April) for fall (September–October) harvest, the country's maize producers should have ample advance time to make basic planning decisions (such as land allocation and crop mix) and to apply for planting loans in time to acquire the necessary inputs. This system of producer pricing has certain obvious built-in disabilities, not the least of which is that the research on the basis of which maize prices are annually determined must be conducted at least a full year in advance of the actual harvest. Such critically important factors as climate and import- and export-parity price levels can only be guessed at. Other important variables, such as the rate of utilization of carryover stocks, can only be roughly approximated, since an undetermined proportion of the country's maize transactions are conducted on the informal market. The system has also been blamed for chronic late announcements, which make it extremely difficult for farmers to prepare the land effectively or to obtain the necessary production credits. Since Kenya's official maize prices are both pan-territorial and pan-seasonal, the system has inevitably been faulted for persistently penalizing efficient, large-scale producers with low transportation costs in order to subsidize less efficient smallholders, whose farms are located at some distance from the country's major urban centers.

Kenya's maize-pricing system has become the subject of heated debate between government officials and some of the country's major donors, such as the World Bank and USAID. The donor critics of the system are often adamant in their insistence that, compared to the free market, it results in lower than shadow-market prices for producers, unnecessarily high prices for consumers, extreme unpredictability in supply (resulting in the need for periodic imports), and consistently lower levels of marketed surplus than would be forthcoming in the absence of governmental intervention.[21] World Bank economists have also condemned the system as inherently prone to widespread corruption, since it places great discretionary authority in the hands of purchasing agents at local buying stations, and for a propensity toward administrative mismanagement and bureaucratic inefficiency. To correct these faults, donors have at some times recommended dismantling the official pricing system and dissolving the NCPB, in order to replace them by a pricing system based wholly on market considerations. In recent years, Kenya's principal donors have advocated more moderate reforms, such as the introduction of a floor-and-ceiling price system, one which would set parameters within which a free market would be allowed to operate.

To understand Kenya's commitment both to maintaining an official system of maize pricing and to implementing the system through the NCPB, it may be helpful to be aware of the government's objectives: The principal goal is not to maximize maize production but, rather, to attain the highest possible degree of self-sufficiency in the country's major food staple. Kenya's agricultural planners are, to a very large extent, motivated by the classic economic principle of comparative advantage. This principle suggests unambiguously that Kenya should maximize the production of coffee and tea while seeking merely to avoid unnecessary imports of maize. Kenyans are profoundly aware of the fact that, compared to countries that regularly export grain in the world market, Kenya is an inefficient and high-cost producer. Its cost of production is generally estimated to be well above export-parity price levels. Thus, if Kenya were maximizing maize production, it would be producing surpluses that could only be disposed of on the international marketplace at a substantial economic loss. More importantly, allowing maize prices to rise to a level that encouraged the production of exportable surpluses would, in all likelihood, drain production inputs away from such crops as coffee and tea, commodities in which Kenya does have a substantial comparative advantage.

Kenyan officials are also deeply skeptical of the reasoning underlying the World Bank's recommendation that the country's maize-marketing system be placed in the hands of private traders. They disagree in particular with the proposition that competition between traders will force the price to the producer upward, while, at the same time, forcing the price to the consumer downward. In their judgment, peasant farmers are highly vulnerable to economic exploitation. Thus, it is at least equally plausible that if private merchants are allowed to operate in Kenya's remote rural areas, they will engage in price collusion, with pernicious effects: lowering the price to the producer while raising the ultimate retail cost to urban consumers. Administrators at all levels of Kenya's agricultural system express the deepest conviction that individual peasant households, producing only small amounts of maize, are highly susceptible to such collusion because they lack bargaining leverage. There is also concern that if maize traders begin to make production loans to peasant families, with land as collateral, they may soon come to possess large amounts of the country's arable land, displacing the original owners and contributing to the country's already sizable problem of urban unemployment.

As Kenyans see it, then, the critical question is not to maintain or dissolve the official pricing system but, rather, to set a price level that will provide the greatest likelihood of an adequate supply of maize for national consumption, without generating surpluses that would need to be exported. To achieve a careful calibration of domestic supply and demand, Kenyans have chosen to set maize prices slightly below import parity. The economic assumptions underlying this pricing strategy are fairly straightforward. If the official price being offered by the NCPB were above import parity, this could be expected to encourage maize imports, either legal or illegal, and the result would be a maize glut, which would quickly make it necessary to reduce the price being offered to the local producer. If the maize price were set substantially below import parity (that is, closer to export parity), this would result in a price level so close to or so far below the cost of production that maize producers would either shift to other crops or withhold their crop from the official market. The result would be a serious shortfall in domestically marketed production, the inevitable growth of a massive informal market in maize, and an increasing need for imports. Kenyan agricultural authorities are deeply aware of the traumatic economic difficulties faced by African countries that have sought to suppress the producer-price levels of their basic food staples and wish desperately to avoid the same experience.

The remarkable feature of maize pricing in Kenya is its consistent success in setting official producer prices close to import parity, and the unsurpassed record of national food self-sufficiency this pricing policy has yielded. Table 6.3 and its accompanying graph compare maize prices in Kenya and Tanzania to the extent to which they approach import parity. Not surprisingly, the difference between the two countries is dramatic. Kenya's adjusted producer prices for maize tend to follow and closely approximate the import-parity price, regularly falling close to the midpoint between export and import parity, an outstanding record of performance in pricing policy. Tanzania's maize prices consistently fall short of this goal.

One characteristic of maize prices in Kenya is that they exceed Tanzania's. Table 6.4 compares Kenya's adjusted producer price for maize with that of Tanzania for the period 1968–1986.

By the mid-1980s, Kenya's adjusted maize prices were regularly three to four times higher than Tanzania's, a difference that, in and of itself, explains Kenya's superior performance in the production of this key commodity.

The same pattern of price differentials can be discerned with respect to other key food-grains as well, including wheat, rice, millet, and sorghum. As Tables 6.5, 6.6, 6.7, and 6.8 reveal, Kenya's grain prices during the late 1970s and early 1980s were consistently several times greater than those of Tanzania. By the mid-1980s, Kenya's adjusted wheat prices had climbed as high as four to six times those of Tanzania, and its rice prices were four to five times higher. Only in the case of the drought-resistant, nonpreferred grains does the pattern of extreme price differentiation break down. Although Kenya's prices for millet and sorghum were generally higher than Tanzania's in the mid-1980s, the difference was not nearly so great. This was undoubtedly due in large measure to Tanzania's determination to place its highest degree of emphasis on drought-resistant grains.

As a result of its grain-pricing policy, Kenya presents a major exception to the proposition that food deficits in Africa are caused by policies intended to lower the price of food staples for urban consumers. As Table 4.9 reveals, Kenya is a food-deficit country only in exceptional years, such as times of drought. During the past decade, for example, Kenya has been compelled to import significant volumes of food-grains on only two occasions, 1980 and 1984. On neither of these occasions do food imports appear to have been the result of poor pricing policy. In 1980, maize was imported because of an unusual combination of circumstances: To cope with a large surplus inventory of maize carried over from a bumper harvest in the fall of 1978 (one so large that it had occasioned maize exports), the government set a particularly low maize price for the fall of 1979. This was intended to reduce NCPB inventories to manageable proportions. Price planners could not have anticipated that 1979 would be a year of serious drought. The result of the coincidence of climatic difficulties and low prices was the need for substantial imports in 1980, only two years after the country had been forced to export in order to handle its surplus.[22]

Kenya was also a heavy maize importer in 1984, a year of such severe drought that this factor alone explains the need for imports. According to most observers, the 1984 drought may well have been the worst to befall the country in this century. There was a virtually complete failure of the rains that spring, when approximately 75 percent of the country's maize was planted. Total maize production dropped by about 40 percent, from an anticipated 2.2–2.4 million tons to only about 1.4 million tons, necessitating imports of approximately 565,000 tons to compensate for the shortfall in the domestically marketed surplus. Indeed, total cereals imports during 1984/85 amounted to nearly 950,000 tons, as Kenya's need for imported wheat also grew substantially because of the shortage of domestically grown maize.

A significant feature of Kenya's 1984/85 cereals imports is that they were obtained, for the most part, through straightforward commercial transactions, rather than as food aid.[23] Kenya's ability to buy food imports is one of the major goals of its national food policy: self-sufficiency. Kenya's agricultural planners make a critical distinction between the goal of self-sufficiency and the idea of being self-supplying, two objectives that involve very different sorts of pricing policy. For Kenyan planners, the idea of self-sufficiency does not imply that a country must be able to supply all of its own cereals needs at all times and under all conditions. Rather, in their view, it is economically preferable to be self-supplying only in average-to-good years and to have a diversified agricultural economy sufficiently buoyant to finance food imports during exceptional years. Kenya's commercial food imports during 1984/85 were made possible largely by the economic strength of its coffee and tea industries.

The most significant feature of Kenya's 1984/85 imports, however, was that they ended in mid-1985, when the country's rainfall pattern returned to normal. Indeed, by the end of 1985, Kenya's maize reserves were so great that plans were being made to export some of the surplus. Kenya's ability to terminate food importation is of importance in revealing the critical difference between Kenya's food imports and those of so many other African countries. Kenya's food imports are not a matter of long-term structural necessity, caused by a policy of price suppression, and it would be unfortunate if Kenya's occasional maize imports were interpreted as evidence of the failure of its pricing system. Kenya's cereals imports are of an episodic and short-term nature. They result naturally from a pricing policy that seeks to be self-supplying only in years of average-to-good weather, lest maize production compete in all years with the production of coffee and tea for export.

Import-Substituting Crops

At the time of independence, Kenya was a heavy importer of four vitally important agricultural commodities: sugar, cotton, barley, and tobacco. Each of these was vital as an industrial input. Sugar is, in fact, doubly important: as industrial input (since it is a key ingredient in the production of soft drinks, candy, and a variety of bakery goods) and as a food staple (since Kenyans drink coffee and tea heavily laced with sugar and milk). Barley is, of course, the key ingredient in the brewing industry; cotton in the manufacture of textiles; and tobacco in the production of cigarettes. If import-substituting industries are to succeed in these fields, it is essential that Kenya be able to supply its own needs for raw inputs, so that scarce foreign-exchange reserves can be freed for the purchase of capital goods and other production inputs that can be acquired only abroad. Kenya's success in increasing its domestic production of these crops has been little short of astonishing and constitutes one of the lesser-known aspects of its agricultural success story. Despite rapid increases in the industrial utilization of these commodities, Kenya became wholly self-supplying in sugar and barley in 1979; in tobacco in 1982, and in cotton by about 1978.[24]

Important questions of pricing policy remain to be resolved for these commodities. The world price of sugar in the 1980s, for example, is only about one-sixth its 1960s level; Kenya could now easily import sugar at far less than its own cost of production. Since sugar and maize are agricultural substitutes, Kenyans have begun to allow the domestic price of sugar to drift downward relative to the price of maize, thereby encouraging, at the cost of modest sugar imports, some conversion of sugar land to maize production. The pace and extent of this changeover are necessarily subjects of intense analysis within the agricultural ministry, especially since Kenya has invested large amounts of capital in the development of a network of sugar-refining factories. Kenya's commitment to a continued expansion of smallholder cotton production has also been questioned, especially by members of the donor community. The further expansion of cotton cultivation will require large-scale and highly expensive irrigation schemes, whose capital costs per household far exceed those in any other developing sector of the agricultural economy. The critical point about this kind of policy decision, however, is that it should be kept in perspective, since it is of a sort that automatically arises in any complex and rapidly maturing agricultural economy, in Africa or elsewhere. The existence of troublesome and unresolved policy issues is a universal feature of all highly developed and market-oriented agricultural systems. The presence of such issues in Kenya is not evidence of fundamental deficiencies in its pattern of agricultural pricing.

Of greater potential long-term importance is the fact that Kenya has reported a consistent downward trend in the agricultural terms of trade (the relationship between agricultural prices and the prices of consumer goods) since the early 1980s. By 1982, for example, the agricultural terms of trade were only about 80 percent of their 1976 level; because the costs of consumer goods continued to rise, the trend continued through 1984, the last year for which figures are presently available.[25] The Kenyan government has summarized this trend as follows:

> The long-term trend of deteriorating terms of trade in agriculture continued in 1984 with the index standing at 94.4 compared with 98.1 in 1983. . . . Despite an improvement in commodity prices, there was no improvement in the terms of trade that was hoped for. While the index on agricultural output prices rose by 9.2 percent between 1983 and 1984, the index for prices paid by farmers increased substantially by 13.5 percent. In spite of a lower rate of domestic inflation in 1984, the agricultural sector, however, remained disadvantaged relative to the rest of the economy.[26]

If this trend should continue, Kenya might face serious difficulties in maintaining agricultural prices at levels that encourage steady increases in the volume of marketed production.

The key feature of Kenya's agricultural performance thus far, however, has been its ability to generate increased real incomes among smallholders, despite the fall in the agricultural terms of trade. By maintaining real producer prices at levels that are as high as possible consistent with border prices, while fostering a continuous increase in yields (and thereby in the volume of marketed goods), Kenya has succeeded in increasing the real income level of its smallholder farmers almost 200 percent since 1972.[27] And, contrary to the experience of a good number of African countries—where there is evidence that rural deprivation is a form of subsidy for urban income levels—there is strong evidence for the belief that Kenya's high level of smallholder income has been achieved, to some degree, by imposing high price levels for agricultural products on urban consumers and on the urban factories that depend on agricultural inputs.

Exchange-Rate Policy

The conventional wisdom holds that African countries overvalue their currencies as a means of propping up the purchasing power of urban wage earners, and that the effect of this policy is to suppress the value of producer prices for both export crops and domestically consumed food staples. Since overvaluation tends to lower the cost of imported goods favored by urban consumers, while indirectly increasing the prices of agricultural inputs required by rural producers, it is generally considered to be a prime factor in shifting the internal terms of trade of African countries against the countryside. The World Bank has commented on this tendency in the following terms:

> The most striking similarity in the trade and exchange rate policies of African governments has been the tendency to let real official exchange rates become overvalued because of higher inflation at home than abroad. [The] statistical evidence along with the increasing use of trade and payments restrictions, the large profit opportunities offered by smuggling, the wide gap between official and black market exchange rates, and the loss of market shares of many traditional exports, all indicate that overvaluation is widespread.[28]

World Bank economists believe strongly that overvaluation creates foreign-exchange scarcities; that these result in one form or another of official rationing; and that when governments responsive to urban interest groups establish rationing systems, these work to the disadvantage of their agricultural populations. Small wonder that currency devaluation is almost invariably among the very first conditions currently attached to loans by both the World Bank and the IMF.

Kenya represents a significant exception to the general African trend toward overvaluation. Since the late 1970s, Kenya has adopted an official policy of flexible exchange-rate adjustments as an integral part of its overall program of structural adjustment.[29] Between 1978 and 1981, for example, Kenya devalued its currency by approximately 40 percent, from U.S. $1 = Shs.(K) 7.4 to U.S. $1 = Shs.(K) 10.3. Since that time, the Kenyan shilling has been devalued an additional 50 percent and now stands at approximately U.S. $1 = Shs.(K) 16. The ultimate barometer of an exchange-rate policy, however, is the ratio between a country's official rate and that existing in shadow markets; i.e., its *de facto*, unofficial rate of exchange. Because unofficial transactions are illegal in Kenya, this differential is intrinsically difficult to measure systematically. But there is strong evidence that Kenya's policy of flexible downward adjustments has been a success. As table 6.9 demonstrates, the unofficial exchange rate for the Kenyan shilling has rarely exceeded the official rate by more than 20 percent. The comparison with Tanzania, where the unofficial rate has sometimes exceeded the official rate by a factor of ten, could not be greater.

Kenya's approach to devaluation differs strikingly from that of other African countries. Many African countries, including Tanzania, tend to make currency devaluation a highly visible political question that becomes a source of open and sometimes ideological confrontation with international lending institutions such as the World Bank or IMF. Indeed, some African leaders have gone so far as to suggest that national pride is at stake in the maintenance of an existing rate of exchange between their currencies and those of Western Europe or the United States. The result of this approach is that currency devaluation becomes extremely difficult to execute. Kenya's ability to sustain a realistic exchange rate results from a different approach, a determination that exchange-rate adjustments will be a matter of low visibility. Its tendency has been to have a series of periodic and modest downward adjustments as these seemed appropriate and necessary, rather than to wait until a major revaluation is called for. When adjustments do occur, they are introduced in such a manner as to garner minimal public attention.

One of the most important outcomes of Kenya's exchange-rate policy has been the country's ability to avoid a hemorrhage of its foreign-currency reserves into illegal channels. In countries where the differential is so great that the national currency is virtually valueless in terms of its real purchasing power, there has been a pervasive tendency for hard-currency earnings to dissipate, through unsanctioned transactions, into private hands. And private individuals who obtain hard currency in this manner will almost inevitably deposit it in overseas accounts. A large proportion of the earnings from agricultural exports in countries with overvalued currency tends to disappear in this manner, with the result that it is unavailable to finance the purchase of needed agricultural or industrial inputs or consumer goods. Thus, there is a close connection between currency overvaluation, on the one hand, and a low rate of industrial-capacity utilization and serious shortage of agricultural inputs, on the other. A shortage of consumer goods can also have a crippling effect on agricultural production, for no amount of increase in the nominal price levels of agricultural products will induce rural producers to sell their commodities on the official marketplace unless the goods they wish to acquire are available for purchase.

Even the most casual observer of Kenya today would conclude that it has been able to avoid most of these problems. Its industrial sector is able to operate at a high percentage of installed capacity, and such constraints as do operate seem to originate from the limited markets available in nearby countries and Europe, rather than from a scarcity of production inputs. Similarly, there have been no reports of shortages of agricultural inputs caused by foreign-exchange constraints. While the officials of donor agencies sometimes comment critically on problems of inefficiency in the national delivery system for such vital inputs as fertilizer, there have been no indications of an inadequate supply attributable to the country's inability to make purchases overseas. And, perhaps most importantly from the standpoint of marketed levels of agricultural production, Kenya has been able to maintain an abundant supply of a wide variety of consumer goods. Whereas it makes sense in many African countries to distinguish carefully between price increases and production incentives, this distinction has little applicability in the Kenyan context. Kenya's agricultural producers can confidently use their income in the national currency to obtain the imported goods they want or need.

In sum, Kenya's consistent maintenance of a realistic exchange rate is an integral feature of its growth-oriented agricultural policies. It has minimized the anticountryside shift in internal terms of trade by assuring rural producers of a high level of purchasing power for their income; it has avoided a disruptive loss of foreign-exchange to overseas accounts, thereby insuring its availability to finance the import of needed production inputs for the industrial and agricultural sectors; and it has helped sustain a sufficiently adequate supply of consumer goods to avoid the emergence of informal markets for agricultural exports. Because the country's official levels of foreign-exchange have been sufficient to permit prompt repayment of foreign debts, it currently enjoys an impeccable reputation for creditworthiness. Thus, Kenya's willingness to adopt a flexible stance on exchange-rate adjustments has also been the basis for a generally cordial relationship between the government and its principal international donors. As a result, it seems likely that should a future economic crisis arise, Kenya will be able to draw on this reputation to obtain emergency credit.

Parastatal Corporations

Analyses of Africa's agricultural decline commonly place heavy emphasis on the poor managerial and financial performance of the continent's all-pervasive parastatal corporations. The following comment, in a study of parastatal agencies prepared for the USAID, is typical of an entire genre of developmental analysis that places much of the blame for the continent's agrarian malaise squarely on these agencies:

> The parastatals impede the development process by creating disincentives to production by small farmers. The government's policies require the parastatals to tax these farmers through artifically low product prices. They discriminate against the farmers through control of production inputs. They use their regulatory powers to reward political support and to punish opposition, thereby rendering the small farmers not only economically disadvantaged, but also politically impotent. . . . The parastatals pricing policies . . . create price distortions in factor and product markets which lead to misallocation of resources and economic inefficiencies.[30]

The authors of this report argue strongly that parastatal corporations are the key tools in the implementation of agricultural policies biased toward urban political interests and that their additional function is to provide rent-seeking opportunities for members of the political elite.

The critics of parastatal agencies are virtually unanimous in their conviction that the source of the problem is the legal monopoly these bodies have over the purchasing, processing, and vending of the commodities under their jurisdiction. Lack of competition means there is no incentive to efficient operation, or to the building of effective working relationships with agricultural producers. Indeed, the very absence of competition is itself seen as an incentive to corruption, overstaffing, and, ultimately, indifference to matters of quality and marketed volume. An additional problem is that, though parastatal agencies are intended to function, in large degree, like independent corporations, they are structured and administered as agencies of the governmental bureaucracy. That is, there is very little, if any, connection between parastatals' profits and losses on the one hand, and their staffing levels and salary structures on the other. As a result, many analysts of Africa's parastatal corporations hold a strong conviction that the continent's agricultural sector would perform immeasurably better if these organizations were abolished or, at the very least, severely curtailed in their powers and functions.

It would be naive to suggest that Kenya's agricultural parastatals are entirely an exception to these generalizations. Certain tendencies noted by parastatal critics are endemic in public-sector bureaucracies, not only in Africa but in the world's most advanced industrial societies; some of these problems can be discerned in Kenya's agricultural bureaucracy. But, against the background of a virtually worldwide agricultural depression, as well as the pandemic agrarian malaise of the vast majority of independent African countries, Kenya's contemporary performance has been commendable. It would be a serious mistake, then, to liken Kenya to other African countries where managerial and administrative problems in the parastatals have emerged as a crippling constraint on agricultural performance. Indeed, Kenya's record of consistent agricultural growth would have been impossible if parastatal mismanagement had been a major economic disincentive.

The quality of Kenya's parastatal system is most visible in the area of agricultural exports, where the record shows continuous increases in the level of marketed production since independence.[31] Kenya's tea parastatal, for example, has been cited by the World Bank as an exemplar in fostering smallholder development:

> The Kenya Tea Development Authority is widely acknowledged to be a remarkably successful institution in two fields—smallholder rural development and public sector enterprise—in which the African experience has often been fraught with difficulties and disappointing experience. In roughly two decades it has organized the planting of about 54,000 hectares of tea by some 138,000 smallholders, and has become a major processor and the largest exporter of black tea in the world.[32]

Kenya's Coffee Board could also be cited as a positive developmental force, for it has consistently returned a high percentage of the world market price to the country's coffee producers, thereby contributing directly to Kenya's emergence as a major coffee exporter. During the period 1971–1975, for example, the nominal coefficient of protection for coffee was .94, a figure that compared favorably with every other important African coffee producer.[33] And though the Coffee Board has returned an average of only about 70 percent of the world price to farmers in recent years, the decrease may reflect more on the extreme fluctuations in the price of coffee, and the difficulty of marketing a sizable proportion of the crop in non-quota countries, than on internal administrative inefficiency.

Although other of Kenya's parastatals have not performed up to the level of its coffee and tea marketing agencies, only one has generated significant controversy: the grain marketing monopoly, NCPB. This massive parastatal was formed in 1979, through the merger of the Maize and Produce Marketing Board and the Wheat Board. The government of Kenya has entrusted the NCPB with truly monumental responsibilties. It is the sole agency legally authorized to purchase maize from the country's growers; it has also been given exclusive authority to import and export maize. To reinforce the NCPB's monopoly, the government has issued a series of supplemental regulations, such as those forbidding transportation of more than certain amounts maize between districts or regions except by the NCPB or its licensed traders. Additional regulations intended to buttress the NCPB's monopoly give great discretionary powers of enforcement to provincial and district authorities. To further entrench itself, the NCPB discontinued the use of licensed traders in 1980 and increased the number of buying depots.

The NCPB has been widely criticized for inefficiency and poor management of the country's major food staple. Some critics have suggested that its high operating margin constitutes an economic disincentive significant enough to lower the amount of maize marketed.[34] Other critics have focused on its basic inability to stabilize the country's maize supply by providing a reliable market for producers or a reliable source for consumers. De Wilde's analysis encapsulates a range of critical analyses:

> The NCPB has been unable to monopolize the market. In the six years 1975/76–1980/81, NCPB purchases amounted to only 20% of the estimated total output, although 35% or more of the total crop is probably marketed. . . . The volume of NCPB purchases has fluctuated widely from year to year, ranging from a low of 131,000 tons in 1979/80 to highs of 552,000 and 536,000 tons in 1975/76 and 1976/77 respectively.[35]

Still other criticisms focus on the inherent impossibility of administering any marketing system based on pan-territorial and pan-seasonal pricing. Since the official producer price for maize remains constant throughout the year, there is no incentive for farmers to withhold a portion of their production, thus taking advantage of seasonal price fluctuations. As a result, deliveries to the NCPB's purchasing depots tend to be concentrated within a fairly short period of time; this inevitably strains the organization's facilities and delays both handling and processing and payments to farmers.

Officials of the government of Kenya staunchly defend the country's grain-marketing system and, while acknowledging the possibility of administrative improvement, insist that the operation of an official monopoly is much preferable to a market dominated by private traders. They believe that the NCPB monopoly is indispensable in fulfilling the government's overall objectives: to regulate the country's maize trade for the benefit of both producers and consumers; and to set price levels that will elicit a sufficient output to meet the country's domestic maize needs, without encouraging production of surpluses, which could only be sold at a loss on the world market. Kenya's agricultural planners approach their country's maize-marketing system with several basic economic assumptions.[36] One is that if maize prices were not carefully regulated, there would be great variation from one season to the next and from year to year; this fluctuation would result in complete uncertainty of supply. Under free-market conditions, they believe, there would be a marked increase in the need for food imports during deficit years and for loss-incurring food exports during surplus years.

Contrary to the view of World Bank officials, who believe that competition among traders would result in the best possible economic treatment of maize farmers, the Kenyans see their smallholder community as so atomized as to be highly vulnerable to price fixing and such extortionary practices as high charges for transportation and processing services. In the opinion of Kenyan agronomists, a free market could well result in very low retail maize prices during periods of abundance; this might well encourage additional dependence on maize, already the country's basic food, setting the stage for enormous urban unrest during periods of scarcity, when the price would inevitably rise to levels unaffordable for the majority of the population. There is no conclusive evidence that a free maize market would result in a lower average price over an extended period of time. Private traders could as easily collude to boost prices at the consumer level as to suppress them for producers. And even if there were a prospective gain in lowering the long-term average price, this would be more than offset by the convulsive and destabilizing effects of extreme short-term price fluctuations. The decision to opt for a carefully controlled maize-pricing system partially reflects a considered judgment about public policy: that long-term price stability for the country's food staple has social and political benefits far outweighing any gains in efficiency that might accrue from privatizing the market.

The most powerful argument for a controlled maize-pricing system, however, is economic and rests on the classic principle of comparative advantage. The goals of Kenya's overall system of producer pricing are to maximize the country's exports of high-quality coffee and tea and to produce self-sufficiency in maize. To achieve these objectives, the Kenyans believe they must be in a position to control the ratio between the country's maize prices and those for its principal agricultural exports. For without such control there is, inevitably, a possibility of an incentive for coffee, tea, and maize producers to shift among these commodities in ways that would not produce the greatest possible benefits for the society as a whole. Since coffee and tea prices fluctuate according to the world market, maize is the only major commodity susceptible to governmental planning. Kenya's agricultural economists are firmly convinced that their country's current system of producer pricing—throughput pricing for export crops and self-sufficiency pricing for maize—facilitates the highest possible level of net export earnings from agriculture. To make this system work, they argue, it is essential that the NCPB continue its role as the designated governmental agency for the implementation of an administered price system for maize.

The Kenyan arguments have found substantial empirical corroboration in the research of Barbara Grosh (University of California, Berkeley). According to Grosh, the NCPB has not operated as conventional stereotypes suggest; that is, it has not suppressed producer prices in order to subsidize urban consumers. She argues that "since the NCPB was created in 1980, producers have been favored over consumers."[37] In surveying agricultural parastatals as group, Grosh finds little evidence to support the views of those who cite their poor performance as a major constraint on development. Her principal conclusion states her position emphatically:

> The first conclusion which stands out is that the current fashion in some circles of speaking in blanket terms of how poorly [agricultural] parastatals perform is ill-founded. In the agricultural sector in Kenya, there have been seven firms which have performed well, some for two decades since independence. All have served large numbers of smallholder farmers, a role which requires a fairly large and complex organization, which makes the success achieved all the more impressive.[38]

Arguing further for a positive overall evaluation, Grosh adds that a number of Kenya's agricultural parastatals have weathered adverse market conditions, both external and internal, and that adverse international circumstances have not generally resulted in institutional decline.

This position has begun to win increasing, if grudging, acceptance among Kenya's major donors; there is now less insistence that the government dissolve the NCPB and move toward a free-market pricing system for maize. Instead, the World Bank presently advocates that Kenya merely employ the NCPB as "buyer and seller of last resort." Such a system, bank officials argue, would enable the government to continue to set a minimal, or floor, price for producers and a ceiling price for consumers. Private traders could then be allowed to operate in the band between these two price levels. The advantage of this system, according to World Bank economists, is that it would enable Kenya to combine the best features of administered and free markets. Traders could not behave exploitively because the NCPB would be prepared to intervene in the marketplace if prices should threaten to drop below or rise above officially designated parameters. But it would be spared the need to maintain the bureaucratically cumbersome apparatus necessary to fulfill its present legal mandate to absorb all the surplus maize offered by producers on the marketplace.

CONCLUSION

Kenya's principal agricultural policies—land, pricing, exchange rate, and marketing—have worked admirably to enable the country to emerge as a major participant in the global trading system for international commodities. It currently ranks tenth in the quotas assigned by the International Coffee Organization and may soon be expected to overtake Uganda and Ethiopia (sixth and eighth respectively), countries whose coffee exports are currently constrained by serious political difficulties. Kenya also ranks among the world's three largest tea exporters, alongside India and Sri Lanka, and enjoys a substantial price premium because of the quality of its tea. In addition, it is generally self-sufficient in basic food staples, importing or exporting only rarely and under unusual conditions. Kenya is, therefore, a major exception to that ensemble of African countries that have had to curtail industrial growth because of falling revenues from agricultural exports. Indeed, Kenya's export earnings from agriculture, combined with those from petroleum re-exports and tourism, continue to sustain a small boom in the development of import-substituting industries, including automobile and truck assembly.

One of the most remarkable aspects of Kenya's agricultural success has been its ability to take advantage of niches of opportunity in the world market for agricultural commodities. In recent years, for example, Kenya has been able to develop a sizable market in horticultural products among the countries of the EEC. And while this market may be somewhat disrupted by Spain's and Portugal's entry into the EEC, the prospects of Kenya's finding alternative consumer countries, possibly in the Middle East, seem good. For the past decade or more, Kenya has been in an exceptionally strong position to take advantage of short-term upward fluctuations in international commodity prices for beverages. It benefitted greatly, for example, from the beverage boom of 1977/78 and has been able to repeat this during the past two to three years. During 1984, Kenya was in a strong position to take advantage of a doubling of international tea prices caused by India's decision to ban tea exports during the first six months of the year. And in 1986, Kenya was extremely well positioned to take advantage of a sizable increase in international coffee prices, caused by severe frost in the coffee-producing regions of Brazil.

The critical questions for Kenya, then, do not have so much to do with the quality of its internal management of a highly complex and rapidly developing agricultural sector, but with the character of the international economic system as it affects countries dependent on the export of primary agricultural commodities. The most critical question is: Precisely what sort of economic future can a country that exports primary agricultural products anticipate? The most authoritative market forecasts available anticipate that world demand for agricultural goods will grow only slowly during the coming decade, while the world market for agricultural goods will become increasingly competitive. As a result, there is likely to be a problem of chronic oversupply, and the price levels of agricultural commodities in real terms may not rise appreciably.[39] Although there could be short-term exceptions to this generalization, such as during the tea boom of 1984 or the coffee boom of 1986, there is little reason to anticipate that the international market for agricultural goods will sustain anything more than the barest increases in GDP. Under these conditions, even well-managed countries such as Kenya may confront the prospect of declining GDP per-capita. If this bleak scenario should transpire, it will be incumbent on the donor community to distinguish carefully between those developing countries whose problems are caused by internal mismanagement, and those whose difficulties arise out of the unavoidable exigencies of the international marketplace.

NOTES

1. According to the World Bank, "total agricultural output grew at an impressive rate of 4.6% per annum from 1964 to 1972 but declined to only 2.0% per annum during 1972–77." The World Bank, *Kenya: Growth and Structural Change,* vol. 1, Annex 2, "Issues in Kenyan Agricultural Development" (Washington, D.C., 1983), p. 325.

2. See Norman N. Miller, *Kenya: The Quest for Prosperity* (Westview Press, Boulder, CO, 1984), pp. 71–78.

3. This point of view pervades the World Bank's most recently published study of Kenya: *Kenya: Growth and Structural Change.* See especially vol. 2, "Issues in Kenyan Agricultural Development," p. 329.

4. The World Bank, *Kenya: Growth and Structural Change,* p. 327.

5. Ibid., Table 3, p. 328.

6. It has been estimated that, between 1964 and 1973, the production of hybrid maize in Kenya grew from approximately 400 acres to about 800,000 acres.

7. The World Bank, *Kenya: Growth and Structural Change,* p. 345.

8. UN, Food and Agriculture Organization, *Food Situation in African Countries Affected by Emergencies: Special Report* (n.p., 1985), p. 28.

9. For an excellent treatment of the land issue during the late colonial period, see David F. Gordon, *Decolonization and the State in Kenya* (Westview Press, Boulder, CO, and London, 1986), especially Ch. 6, "Peasants Vs. Settlers: Land and Agricultural Policies."

10. See E. A. Brett, *Colonialism and Underdevelopment in East Africa: The Politics of Economic Change* (Heinemann, London, 1973), Ch. 6, "Kenya—Settlers Predominant," pp. 165–216.

11. For a full discussion of this project, see Christopher Leo, *Land and Class in Kenya* (University of Toronto Press, Toronto, 1984). See especially Chs. 5–7.

12. Kenya, *Sessional Paper Number 10: African Socialism and its Application to Planning in Kenya* (Government Printer, Nairobi, 1965), p. 28.

13. Michael Blundell, *So Rough a Wind: The Kenya Memoirs of Sir Michael Blundell* (Widenfeld and Nicolson, London, 1964), p. 217.

14. Kenya, Ministry of Planning and National Development, *Statistical Abstract* 1985 (Central Bureau of Statistics, Nairobi, n.d.), p. 3.

15. Kenya, *Development Plan 1984–1988* (Government Printer, Nairobi, 1983), p. 187.

16. There are two classic examples of this intellectual genre: The World Bank, *Accelerated Development in Sub-Saharan Africa: An Agenda for Action* (Washington, D.C. 1981); and Robert Bates, *Markets and States in Tropical Africa* (University of California Press, Berkeley and Los Angeles, 1981).

17. Cathy L. Jabara, "Agricultural Pricing Policy in Kenya," *World Development* 13, no. 5, (May 1985), p. 624.

18. The Kenyan government also imposes a fixed export tax when the world market price rises above a certain level.

19. Based on interviews conducted in the Ministry of Agriculture, Planning Section, during the summers of 1984 and 1985.

20. John de Wilde, *Agriculture, Marketing and Pricing in Sub-Saharan Africa* (Crossroads Press for African Studies Association and African Studies Center, Los Angeles, 1984), p. 17.

21. For a fuller discussion of these propositions, see Robert Bates, "The Maize Crisis of 1979/80: A Case Study and Update" (Unpublished ms., 1985), and Christopher D. Gerrard and Greg Posehn, "Government Interventions in Food Grain Markets in Kenya: An Update" (Unpublished ms., 1985).

22. In his case study of maize pricing in Kenya, Robert Bates has suggested that there is a policy-induced maize cycle, triggered by the fact that import-parity pricing tends to generate periodic surpluses. To manage these surpluses, the government is compelled to reduce the maize price drastically, and, when this happens to occur when there is a drought or serious rainfall deficit, the result is an abrupt oscillation from surplus to deficit in the country's maize supply. See Bates, "The Maize Crisis of 1979/80: A Case Study and Update."

23. FAO, *Food Situation,* p. 30–31. According to this document, Kenya imported 945,600 tons of cereals in 1984/85. Of this amount, 519,700 tons were obtained as commercial purchases and 425,900 tons as food aid.

24. Jabara, "Pricing Policy," p. 613.

25. Kenya, Ministry of Finance and Planning, *Economic Survey 1984* (Nairobi, 1984), p. 113; and Ministry of Finance and Planning, *Economic Survey 1985* (Nairobi, 1985), p. 109.

26. Kenya, *Economic Survey 1985,* p. 109.

27. Jabara, "Pricing Policy," Table 6, p. 623.

28. World Bank, *Accelerated Development,* pp. 24–25.

29. Kenya, *Development Plan, 1984–1988* (Government Printer, Nairobi, 1983), pp. 31–32.

30. Keene, Monk & Associates Inc., *Agricultural Parastatals* (Unpublished ms., Alexandria, Virginia, September, 1984), p. i.

31. See de Wilde, *Agriculture, Marketing and Pricing,* Table 2.1, p. 14.

32. Geoffrey Lamb and Linda Muller, *Control, Accountability, and Incentives in a Successful Development Institution: The Kenya Tea Development Authority* (The

World Bank, Washington, D.C., 1982), p. 1.

33. Keene, Monk & Associates, *Agricultural Parastatals*, Table 1, p. A-19. The nominal coefficient of protection is the price paid to the producer divided by the amount that would have been received in a pure throughput system; that is, the world price minus transport, processing, and marketing costs.

34. See, for example, David Sunding, "Supply Response and the Impact of Marketing Boards on Agricultural Production in Kenya's Rift Valley," (unpublished ms., Berkeley, California, 1985).

35. De Wilde, *Agriculture, Marketing and Pricing*, p. 17.

36. The author wishes to thank the members of the staff of the Planning Section of the Ministry of Agriculture and Livestock Development, who graciously consented to lengthy interviews on this subject during the summers of 1984 and 1985.

37. Barbara Grosh, "Agricultural Parastatals Since Independence: How Have They Performed?" Working Paper no. 435 (University of Nairobi, Institute for Development Studies, 1986), p. 44.

38. Ibid., pp. 45–46.

39. See, for example, *Commodity Trade and Price Trends* (The World Bank; Distributed by Johns Hopkins University Press, Baltimore and London, 1985); Ronald Duncan, ed., *The Outlook for Primary Commodities, 1984 to 1985* (The World Bank, Washington, D.C. 1984); and, The World Bank, *The Outlook for Primary Commodities, World Bank Staff Working Paper* no. 9 (Washington, D.C., 1983).

TABLE 6.1 Coffee Prices in Kenya, 1966/67–1979/80; and Ratio to Prices in Tanzania

Year	CURRENT PRODUCER PRICES in Sh/Ton		ADJUSTED PRODUCER PRICES Prices in Constant (1967) U.S.$ Adjusted to Parallel Market Exchange Rates		RATIO OF ADJUSTED PRICES Kenya to Tanzania
	Amount	Index	Amount	Index	
1966/67	6546	100	779.63	100	1.45
1967/68	5830	89	671.62	86	1.38
1968/69	6404	98	745.43	96	1.45
1969/70	6340	97	634.00	81	1.72
1970/71	7478	114	659.56	85	1.29
1971/72	6365	97	576.03	74	1.60
1972/73	7789	119	600.53	77	1.49
1973/74	9207	141	709.86	91	1.34
1974/75	9835	150	773.03	99	2.19
1975/76	10690	163	741.89	95	1.72
1976/77	25240	386	1600.22	205	3.21
1977/78	39750	607	2683.13	344	4.27
1978/79	28180	430	1780.98	228	3.49
1979/80	27860	426	1543.44	198	3.56

SOURCE: U.S. Department of Agriculture, Economic Research Service.

TABLE 6.2 Tea Prices in Kenya, 1966/67–1979/80; and Ratio to Prices in Tanzania

Year	CURRENT PRODUCER PRICES Official Rates in Sh/Ton		ADJUSTED PRODUCER PRICES Prices in Constant (1967) U.S.$ Adjusted to Parallel Market Exchange Rates		RATIO OF ADJUSTED PRICES Kenya to Tanzania
	Amount	Index	Amount	Index	
1966/67	7800	100	929	100	1.09
1967/68	7830	100	902	97	1.10
1968/69	5850	75	681	73	0.87
1969/70	6189	79	619	67	0.97
1970/71	6783	87	598	64	1.19
1971/72	6505	83	589	63	2.11
1972/73	6015	77	464	50	2.08
1973/74	5927	76	457	49	1.86
1974/75	7206	92	566	61	1.72
1975/76	7909	101	549	59	3.17
1976/77	10570	136	670	72	2.69
1977/78	21490	276	1451	156	3.32
1978/79	15832	203	1001	108	2.82
1979/80	13567	174	752	81	2.48

SOURCE: U.S. Department of Agriculture, Economic Research Service.

TABLE 6.3 Corn Producer Prices Compared to World Prices: Kenya and Tanzania, 1968-1985 (Prices in Current U.S.$ at Parallel Market Rates)

Year	Tanzania	World	Kenya
1968	$32.12	$60.90	$37.33
1969	$27.47	$66.10	$30.33
1970	$23.83	$68.90	$28.31
1971	$16.87	$66.70	$36.59
1972	$17.79	$71.60	$37.68
1973	$22.97	$119.30	$40.00
1974	$35.71	$158.70	$53.95
1975	$30.00	$154.10	$77.99
1976	$39.22	$138.90	$82.81
1977	$56.11	$114.40	$109.08
1978	$72.26	$132.50	$109.75
1979	$74.07	$154.80	$93.37
1980	$37.74	$210.30	$120.48
1981	$61.60	$181.00	$84.40
1982	$60.03	$137.40	$87.52
1983	$44.00	$162.20	$98.77
1984	$22.22	$167.30	$91.21
1985	$28.89	$134.40	$99.69

SOURCE: Producer prices provided by U.S. Department of Agriculture. World prices from World Bank, Commodity Trade and Price Trends (Johns Hopkins University Press, 1986), Section 5.

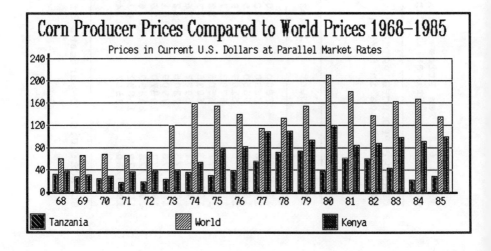

Corn Producer Prices Compared to World Prices 1968–1985
Prices in Current U.S. Dollars at Parallel Market Rates

TABLE 6.4 Corn Prices in Kenya, 1966–1986;
and Ratio to Prices in Tanzania

Year	CURRENT PRODUCER PRICES Official Rates in Sh/Ton		ADJUSTED PRODUCER PRICES Prices in Constant (1967) U.S.$ Adjusted to Parallel Market Exchange Rates		RATIO OF ADJUSTED PRICES Kenya to Tanzania
	Amount	Index	Amount	Index	
1966	401	130	47.76	133	*
1967	353	115	40.67	113	*
1968	308	100	35.85	100	1.16
1969	276	90	27.60	77	1.1
1970	276	90	24.34	68	1.16
1971	333	108	30.14	84	2.16
1972	390	127	30.07	84	2.11
1973	390	127	30.07	84	1.74
1974	464	151	36.47	102	1.51
1975	698	227	48.44	135	2.6
1976	766	249	48.56	135	2.11
1977	889	289	60.01	167	1.94
1978	889	289	56.18	157	1.51
1979	775	252	42.94	120	1.25
1980	1000	325	48.80	136	3.18
1981	1055	343	31.02	87	1.36
1982	1444	469	30.18	84	1.46
1983	1600	519	35.20	98	2.25
1984	1733	563	33.79	94	4.02
1985	1944	631	38.49	107	3.52
1986	2089	678	42.20	118	2.9

*Tanzanian producer prices not available for 1966 or 1967.
SOURCE: U.S. Department of Agriculture, Economic Research Service.

TABLE 6.5 Wheat Prices in Kenya, 1966–1986; and Ratio to Prices in Tanzania

Year	CURRENT PRODUCER PRICES Official Rates in Sh/Ton		ADJUSTED PRODUCER PRICES Prices in Constant (1967) U.S.$ Adjusted to Parallel Market Exchange Rates		RATIO OF ADJUSTED PRICES Kenya to Tanzania
	Amount	Index	Amount	Index	
1966	523	100	62.29	100	0.88
1967	545	104	62.78	101	0.95
1968	568	109	66.12	106	0.98
1969	563	108	56.30	90	1.04
1970	545	104	48.07	77	1.14
1971	451	86	40.82	66	1.34
1972	506	97	39.01	63	1.32
1973	506	97	39.01	63	1.22
1974	567	108	44.57	72	1.2
1975	804	154	55.80	90	2.25
1976	1047	200	66.38	107	1.93
1977	1203	230	81.20	130	1.79
1978	1333	255	84.25	135	1.55
1979	1333	255	73.85	119	1.61
1980	1436	275	70.08	113	2.78
1981	1667	319	49.01	79	1.48
1982	1777	340	37.14	60	1.26
1983	2167	414	47.67	77	2.03
1984	2690	514	52.46	84	5.55
1985	2933	561	58.07	93	3.84
1986	3178	608	64.20	103	2.85

SOURCE: U.S. Department of Agriculture, Economic Research Service.

TABLE 6.6 Rice Prices in Kenya, 1966-1986; and Ratio to Prices in Tanzania

Year	CURRENT PRODUCER PRICES Official Rates in Sh/Ton		ADJUSTED PRODUCER PRICES Prices in Constant (1967) U.S.$ Adjusted to Parallel Market Exchange Rates		RATIO OF ADJUSTED PRICES Kenya to Tanzania
	Amount	Index	Amount	Index	
1966	465	102	55.38	105	*
1967	441	97	50.80	96	*
1968	455	100	52.96	100	0.96
1969	458	101	45.80	86	0.86
1970	459	101	40.48	76	0.81
1971	507	111	45.88	87	1.52
1972	484	106	37.32	70	1.22
1973	508	112	39.17	74	1.22
1974	501	110	39.38	74	1.31
1975	586	129	40.67	77	1.64
1976	1045	230	66.25	125	2.31
1977	1369	301	92.41	174	2.12
1978	1369	301	86.52	163	1.65
1979	1449	318	80.27	152	1.57
1980	1508	331	73.59	139	2.75
1981	1508	331	44.34	84	1.28
1982	1700	374	35.53	67	1.00
1983	2700	593	59.40	112	2.09
1984	3250	714	63.38	120	5.03
1985	3400	747	67.32	127	4.01
1986	3750	824	75.75	143	3.44

*Tanzania rice prices are not available for 1966 or 1977.
SOURCE: U.S. Department of Agriculture, Economic Research Service.

TABLE 6.7 Millet Prices in Kenya, 1966–1983; and Ratio to Prices in Tanzania, 1968–1983*

Year	CURRENT PRODUCER PRICES Official Rates in Sh/Ton		ADJUSTED PRODUCER PRICES Prices in Constant (1967) U.S.$ Adjusted to Parallel Market Exchange Rates		RATIO OF ADJUSTED PRICES Kenya to Tanzania
	Amount	Index	Amount	Index	
1966	370	93	44.07	95	**
1967	380	95	43.78	94	**
1968	400	100	46.56	100	0.91
1969	390	98	39.00	84	1.01
1970	380	95	33.52	72	0.78
1971	320	80	28.96	62	1.01
1972	350	88	26.99	58	1.01
1973	350	88	26.99	58	0.93
1974	400	100	31.44	68	1.07
1975	560	140	38.86	83	1.84
1976	730	183	46.28	99	1.69
1977	730	183	49.28	106	0.67
1978	760	190	48.03	103	0.55
1979	930	233	51.52	111	0.75
1980	930	233	45.38	97	1.90
1981	1,116	279	32.81	70	1.45
1982	1,228	307	25.67	55	1.45
1983	1,350	338	29.70	64	2.09

* Kenya millet prices not available after 1983.
** Tanzania millet prices not available for 1966 or 1967.
SOURCE: U.S. Department of Agriculture, Economic Research Service.

TABLE 6.8 Sorghum Prices in Kenya, 1966-1985; and Ratio to Tanzania Prices

Year	CURRENT PRODUCER PRICES Official Rates in Sh/Ton		ADJUSTED PRODUCER PRICES Prices in Constant (1967) U.S.$ Adjusted to Parallel Market Exchange Rates		RATIO OF ADJUSTED PRICES Kenya to Tanzania
	Amount	Index	Amount	Index	
1966	304	92	36.21	95	**
1967	316	96	36.40	95	**
1968	329	100	38.30	100	1.11
1969	326	99	32.60	85	1.08
1970	316	96	27.87	73	0.91
1971	262	80	23.71	62	1.29
1972	293	89	22.59	59	1.10
1973	293	89	22.59	59	1.09
1974	328	100	25.78	67	0.96
1975	465	141	32.27	84	1.73
1976	620	188	39.31	103	1.52
1977	620	188	41.85	109	1.15
1978	680	207	42.98	112	0.99
1979	770	234	42.66	111	1.25
1980	770	234	37.58	98	2.46
1981	925	281	27.20	71	1.80
1982	1,017	309	21.26	56	1.13
1983	1,119	340	24.62	64	1.73
1984	*	*	*	*	*
1985	1,400	426	27.72	72	3.30

* Kenya sorghum prices not availab for 1984.
** Tanzania sorghum prices not available for 1966 and 1967.
SOURCE: U.S. Department of Agriculture, Economic Research Service.

**TABLE 6.9 Official and Parallel Market Exchange Rates
(Kenya Shilling)**

Year	Official Rate	Parallel Rate	Ratio: Parallel to Official
1965	7.14	8.52	1.19
1966	7.14	8.64	1.21
1967	7.14	8.68	1.22
1968	7.14	8.25	1.16
1969	7.14	9.10	1.27
1970	7.14	9.75	1.37
1971	7.14	9.10	1.27
1972	7.14	10.35	1.45
1973	6.90	9.75	1.41
1974	7.14	8.60	1.20
1975	8.26	8.95	1.08
1976	8.31	9.25	1.11
1977	7.95	8.15	1.03
1978	7.40	8.10	1.09
1979	7.33	8.30	1.13
1980	7.57	8.30	1.10
1981	10.29	12.50	1.21
1982	12.75	16.50	1.29
1983	13.70	16.20	1.18
1984	15.78	19.00	1.20
1985	16.28	19.50	1.20
1986	16.22	19.50	1.20

SOURCES. Official and Parallel exchange rates
1965-1984: Philip P. Cowitt (ed.), World Currency
Yearbook (International Currency Analysis, Brooklyn,
N.Y., 1985) p. 738; Franz Pick, Pick's Currency
Yearbook 1976-1977, p. 571; and Pick's Currency
Yearbook, 1970, p. 485. Exchange rates for 1985
and 1986: by interview in Nairobi.

·PART 3·

·7·

Roots of Policy:
Kenya's Farmer Elite,
Tanzania's Urban Elite

The essential policy differences between Kenya and Tanzania, and their attendant economic consequences, have probably been broadly familiar to most readers of this volume for some time. These two countries have been intensively studied by scholars of African development. It is surprising, given their relatively high degree of familiarity, that there have been so few efforts systematically to contrast these countries. Indeed, with the possible exception of the excellent *Politics and Public Policy in Kenya and Tanzania,* edited by Joel Barkan, there have been virtually no efforts to subject these countries to side-by-side comparison.[1] The absence of such comparison reflects the fact that the academic literature has consisted almost entirely of case studies of one or another aspect of Kenya or Tanzania.

During the 1970s, preoccupation with the "dependency" debate stimulated the publication of Colin Leys' now classic study, *Underdevelopment in Kenya,* and its equally classic rejoinder, Nicola Swainson's *The Development of Corporate Capitalism in Kenya 1918–1977.*[2] The central theoretical question in the dependency debate has been the nature of Kenya's dominant class. Pro-dependency theorists have seen this class as essentially *comprador* or auxiliary—inextricably beholden to Western economic interests. Those critical of this position, including Swainson, have seen Kenya's dominant class as a national bourgeoisie, involved in its own process of capital accumulation and investment.

Tanzanian studies have also resonated to this debate, most particularly Issa Shivji's widely read *Class Struggles in Tanzania.*[3] Indeed, since dependency theory in one guise or another has permeated the intellectual atmosphere of the University of Dar es Salaam, it is not surprising that this concern has dominated so much of the literature on the country. But Tanzanian studies have also had another focus: Tanzania's socialist strategy of development, and the factors that might help or impede its successful implementation. Among the outstanding works in this genre are Dean E. McHenry Jr.'s *Tanzania's Ujamaa Villages,* and the edited volume by Bismarck Mwansasu and Cranford Pratt, *Towards Socialism in Tanzania.*[4] The discussion of socialism in Tanzania has been somewhat influenced by

185

the dependency debate, with questions being raised as to whether the failure of the strategy might be explained by the intervention of Western economic interests. But the principal focus of attention has been on the question of whether peasant society is amenable to a collective mode of social organization, a topic that is currently dominated by Goran Hyden's controversial book, *Beyond Ujamaa*.[5]

As a study of economic policy and its effects, this volume is rooted in a different intellectual genre: the literature on state interventions in the marketplace and their consequences for economic growth. Its intellectual debt is to Michael Lipton's seminal volume, *Why Poor People Stay Poor*, and to Robert Bates' work on African agriculture, most particularly his book, *Markets and States in Tropical Africa*.[6] Lipton and Bates were among the first social scientists to show the extent to which the agricultural policies of modern African nations are dominated by the economic interests of urban social classes. Their work demonstrates the degree to which urban groups, customarily pitted in an adversarial relationship with groups such as industrialists and industrial workers, find common cause in policies that produce cheap food and that impose a disproportionately heavy tax burden on the countryside.

This author shares with Lipton and Bates the assumption that public policies can be persuasively explained on the basis of the kinds of pressures exerted by various interest groups on the policymaking elite. No other assumption provides as fruitful a starting point for understanding why Kenya and Tanzania, two countries that appeared to share so many similarities on the eve of independence, should have pursued such widely divergent policy paths during the past twenty-five years. Chapter 3 of this volume sets out the analytical paradigm that grows out of this assumption. The internalist approach to agricultural policy in Africa is rooted in the conviction that Africa's political elites have, time and time again, responded to the political volatility of urban pressure groups, shaping their countries' rural policies in ways that extract resources from the countryside in order to subsidize urban residents.

The urban bias–weak state paradigm links the concepts of urban bias and the weak state by suggesting that the basic reason for this ongoing accommodation to urban pressures is the imperative of political survival. The survivalist strategy leads inexorably to the implementation of policies that have short-run political benefits, but long-term economic costs. Taken all together, these measures demonstrate the use of state policy as a vehicle for the transfer of economic surplus from the countryside to the city.

THE ROOTS OF POLICY

This book seeks to demonstrate that the urban bias–weak state paradigm provides a perfectly plausible explanation for the agricultural policies pursued by the Tanzanian government since independence, but that Kenya's agricultural policies are clearly exceptional. The challenge, then, is not so much to explain why Tanzania has implemented an agricultural policy that has led to sectoral stagnation, but why Kenya has not. In a nutshell, why is Kenya different?[7]

The answer to this question is complex but does not involve any major qualification of our operative assumption (developed in Chapter 3) about the inextricable linkages among social pressures, the political interests of the governing elite, and public policy. It does, however, require a more careful and complex formulation of the urban bias–weak state paradigm. This paradigm, as articulated by both Lipton and Bates, depends heavily on the presupposition that, throughout independent Africa, rural producers and political elites are different social groupings that do not share any significant economic interests. It stipulates an irreducible adversarial relationship between urban consumers' desire for cheap food and imported goods on the one hand, and rural producers' desire for high commodity prices on the other. Despite the pervasiveness of crosscutting ties of a noneconomic nature, such as ethnicity, language, and religion, the distinct and separate economic interests of urban dwellers are assumed to be sufficiently powerful to propel public policy.

To explain agricultural policy in Kenya, it is vital to understand that this is simply not the case. The commonplace notion of a socioeconomic distinction between farmers and governing political elites, so critical as an explanatory point of departure elsewhere in Africa, makes substantially less sense in the Kenyan context. The critical difference does not lie in the fact that Kenya's governing elite shares important cultural, ethnic, and religious ties with the countryside; in this respect, Kenya is not significantly different from most African countries. Rather, it lies in the extent to which Kenya's elite has economically invested in the rural areas, typically deriving an important portion of its income from ownership of agricultural land. It would involve only the slightest oversimplification to suggest that Kenya's political leaders are also farmers, and that Kenya's farmers are—from the standpoint of social class—also its political leaders.

Elite land acquisition has both ancient and modern historical roots. It depends first and foremost on a system of land tenure that features private ownership, with virtually unrestricted latitude for individuals to purchase and sell parcels of land. This system, so rare elsewhere in Africa, can be traced historically to Kenya's earliest era. According to anthropological evidence, the private purchase of land, for individual or group freehold, has roots that extend to the earliest arrival in this region of the Kikuyu people. John Middleton and Greet Kershaw have shown that the Kikuyu of Kenya first began to acquire land by purchasing it from its original holders, the Dorobo. By the time the colonial era began, the system of acquiring land through purchase had become widely diffused throughout the central highlands.[8] Although an individual's right to sell or acquire land was somewhat circumscribed by broader familial obligations, it would involve no exaggeration to suggest that, in this part of Kenya, the traditional system of landholding bore a remarkable resemblance to fee-simple ownership.

The tradition of individual land ownership was powerfully reinforced by colonial policy. Well before independence, it became the policy of the Kenyan government to allow—indeed, to encourage—Africans to acquire land on a freehold basis. The most powerful thrust in this direction derived from the policy of land consolidation and adjudication initiated by the colonial administration in the early 1950s. The official justification for wholesale conversion of the country's pattern of land ownership from communal tenure to individual title was economic. Credit depended on the individual being able to offer the land as collateral, and this could not occur unless the form of title allowed the farm to be bought and sold openly in the marketplace. The real motivation, however, was at least equally political: to stabilize the colonial presence by creating an elite class of African farmers with a stake in the nation's system of private land ownership. The ultimate goal was to produce an African government that would be dominated by persons with an economic stake in private land ownership, and whose policies would fully reflect that interest.

It would be difficult to overestimate the contemporary political impact of the Swynnerton plan. One measure of its significance is that it was taken over virtually intact as a cornerstone of rural policy by the postindependence government of Kenya. The program, renamed land adjudication, is now administered by the Ministry of Lands, Settlement and Physical Planning. The principal difference between the present policy and the earlier program of land consolidation and adjudication is that the consolidation aspect has been dropped as too cumbersome. Land adjudication, since independence, simply requires that an individual's land holdings be carefully demarcated, and that traditional entitlement be fully established, before title is awarded. Under this system, further consolidation of small land units into economically viable farms is left to the operation of the marketplace.

Much of this land has been acquired by government officials. Since the first steps to implement the country's program of land registration and adjudication, elite land acquisition has been abetted by a variety of institutional and economic forces. These include both private banks, which view government salaries as secure collateral for farm mortgages, and state lending agencies, such as the Agricultural Finance Corporation, whose purpose is to make loans to Kenyans who wish to acquire agricultural land. It has been further stimulated by special arrangements for elite participation often built into programs for land resettlement. Perhaps most importantly, land acquisition by the country's political and administrative elites is facilitated by the operation of the marketplace itself. Individuals who receive government salaries are, quite simply, in a stronger position than most other Kenyans to outbid competitors for agricultural land and, having acquired it, to make the mortgage installment payments necessary to maintain ownership.

The exact profile of land ownership by the Kenyan political elite is not well known, for there have been few detailed studies of such land acquisition.[9] But firsthand observers of the Kenyan scene suggest that the amount of land owned by individual political officials is, in most cases, roughly proportional to governmental rank. High-ranking politicians and administrators probably own one or more fairly large farms, more likely than not in a high-potential region of the country and devoted in large part to the production of exportable commodities. Middle-ranking political figures and civil servants undoubtedly own lesser amounts of land, possibly in slightly less desirable locations, and perhaps given over in somewhat larger measure to the production of food staples, such as maize. It is impossible to calculate the amount of agricultural land owned by Kenyan politicians and civil servants, but the number of government officials who own farmland probably reaches well into the thousands, possibly higher.

One of the remarkable features of this pattern is the degree to which it incorporates public officials at the very lowest levels of the system—such as primary school teachers, road workers, customs and immigration officers, and custodial personnel—as well as the country's highest-ranking administrators and political leaders. The end product of policies that encourage governmental personnel to acquire land, and that provide them both credit and opportunity, is that administrators and politicians from the highest to the lowest levels have heavily invested in the agricultural sector. As a result, agricultural interests have attained a formidable degree of influence over government policy. Indeed, land ownership by state officials is so all-pervasive that it would be inaccurate to conceptualize farming interests as a lobby outside the government. It would be far more accurate simply to state that, so far as agricultural matters are concerned, Kenya's government is one of farmers, by farmers and for farmers.

The theoretical implication of Kenya's pattern of elite land ownership, and of agricultural policies it has induced, is considerable. At the very least, the concept of urban bias must be treated with utmost caution and applied with great selectivity. Joel Barkan has usefully stated that urban bias is not an *a priori* feature of political systems throughout Africa but, rather, a highly variable factor, whose salience can vary considerably from one country to the next as well as over time within countries:

> Any discussion of the incidence of 'urban bias' in selected Third World states must first consider the structure of political conflict and the balance of power between the countryside and the state. Questions as to why prices and the marketing structure confronting peasant producers are what they are, or why peasant access to state welfare services is rising or falling cannot be fully answered without first determining the extent and kind of influence residents of the rural areas exert on the policy-making process.[10]

Since urban bias is intended to treat the politicoeconomic advantage gained from sheer physical proximity to political power, it might be more useful at the outset to state that the concept really refers principally to "capital city" bias. This is of special importance in the African context, where physical, population, and infrastructural disparities between national capitals and other cities are typically enormous. For Kenya and Tanzania, the notion of urban bias really refers to the political influence of the populations of Nairobi and Dar es Salaam. It would be virtually ludicrous to claim that the political weight of the populations of such economically important, but nevertheless politically secondary, cities as Mombasa, Tanga, Kisumu, or Mwanza comes even close to that of those of the two capitals.

As utilized by Lipton, the theory of urban bias is intended to provide a diffuse and highly comprehensive explanatory instrument, one that sheds light on a whole range of government policies. This is far too broad a claim. The pattern of agricultural and nonagricultural policies in Kenya suggests that the notion of urban bias may be a useful tool to explain certain policy areas but not others. Urban bias is notably absent from Kenyan agricultural policy, for example, but this is not to say that the theory does not shed useful light on other governmental programs. The dense concentration of the country's medical, educational, welfare, and other services in Nairobi can be viewed as a governmental response to the needs, interests, and influence of the residents of its capital city. Certain specific features of Kenya's agricultural policy can also be viewed as a response to urban interests. The intermittently applied ban on private sales of maize between districts, for example, is part of a clear effort to see that the maize requirements of Nairobi and other large cities are satisfied before those of the more remote rural regions.

In sum, the political and economic interests that influence Kenya's governing class are highly complex, comprising a mixture of both urban and rural factors. Like other elites in Africa, Kenya's leaders must deal with the volatility of the country's urban centers and, most particularly, the capital city. Their economic interests in the overall prosperity of the country's agricultural sector significantly differentiates the Kenyan political elite from the vast majority of governing elites in African countries. As politicians concerned with the stability of their government, Kenya's political leaders may benefit from policies that provide an artificial boost for the material conditions of urban residents at the expense of agricultural producers, but as farmers, they have a clear interest in ensuring that the rural sector receives an equitable share of the nation's economic resources. *Rural bias* thus provides a far better explanation of Kenyan agricultural policy than does urban bias.

To pursue their personal economic interests, Kenya's political leaders must adopt and implement policies that benefit farmers as a group. This accounts, for example, for the fact that Kenya has adopted a prudent and realistic exchange-rate policy.[11] A prudent exchange rate helps insure a high return on investments in coffee and tea farming. Kenya's political elite benefits in exactly the same way from pricing policies that pass on to the growers a very high proportion of the world-market price for exportable commodities, and that provide a high percentage of the domestic retail price for food staples such as maize. Similarly, though elite politicians may benefit from using parastatal corporations as sources of political patronage and as vehicles for the extraction of political rents, they benefit as farmers when these corporations function responsibly and at low levels of operating overhead. This explains why Kenya's agricultural parastatals have generally displayed a remarkable degree of fiscal and administrative responsibility, in contrast to those of other African countries.[12]

The contrast with Tanzania is particularly vivid. The land policies of the Tanzanian government have been exactly opposite to those of Kenya, and intended to prevent politicians and administrators from investing in land. The result, as David Leonard has observed, has been that "no massive transfers of land to individual Africans were organized and Tanzania's senior civil servants did not buy into capitalist agriculture to any significant degree."[13] After the promulgation of the Arusha declaration in early 1967, the Tanzanian government nationalized the country's land, thereby preventing the development of a farming system based on private land ownership. At the same time, the government issued a leadership code of conduct that declared it improper for any official of the Tanzanian state to have secondary sources of income. The effect of this code was, for all practical purposes, to cut off any possibility that political or bureaucratic leaders might invest in agricultural land. Although a small number might be able to sustain a certain amount of farming activity, this necessarily had to be indirect and extremely limited.

The divorce between those who held land and made their living by farming it, and those who controlled the Tanzanian state and formulated its agricultural policies, could not have been more complete. The principal (if not exclusive) source of income for members of the Tanzanian elite was their governmental salaries. The alienation of governmental office from land ownership helps explain better than does any other factor the character of the Tanzanian government's rural policies. Despite the leadership's rhetorical commitment to the construction of a socialist agricultural system that would insure the well-being of the peasant population, the agricultural policies of the Tanzanian government were framed and implemented by politicians whose political and economic base was exclusively urban. Tanzania's agricultural policies thus provide one of Africa's clearest examples of a system designed to transfer economic resources from the countryside to the city.

The theoretical implication of urban-versus-rural bias for the distinction between strong and weak states is less clear. If the tendency to accommodate agricultural policy to urban interests goes hand in hand with the political weakness of African states, does the tendency toward rural bias indicate that a state is strong? An argument to support this position would suggest that such a state must necessarily be strong enough to resist and control the various urban pressures and forces that so successfully impose their will on governments elsewhere. This interpretation finds considerable empirical substantiation in the Kenyan government's consistent record of success in squelching extraconstitutional challenges to its authority, whether by dissident military units or underground political movements. The strong-state interpretation of Kenya is also supported by the argument in Chapter 6 of this volume: that much of Kenya's agrarian success is based on the government's capacity to pursue "hard-option" agricultural strategies, especially in the immediate postindependence period.

An alternative interpretation, however, suggests that the presence of a rural bias in Kenya's agricultural policy is not persuasive evidence of a strong state. An argument to this effect would suggest that Kenya may simply be a weak state responding to the considerable force of rural, rather than urban, interests. In this view, the location of a country's most powerful interest groups has no bearing whatsoever on the strength or weakness of its state institutions: Some weak states are compelled to respond to urban interest groups, others to rural ones.[14] This theoretical dilemma may not be susceptible to final resolution, for the conceptual underpinnings of the distinction between strong and weak states may ultimately be too imprecise to sustain an equation that associates rural bias with political strength. The nature of a country's agricultural policy offers an excellent guide to the rural or urban orientation of its politicians. It is a less perfect indicator of the strength or weakness of state institutions.

A partial answer to this dilemma lies in the contrasting political styles of Kenya and Tanzania. As Joel Barkan has demonstrated, Kenya's political system features a highly open, pluralistic governing party, which provides a great deal of scope for rural interests to gain influence at the national level. This is possible because the government seeks, from time to time, to renew itself and its mandate to govern by holding genuinely competitive national elections. Barkan's description is instructive:

> [In Kenya and the Ivory Coast] . . . rural communities and especially rural elites have a means to pressure the state to provide a measure of services to the local community. Political careers rise and fall on the ability of elected officials to extract services from the center. In this context, urban based central planners may not always allocate a "fair share" of state resources to the rural areas . . . but their freedom to pursue urban based policies is sharply curtailed.[15]

In Kenya, free elections afford rural political leaders the opportunity to compete among themselves on the basis of their relative influence at the national level. And for the constituents and supporters of those representatives, this influence is measured by the extent to which governmental policies accommodate the economic interests and needs of small-, medium-, and large-scale farmers.

The Tanzanian political system, by contrast, offers little opportunity for the effective expression of rural interests. As Barkan points out, rural political demands in Tanzania must be articulated through a complex hierarchy of village, district, and regional development committees, "each of which is dominated by officials of the ruling party."[16] Although this system has been consistently hailed by outside observers as evidence of Tanzania's commitment to participatory democracy, its real effect is to insulate the political center from demands from below. Most of the real work of these committees consists of reviewing the recommendations of lower-level committees, to ensure that they are consistent with centrally approved economic programs. The net effect of this policymaking process is to deprive rural representatives to the Tanzanian National Assembly of any effective influence. The political influence of rural representatives in Tanzania is further reduced by the fact that, under the Tanzanian constitution, the National Assembly is politically subordinate to the national executive committee of the governing party. Since the National Assembly is rarely in session in any case, there is an even greater tendency for the system to devolve wide decisionmaking authority onto urban bureaucrats.

The relationship between democracy and development is beyond the scope of this volume. But the force of these observations aligns strongly with Richard Sklar's argument that democracy is far more conducive to development than is its authoritarian alternative. Sklar's essay challenges the "prevalent belief that mass political participation would be detrimental to social savings or capital accumulation for productive investment." [17] In Kenya, a political system open to effective participation by the representatives of rural communities has been integral to the formulation and implementation of agricultural policies contributing to a high rate of investment and consistent economic growth in the agricultural sector. Tanzania's more closed and bureaucratic political system, on the other hand, has facilitated the formulation and implementation of policies exploiting the rural sector and contributing to high levels of consumption by the country's bureaucratic elite.

WEAKNESSES OF DEVELOPMENT POLICY

It is one of the great ironies of contemporary African political history that the continent's most famous program of rural socialism was formulated and implemented by political leaders who had become an urbanized elite, both in lifestyle and in their dependence on wage income. As urban salary earners, Tanzania's leaders benefitted from the implementation of precisely the economic policies that Michael Lipton, Robert Bates, and the World Bank have condemned. They were able, for example, to inflate the purchasing power of their salaries by overvaluing the nation's currency. And since they were not deterred from this policy by countervailing commitments to rural economic interests, the process of overvaluation proceeded to the point where there was virtually no relationship between the country's official and unofficial exchange rates. Similarly, industrialization through import substitution offered the prospect of politically captive industries, which would, because they depend on the state for economic protection, be available for political patronage and other corrupt practices.

As urban dwellers, Tanzania's leaders also benefitted from policies that suppressed the prices of agricultural commodities. Low producer prices for foodstuffs, for example, helped to reduce their cost of living and further inflated the purchasing power of governmental wages. Tanzania's political elite had numerous reasons for suppressing the prices of exportable commodities. The difference between the world-market price of coffee, tea, and sisal, when skimmed off by the government's parastatal corporations, could be used to finance the importation of consumer goods for the urban middle classes or to provide political clients with positions on the payrolls of government agencies. Even as the country's export earnings declined as a result of stagnating production, there was no impetus to correct this policy by increasing the real producer price to export farmers. The export-oriented farmers did not have political influence; those with political influence did not have farms.

The government's reaction to the economic crisis caused by soaring balance-of-payments deficits seems to have been to intensify the level of rural exploitation, as a means of insuring continued urban political tranquility. As Tanzania's economy declined in absolute terms, everyone suffered. But those in charge of the parcelling out of economic resources, preoccupied with the political atmosphere in the nation's capital, were able to see to it that those in Dar es Salaam suffered less than did those in the country's rural areas. Firsthand observers of the Tanzanian scene have professed bewilderment at the lack of overt urban political dissent during the years of economic deterioration; there was not a single major riot or demonstration against the government's economic policies throughout the 1970s or early 1980s.

The reasons for urban peace are not difficult to discern. By using its economic policy instruments to subsidize urban dwellers, the Tanzanian elite has been able to see to it that the impact of the country's economic decline on the urban population was gradual, rather than abrupt. There has been no single episode, such as the removal of a food subsidy, that provided a flashpoint for urban unrest. In addition, Tanzania's urban residents have had no occasion to feel a sense of relative deprivation, a mood that has so often provoked urban unrest in other African countries. However badly they have suffered from the lack of goods and services, Tanzania's urban dwellers have been immeasurably better off than their rural counterparts. The standard of comparison for residents of Dar es Salaam is not the affluence of Nairobi, but the extreme poverty of their own countryside. As a result, many have been inclined to feel comparatively privileged within the context of a downward-spiralling system.

The absence of serious upheaval testifies to the political effectiveness of Tanzanian policy. The economic strategies pursued by urban political elites—concerned to protect the stability of a system that insured them a disproportionate share of the nation's resources—did exactly as they were intended. They provided Tanzania with more than twenty-five years of urban political peace. But the economic and social costs of this peace are beyond reckoning. It would be impossible to sum up the cost to the Tanzanian people of reduced social well-being: failing education and health systems; absolute shrinkage of opportunity for productive employment in agriculture, industry, and trade; and the emotional toll of living in a society increasingly cynical and corrupt. Suffice it to say that an entire generation of Tanzanians has had to endure severely diminished material circumstances as a result of the government's inflexible commitment to policies that made sense politically but were inappropriate for the stimulation of economic growth.

The principal implication of the forgoing analysis, which stresses the pivotal importance of the relationship between political elites and agricultural land, is the relative strength of the impetus for policy reform. In Kenya, where governmental officials have heavily invested in land, the impetus for a growth-oriented set of agricultural policies arose early and has been a powerful and constant feature of the political process since the early 1970s. In Tanzania, where the governing class has separated its well-being from the productivity of the agricultural sector, there has been very little domestic impetus for policy reform. The most significant pressure to change the country's agricultural policies has come from international agencies—such as the World Bank and IMF—which, through conditional lending, have sought to push the Tanzanian government toward policy reform.

To contrast the timing of policy adjustment in the two countries, it is useful to recollect that, immediately after independence, both Kenya and Tanzania, like many other newly independent African nations, adopted industrial strategies based on the principle of import substitution. Development economists writing during this period offered compelling reasons for this strategy. They generally viewed import subsitutition as a means of conserving foreign exchange, and as an effective way to initiate the development of an industrial sector. The measures needed to sustain the new industries—such as protective tariffs or quantitative restrictions on imports—were generally considered temporary: They would be essential only until the infant industries matured and became self-sufficient. The social arguments for import substitution were also strong: It offered a means of alleviating the growing problem of urban unemployment.

Import substitution, however, imposed a severe burden on agriculture. As Chapter 3 of this volume shows, it worsened the internal terms of trade, by forcing Africa's rural populations to pay artificially high prices for domestically produced goods that were protected from foreign competition. It also required an exchange-rate policy that severely disadvantaged agricultural exporters. Since overvaluation made it possible for the new industries to import capital goods and raw materials cheaply, it resulted in lower producer prices for exportable commodities and, therefore, discouraged export-oriented farmers. Moreover, since there was a tendency to use a large percentage of foreign-exchange earnings to satisfy the capital needs of the new industries, there was a commensurate tendency to starve the countryside of capital. The inadequacy of rural infrastructure, and the critical shortages of facilities for transporting, preserving, and storing agricultural goods, were, in many respects, the inevitable outcome of an economic policy that provided a forced draft of resources for the industrial sector.

The policy of import substitution further handicapped the agricultural sector by increasing its operating costs. Consumer-goods industries that functioned within a protective cocoon of high tariffs and other import restrictions could afford to offer relatively high wages to attract workers, without concern that this would lessen their competitiveness with goods imported from abroad. In small African economies, this raised the overall level of labor costs and, therefore, resulted in higher wage costs for the agricultural sector, which had to compete in the same labor market. Protected industries could afford to bid up the costs of other production inputs, such as energy, transportation, and locally produced raw materials. And this, too, resulted in increased operating costs for agricultural producers. The burden has been especially heavy for agricultural exporters, who were competing in the international marketplace. Stated bluntly, import substitution and neglect of the agricultural sector went hand-in-hand, were cause and effect. It soon became clear that one of the major preconditions for stimulating agricultural growth, and especially the growth of agricultural exports, was the reform of industrial policy.

The most visible symptom of the economic crisis caused by import substitution was acute balance-of-payments difficulties. It is significant that both Kenya and Tanzania began to suffer from severe shortages of foreign exchange several years before the oil-price increase of late 1973, which is commonly blamed for this problem. Import substitution had contributed to the crisis in several different ways. It lessened the foreign-exchange earnings from agricultural exports and, by diminishing the volume of domestic food production, required the expenditure of foreign exchange on food imports. Most importantly, prodigious amounts of hard currency were consumed to satisfy the input requirements of industries that, themselves, earned almost nothing abroad. The balance-of-payments difficulties of African countries are, of course, the product of numerous external as well as internal factors, and it would be incorrect to place sole responsibility on import substitution. But the fact is that of the internal factors amenable to governmental corrective measures, import substitution was undoubtedly the most significant.

The real result of the industrial strategy of import substitution, however, was the continuing tendency to starve the agricultural sector of vital capital inputs. During the second half of the 1970s, there was an ongoing shift in Tanzania's investment emphasis from agriculture to import-substitution industry. Kenya took exactly the opposite course of action. Because its economic policies were framed and implemented by political leaders who had a personal stake in agricultural growth, the government acted swiftly and decisively to correct its anti-rural bias and was soon embarked on a comprehensive process of policy reform intended to stimulate agricultural growth.

DEVELOPMENT AND EQUITY

There is a commonplace convention in African development studies that holds that Kenya represents one of Africa's clearest examples of economic growth achieved at the expense of great social inequality, whereas Tanzania has achieved an equalitarian social structure but at the expense of economic development. According to this convention, Kenyan society suffers from extreme income differentiation: Landlessness, destitution, and unemployment at the bottom of the social ladder contrast sharply with affluence at the top. In Tanzania, on the other hand, the extremes of wealth and poverty are said to have been eliminated by a strict incomes policy for state officials combined with a rigorously progressive tax system. These institutions, along with such other progressive measures as the abolition of private land ownership, are credited with having fostered a society in which the socioeconomic distance between the rich and the poor is very narrow.

Journalistic and academic visitors to these countries have seen much evidence to confirm these impressions. Kenya's politicoeconomic elite has not concealed its affluence from public view. In Nairobi and the areas that surround it, conspicuous consumption and extreme poverty both have high visibility. Kenya leaves little doubt that the opulent material lifestyle once enjoyed exclusively by the European settler class has been adopted with alacrity by the new power elite. Not only do Nairobi's wealthiest citizens enjoy great personal wealth, but they have created a lifestyle in which lavish entertaining, expensive automobiles, and luxurious homes play an important part. Indeed, elite suburbs of Nairobi, such as Muthaiga and Karen, display a level of private prosperity that is astonishing in a basically poor agricultural country. And, if additional confirmation of vast inequality is needed, there is a constant barrage of rumors and speculative reports about the landholdings of the wealthiest members of the political classes and their business dealings—both legal and illicit.

Nor are the poorer segments of society at all hidden from public view, for Kenya has also the quality of making its poverty visible and accessible. The squatter slums of Mathari Valley, Jericho, and Eastleigh, which provide domiciles for untold thousands of unemployed and underemployed squatters, are only a short distance from the center of the city. Similarly, some of Kenya's poorer rural areas are only a short distance from the city limits, and, because the country's road system is well maintained, easily accessible by automobile. Kenya's social contrasts are readily apparent and, as a result, have become the subject of voluminous journalistic commentary, much of it sensationalist.[18]

Tanzania, on the other hand, creates an exact opposite impression. Dar es Salaam is a poor and somewhat run-down city. Even its wealthiest section, Oyster Bay, does not somehow seem terribly distant in social terms from the vast subdivisions along the Morogoro road. Nor does Dar es Salaam have any of the glitter of Nairobi: no international-class hotels or restaurants; no shops offering expensive cameras, watches, and jewelry; and virtually no tourist economy to generate a demand for such expensive services as automobile rentals or safaris. Because of the shortage of foreign exchange, imported goods are practically unavailable off the informal market. Since luxury goods can only be purchased at high cost in illicit markets, this alone is a great incentive to keep them well concealed. The tendency to conceal wealth is further reinforced by Tanzania's tax system, which is highly confiscatory at upper-income levels. Any conspicuous consumption is *prima facie* evidence of tax evasion or some other illegal activity. Concealing personal resources from public view is partly accomplished by maintaining hard-currency accounts overseas.

If visual evidence alone were sufficient, the conventional stereotypes of social structure in Kenya and Tanzania would be solidly established, but there are many reasons to doubt the commonplace viewpoint. The first of these is that neither Kenya nor Tanzania has been the subject of a systematic study of income distribution. The fact is that the basic patterns of income distribution for these two countries are simply unknown. Our ignorance of income distribution for Tanzania is further compounded by the notorious unreliability of virtually all statistical materials on that country, including those that provide gross comparisons of rural and urban incomes and those that establish the country's physical-quality-of-life index. The absence of reliable empirical evidence is extremely frustrating, for it means that the answer to one of the most basic questions about development—whether capitalist and socialist strategies have differential impacts on social inequality—is simply unavailable.

There are theoretical reasons to believe that the common stereotypes are misleading. Kenya, for example, has achieved a substantial degree of income-flattening that does not readily meet the eye. As a result of its rural-policy emphasis on the development of the smallholder sector, Kenya has done a great deal to widen the possibilities for land ownership and to measurably increase income among mid-sized landowners. Indeed, University of Nairobi political scientist Michael Chege has argued that the most significant social trend in the Kenyan countryside today is neither massive land acquisition by the political elite nor the further dispossession of Kenya's marginal peasantry, but rather the income-flattening effect created by the steady increase in the number of smallholder cash-crop farmers.[19]

Critics absorbed with recording the extensive landholdings of Kenya's wealthiest families, and with their potential for generating political unrest, have generally failed to document the socioeconomic importance of the government's enormous commitment to the development of smallholder agriculture. The extent of large landholdings by the very wealthy is easily susceptible to exaggeration. Kenya has by no means moved in the direction of large-scale plantation holdings (common throughout Latin America). The production of smallholder farmers has grown far more rapidly than that on large farms and, since the early 1970s, has consistently accounted for more than 50 percent of marketed output. Kenya's political leaders have served their long-term interests by fostering a high degree of prosperity among Kenya's approximately 1 million smallholders, who have farms of between one-half hectare (1.24 acres) and 5 hectares (12.4 acres) in size.

The socioeconomic implications of smallholder development are considerable. There is evidence to reject the rural-immiseration thesis advocated by some researchers. Chege, for example, believes that smallholder development has contributed to a gradual process of rural social equalization in Kenya's Central Province.

> We are therefore left with a situation in which neither the income share of larger landowners nor that of the smallest holdings is increasing, as opposed to that of the medium landholdings. . . . It is evident . . . that the middle income have fared better overall than either the richest or poorest strata, having increased both their share of current income and consumption.[20]

Chege cites Paul Collier and Deepak Lal, development economists, to show that the poorest 40 percent of the rural population have maintained a basically constant share of consumption, while the richest farmers have lost part of their share to the middle-income group.[21] Far from contributing to rural immiseration, then, Kenya's land and agricultural policies have, at the very least, stabilized the consumption share of Kenya's poorest agriculturists.

Collier and Lal do acknowledge that Kenya's pattern of income distribution became increasingly unequal during the period they examined. Between 1963 and 1974, the share of national income going to the poorest 40% dropped from about 25% to about 18%, while that going to the wealthiest 30% increased from about 50% to almost 56%.[22] This trend, however, was mitigated by two countervailing tendencies. First, as Chege shows, the consumption share of the poorest 40 percent remained stable, even as its income share dropped. The reason for the apparently divergent trends of income share and consumption share is that smallholders, contrary to widespread stereotypes about risk aversion, have adopted innovations involving them in a greater degree of crop risk. Collier and Lal explain the result of this pattern:

> This would have the effect of increasing the dispersion of current income more than that of permanent income, so that snapshots of annual income would show a worsening of distribution even if the true distribution, as reflected by consumption, has not deteriorated.[23]

Perhaps most importantly, however, the decreasing share of national income going to Kenya's poorest 40 percent was dramatically offset by the fact that, as a result of economic growth, this stratum of the population enjoyed an increase in real per-capita income of almost 10 percent.

Tanzania's economic programs may, indirectly, have had far more perverse effects. By fostering the emergence and rapid proliferation of the informal economic sector, Tanzania's agricultural policies have certainly contributed to widening rural inequalities. For the informal sector is, almost by definition, exempt from the income controls and progressive tax programs that govern official economic life. Informal economic transactions are not only tax-free, but free of all other official income restraints. Tanzanians who have prospered by conducting large volumes of informal trade have almost certainly amassed considerable personal fortunes, both in local currency and in foreign exchange. Their tendency to maintain a low personal and group profile makes it impossible even to estimate the degree to which an informal bourgeoisie has emerged. But many close observers believe that political pressures exerted by this group are a major influence in maintaining the current economic system. So long as Tanzania continues to uphold an official economy that fails to provide vitally needed goods and services to its population, private fortunes will continue to be made by those who are able to operate in the informal sector.

Even if Tanzania is more egalitarian than Kenya in its pattern of income distribution, the issue of development and equity would remain an open one. Even the country's most ardent defenders acknowledge that, with the sharp drop in the country's real GDP during recent years, real per-capita incomes have fallen considerably at all levels of society. Frances Stewart, for example, has calculated that the real purchasing power of the minimum wage in 1979 was only about half that in 1969.[24] This contrasts most dramatically with Kenya, where the real purchasing power of the poorest segments of the population has risen during the period of independence, even if it has not risen as rapidly as that of the highest income levels in the society. The socioeconomic contrast between Kenya and Tanzania cannot be reduced to simplifications about equality versus inequality. For with all its alleged inequality, Kenya has succeeded to a measurable degree in improving the conditions of the poor. For all of its presumed equality, Tanzania has not.

The purpose of these observations is to question, not rebut, the conventional orthodoxy about capitalist and socialist development strategies. Until more persuasive income surveys are available, observations about the changing profiles of real income distribution in Kenya and Tanzania will remain somewhat speculative. For the time being, however, the standard view that Kenya has attained growth without development, while Tanzania features development without growth, seems largely ideological. It is at least equally plausible that Kenya has achieved growth with development while Tanzania has attained neither.

NOTES

1. Joel Barkan, ed., *Politics and Public Policy in Kenya and Tanzania* (Praeger, New York, 1984).

2. Colin Leys, *Underdevelopment in Kenya: The Political Economy of Neo-Colonialism* (University of California Press, Berkeley and Los Angeles, 1974), and Nicola Swainson, *The Development of Corporate Capitalism in Kenya 1918–1977* (University of California Press, Berkeley and Los Angeles, 1980).

3. Issa G. Shivji, *Class Struggles in Tanzania* (Monthly Review Press, New York and London, 1976).

4. Dean E. McHenry, Jr., *Tanzania's Ujamaa Villages: The Implementation of a Rural Development Strategy* (Institute of International Studies, University of California, Berkeley, 1979), and Bismarck U. Mwansasu and Cranford Pratt, eds., *Towards Socialism in Tanzania* (University of Toronto, Toronto,1979).

5. Goran Hyden, *Beyond Ujamaa: Underdevelopment and an Uncaptured Peasantry* (University of California Press, Berkeley and Los Angeles, 1980).

6. Michael Lipton, *Why Poor People Stay Poor* (Harvard University Press, Cambridge, MA, 1976), and Robert Bates, *Markets and States in Tropical Africa: The Political Basis of Agricultural Policies* (University of California Press, Berkeley and Los Angeles, 1981).

7. The discussion that follows draws heavily on David K. Leonard, "Class Formation and Agricultural Development," in *Politics and Public Policy in Kenya and Tanzania,* ed. Joel D. Barkan.

8. John Middleton and Greet Kershaw, *The Kikuyu and Kamba of Kenya* (International African Institute, London, 1965). See especially pp. 25ff.

9. The principal exception is the doctoral dissertation of Apollo I. Njonjo, *The Africanisation of the White Highlands: A Study in Agrarian Class Struggles in Kenya 1950–1974* (Ph.D. diss., Department of Politics, Princeton University, Princeton, NJ, 1977).

10. Joel D. Barkan, "'Urban Bias,' Peasants and Rural Politics in Kenya and Tanzania," Occasional Paper no. 1 (Department of Political Science, University of Iowa, Ames, 1983), p. 4.

11. For an especially favorable evaluation, see K. Toh, "Assessment of Exchange Rate Policy in Kenya" (USAID, Nairobi, 1986).

12. For an extremely positive evaluation, see Barbara Grosh "Agricultural Parastatals Since Independence: How Have They Performed?" Working Paper no. 435 (Institute for Development Studies, University of Nairobi, 1986).

13. Leonard, "Class Formation," p. 151.

14. This discussion owes much to Geoffrey Bergen of the Political Science Department, University of California, Los Angeles.

15. Barkan, "Urban Bias," p. 5.

16. Ibid., p. 6.

17. Richard Sklar, "Developmental Democracy," *Comparative Studies in Society and History* 29, no. 4 (October 1987), p. 709. Also see Sklar's African Studies Association Presidential Address, "Democracy in Africa," 1982 (African Studies Center, University of California, Los Angeles).

18. For one example of such reporting on Kenya, see John Barry, "Kenya on the Brink: The Tensions and Greed Which Threaten Kenya," *Sunday Times* (London), August 10, 17, and 24, 1975.

19. Michael Chege, "The Political Economy of Agrarian Change in Central Kenya" (Paper prepared for a conference on the Political Economy of Kenya, Johns Hopkins University, Baltimore, MD, April, 1986), pp. 26ff.

20. Michael Chege, "The Political Economy of Agrarian Change in Central Kenya," in *The Political Economy of Kenya,* ed. Michael G. Schatzberg (Praeger, New York, Westport, and London, 1987), p. 111.

21. Paul Collier and Deepak Lal, "Why Poor People Get Rich: Kenya 1960–79," *World Development* 12, no. 10 (1984), pp. 1007–1018.

22. Ibid., Table 1, p. 1009.

23. Ibid., p. 1008.

24. Frances Stewart, *Planning to Meet Basic Needs* (Macmillan, London and Basingstoke, 1985), p. 193.

·8·

Policy Reform: Implications for the Future

THE NEED FOR POLICY REFORM

Taken cumulatively, the patterns of policy intervention pursued by African governments toward their rural sector have resulted in shifting the internal terms of trade against the economic well-being of the rural sector. Driven by powerful coalitions of urban-based interest groups, African political leaders—who are themselves an important component of these coalitions—have adopted economic measures that cater to the economic needs of city dwellers at the expense of rural social groups, especially smallholder farmers. There is an important theoretical point here, one that merits at least brief elaboration. Urban social groups, like rural ones, vary greatly in their access to and exercise of political power. It would be absurd on the face of it to suggest that the political influence of urban workers or the urban underemployed is in any way commensurate with the political power of high-ranking politicians, wealthy industrialists, or members of the top administrative cadres.

Economic policies based on short-term political expediency can now be shown to have disastrous long-term effects. In present-day Africa, rural poverty and rising levels of urban unemployment are the outcome of a set of agricultural policies designed to subsidize the cost of living of urban consumers at the expense of rural producers. Today, observers at virtually all points on the political spectrum strongly agree that the major starting point for agricultural recovery must necessarily be the implementation of a set of measures that will shift the internal terms of trade back toward the rural sector and improve real economic incentives for agricultural producers.

Price Reforms

The first step should be a substantial, indeed radical, improvement in producer prices. For unless farmers' incomes are dramatically increased, the current trend toward deteriorating per-capita productivity in both the food- and export-crop sectors will only continue. An improvement in the price structure for basic food crops is especially essential since the decline in food production is directly related to famine conditions of deepening severity; these conditions, in turn, have created a need for food imports so great as to crowd out the importation of goods vitally necessary for the industrial sector. The impact of increasing food prices on political stability must be addressed squarely, for African governments that view this policy reform as politically suicidal are extremely unlikely to undertake it.

The evidence that rising food prices lead directly to urban unrest, and indeed, to critical problems of regime stability, is overwhelming. The list of African cities where heightened food costs have been directly related to major recent episodes of political instability now includes such disparate locales as Khartoum, Lusaka, Cairo, Tunis, Rabat, Kampala, Nairobi, and Monrovia. The relationship between urban inflation and political instability is so direct that it is not surprising so few African governments have contemplated serious reforms in their food-pricing systems. Governments that place a value on their own political survival find it far easier to cite factors beyond their control as the source of the problem and to use the famine conditions that result from poor policy as a source of leverage on the donor community's food assistance. While this strategy may help assure day-to-day political survival, it is valueless for long-term economic recovery.

The critical question, then, is how to induce reforms in the pricing system that do not fundamentally threaten the political security of governing elites. There is no simple answer to this question, and those, such as Africa's more monetarist donors, who urge the full and immediate adoption of a free-market pricing system simply avoid the political ramifications of this remedy, and therefore the issue of its practical feasibility. Persistent prescriptions for free-market pricing doubtless reflect to some extent the frustration of donor officials and development economists, who have long since grown impatient at the seeming intractability of Africa's commitment to governmental determination of food prices. But the experiences of numerous African countries have shown that prudence and gradualism are the essential preconditions for the long-term viability of a policy-reform program. It is thus regrettable that so much of the debate about producer pricing in Africa has been cast in terms of a bipolar distinction between controlled and free-market pricing.

A wholesale changeover from controlled pricing to free-market pricing could also be questioned on economic grounds. Bienefeld offers strong echoes of Hollis Chenery when he cautions that current free-market prices are not the best guide to a society's long-run comparative advantage:

> Even the most ardent neo-classical economists must accept that the fashioning of an economy's future comparative advantage will require investments in infrastructure, industry, technology, education and many other areas, which cannot be determined by current prices; whose 'payoff' will often be long deferred and obtained in the form of benefits that are not project specific and difficult to quantify.[1]

Agriculture can be expected to bear a fair share of the burden of providing these benefits; thus free-market pricing may not only be politically unfeasible, it may well be economically undesirable.

The real-world policy choice is far more difficult and sensitive than a decision to remove controls and allow free-market forces to set producer prices. It involves the more complex issue of how to restore price incentives while, at the same time, utilizing agriculture, like other sectors, as a source of tax revenue to provide broader social benefits. The difficulty of formulating a pricing policy that will help realize both these objectives is rendered infinitely more difficult by the fact that the economic information on the basis of which to make such choices is frequently unavailable or very sketchy. As a result, it would be only realistic to develop a course of action that, by combining partial and gradual solutions, achieved an element of political practicality. The essential presupposition underpinning a gradualist strategy is recognition that today's agricultural crisis is the product of many years of questionable agricultural policies, and that, precisely for this reason, it is not amenable to easy remedies. The proponents of producer-price increases must recognize that the problem cannot be addressed on a piecemeal basis. A system of agricultural producer prices is a fragile and delicately balanced mosaic of individual crop prices; abrupt changes in any one of these could easily have unintended and unwanted consequences for the productivity of others.

A workable strategy of pricing reform would probably need to have a number of components. Pricing changes would need to be gradual, not only so as to avoid an inflationary shock in the cities, but so as to provide opportunity to assess the effect of change in any one sector of the agricultural economy on the productivity and vitality of other sectors. Massive increases in producer prices for food staples that simply lead to the wholesale substitution of food crops for export crops are not really a solution to the problem. During a transitional period of pricing reform, the donor community would have a critically important role to play. To help hold down the rate of urban inflation, donors would need to be prepared to continue to supply food assistance, much of it on concessional terms. But the precise level of food assistance would need to be carefully calibrated so that food aid would not constitute a disincentive to local production. Food aid could be an important political condition for local pricing reform, but it would also be essential to reduce the level of food assistance as increased producer prices triggered an increase in the level of marketed domestic production.

An additional ingredient in a politically workable program of price reform is the willingness of the donor community to provide capital assistance for the industrial sector. Industrialization by import substitution may have been a flawed strategy from its inception, but these industries do offer an important vehicle for quickly regenerating urban employment. This is not only economically essential, but, insofar as an increase in employment provides additional basis for political stability, it is a vital part of the broad assurance to African governments that willingness to engage in policy reform need not be self-endangering. Most importantly, the regeneration of the consumer-goods sector is integral to the success of pricing reform. Unless a supply of consumer goods to the countryside can be reestablished, price increases are meaningless. In some African countries, economic decline has gone so far that such essential consumer items as soap, cloth, sugar, radio batteries, bicycle tires, and cooking oil have simply disappeared from the countryside. Where this has occurred, farmers have no incentive to respond to price increases, because an improvement in cash income does not really produce an improvement in living conditions.

Currency Devaluation

Currency devaluation is a precondition of agricultural recovery. No other single policy so conspicuously reflects the urban bias of African governments or so drastically tilts the internal terms of trade against rural producers as the imposition of an overvalued currency. By facilitating the tendency toward conspicuous consumption in the cities and by draining the rural sector of foreign exchange to finance the needs of import-substituting industries, currency overvaluation deprives agriculture of badly needed capital. It is causally related to agricultural decline because it is an integral feature of pricing systems that suppress production by lowering the real returns to agricultural producers. This is especially evident in the case of export crops, which are, in effect, "taxed" by the amount of the overvaluation, but it is also operative in the food-crop sector, where prices are typically set sufficiently low as to minimize any possible tendency to substitute food crops for cash crops in the rural areas.

The precise importance of devaluation is sometimes missed by critics who argue that it is not likely to stimulate exports by reducing their prices on world markets. Those who hold this view point out, quite correctly, that the world-market prices for agricultural commodities are set in hard currencies, typically the U.S. dollar, and that devaluation does not have any effect on these prices. The purpose of devaluation, however, is not to lower export prices, but to facilitate a substantial increase in the domestic producer price, which is paid in local currency. Devaluation would permit an increase in the local producer price of an exportable commodity and, in this way, help to stimulate marketed production. Since one of the major symptoms of Africa's agricultural decline has been a falling share of world markets for key commodities, devaluation provides a direct means of reestablishing its former market position.

As do other strategies that seek to address the problem of agricultural decline by shifting the internal terms of trade to favor the countryside, currency devaluation poses a serious political problem because of its potential for inflationary impact on the urban population. The critical question with respect to this reform, then, as with respect to reform of producer prices, is how to achieve an economic goal while minimizing the political strain it imposes. The answer is not radically different. Currency devaluation is not an "all-or-nothing" proposition; it can be achieved in a sequence of phased steps so as to reduce the impact at any given moment. Devaluation can also be accompanied by other measures, such as wage increases or tax reduction, that are intended to yield a partial offset of its effects, especially on poorer segments of the urban population.

If donor nations cooperate by making financial assistance available during the difficult period of transition to a realistic exchange rate, the inevitable increase of urban discontent should not be so great as to destabilize governments intent on the reform process. Much may depend, ultimately, on the character of the specific government in question: Those that have a democratic base and that seek to distribute the burdens of reform equitably may have a greater chance of survival than those that seek to maintain the privileges of the few while lowering the standard of living of the majority of the population. The contemporary political history of the vast majority of African nations suggests that very few African countries have exhibited tendencies toward sustained democratic political practices. Since the maintenance of economic privileges at the top appears to be the rule rather than the exception in modern Africa, the most likely prospect is that the price of this policy reform, like others, will be paid by the poorer segments of society.

The Parastatal Sector

The third broad area where policy reform is essential to economic recovery has to do with the continent's ubiquitous agricultural parastatals. It is extremely doubtful that a process of agricultural recovery can be launched so long as state corporations continue to hold legalized monopolies over the purchasing, processing, and vending of major commodities. These corporations have few, if any, incentives for efficiency or economy of operation; they have become the subject of gross political abuse, including rampant corruption and nepotism; and, perhaps most importantly, they have generated an atmosphere of cynicism and mistrust among their producer clienteles. Under these conditions, it would be tempting to conclude that the most fruitful course of action would be to abolish the parastatals altogether. Parastatal performance in Africa has been so dismal that genuinely moderate observers have sometimes been driven to this conclusion along with ardent proponents of the free-market.

Abolishing parastatals, like other radical remedies, does not fully address the political and economic complexities of the present situation. Because of their substantial resources, large numbers of personnel, and organizational linkages throughout society, parastatal corporations wield enormous political power. African political elites typically regard the parastatal sector as a key source of political support and are understandably reluctant to contemplate a policy change that might alienate this powerful constituency. Moreover, certain of the economic functions assigned to the parastatals remain of great importance, even if the parastatals as currently constituted do not perform them very well. The central question, then, is: What sort of policy might make it possible to reform the parastatal system in order to achieve some of the efficiency and economy-of-operation of the private sector and, at the same time, maintain a mechanism to provide important economic services that are not likely to be delivered by the private sector?

Defenders of the parastatal system point out that these organizations are given a virtually impossible job, that they are required to operate within a framework beyond their jurisdiction. Agricultural parastatals, for example, are expected to stabilize financial returns to the farmers—a goal that almost no agricultural system in the world has been able to achieve—but they are given almost no control over the pricing system. The prices at which they must buy and sell the commodities they are responsible for are generally set at the cabinet or ministerial level. Parastatal corporations are also characteristically required to purchase whatever supplies of a given crop are offered to them rather than to operate on the basis of their own judgment about what the market can absorb at a given time. Parastatal supporters point out, as well, that the operating costs of these organizations are entirely out of their control; decisions about staffing levels and salary scales are also made externally, by members of the cabinet or special cabinet committees. The managers of export parastatals operate under a particularly severe disability because the prices they can pay to growers are a function of officially set exchange rates, and they are unable to avoid the downward distortion of producer prices that ensue where currency overvaluation is a serious problem.

The ultimate defense of the parastatal system rests on an implicit comparison with the performance of the private sector. While acknowledging that corruption and inefficient performance are extremely serious matters, supporters of agricultural parastatals argue that a system of state control ultimately provides far more benefits for peasant farmers than would a free-market. There is an intense conviction that private merchants, who might in many cases be racially different from their farmer-producers, would behave far more exploitively than do the parastatals as regards pricing, and that the private sector would fail altogether at such vital goals as price stabilization or crop research.

The debate over the appropriate role, if any, for agricultural parastatals is as intense as any in the field of African development today. Numerous critics of the parastatal system tend to believe that its problems are inherent in the very concept of official monopoly and argue strongly for thoroughgoing privatization of the agricultural sector as the only solution to today's crisis. Others tend to believe that a more workable and politically feasible solution lies in creating a formula that will combine the best features of competitive private trading with retention of parastatals to guarantee the carrying out of certain functions that only state institutions are well equipped to provide. Those who propose a more mixed system tend to argue that parastatals should be buyers and sellers of last resort, establishing a price band within which private traders could operate freely. They also tend to believe that only state institutions have the capacity to carry out such important functions as: (a) monitoring the behavior of the private sector; (b) creation of a strategic food reserve; (c) the dissemination of food aid to especially needy regions; and (d) the conduct of agricultural research and dissemination of its results. It is a measure of the failure of the present parastatal system that virtually no one defends its retention without major reform.

The Industrial Sector

It is not to Africa's long-term advantage to retain an industrial strategy based on import substitution. Industries based on this principle seem inherently prone to inefficient and high-cost operation. Industrial managers who can depend on protected markets buffered by high tariff barriers and outright import restrictions have neither the incentive nor the impetus to improve their industrial processes. Rather, they tend to focus their efforts on maintaining the good will of the politicians in whose power it is to maintain the protectionism that guarantees profitability. Moreover, as a result of protectionism, industries based on import substitution compete unfairly for labor and other inputs with industries that are export-oriented and might make an economic contribution by adding to a country's foreign-exchange earnings.

African governments inclined to withdraw their support from heavily protected industries face a difficult conundrum, for, in the midst of the current crisis, these industries do offer an excellent prospect of increasing urban employment and of improving the availability of consumer goods. And, in the absence of a viable alternative, governments that withdraw their support from import-substituting industries run the immediate risk of having no industrial sector at all. On the other hand, governments that continue their support for import substitution will continue to find themselves drained of foreign exchange and burdened with a high-cost, low-productivity industrial sector inherently prone to corruption and unable to compete in foreign markets. Those governments will, therefore, be chronically short of the financial reserves necessary to replenish the agricultural realm. The most difficult question about policy reform poses itself once again: how to disengage from a failed policy of import substitution in such a way that the disengagement itself does not worsen the problem of economic malaise.

The only workable answer to this question is that the process of economic disengagement from import substitution must be characterized by the same prudent gradualism that must mark the process of reform in other policy areas. Industries that have enjoyed a long period of protection cannot be expected to adjust overnight to economic competition from the world's most efficient industrial exporters. A certain number of the protected industries may never be able to compete on the basis of their productive efficiency. The process of ending the protectionist policies that encourage infant industries never to mature is one of endless difficult choices: how quickly to end tariff protection and where; how quickly to allow foreign imports to invade domestic markets and precisely which ones; and whether there might be certain protected industries that, despite their economic inefficiencies, merit continued protection for other than purely economic reasons. The movement away from import substitution is one that calls for continuous and meticulous empirical research.

The decision to curtail import substitution could be taken to imply acceptance of the view that there is an alternative, export-led growth strategy available, and that this strategy has greater potential for improving the material conditions of the African peoples. This is an issue that merits full exploration before a final rupture with the strategy of import substitution is implemented, for even World Bank economists have begun to cast doubt on the feasibility of the export-led growth model. In recent years, the prices of primary agricultural commodities have declined sharply in world markets, and, given the intense competition among primary agricultural exporters as well as the relatively slow growth in world demand for these products, it is unrealistic to expect the prices of primary commodities to rebound in the near future.[2] The processing of these commodities also has limitations as a means of levering an improved position in the world economy, because, in an effort to maintain their own industrial base, the world's industrial nations have erected systems of protectionism to discourage the import of finished goods.[3] The export-led strategy has many possibilities for stimulating economic growth in Africa, but an important precondition for its success is the political and economic cooperation of the world's advanced industrial societies.

The selection and implementation of a strategy of policy reform is an extraordinarily difficult and complex problem. Not even the most zealous advocates of policy reform would suggest that these remedies alone can elicit a greater supply response from Africa's peasant farmers. Attention must be paid, as well, to improving the physical infrastructure, to removing the innumerable petty bureaucratic restraints on production (such as bans on the interdistrict movement of goods), and to providing greater physical security in the countryside. One of the greatest constraints on fuller farmer participation in the marketplace is the sheer physical difficulty of moving goods from the farm to the nearest market or transportation center; another is the danger of robbery by criminal gangs or extortion by corrupt local officials.

If policy reform is undertaken successfully, however, Africa may well be in a strong position to regenerate agricultural production as a whole. Internalists believe strongly that an improved policy environment will benefit both cash-crop and food-crop production. The key issue is not whether resources are directed to export-crop production or food-crop production, but rather the need to redirect economic resources away from the urban milieu to the countryside. If this is accomplished, Africa will not only be able to recapture some of its former share of world trade in key agricultural commodities but to achieve a heightened degree of food self-sufficiency. Indeed, food self-sufficiency would appear to be well within the grasp of the majority of African countries that are now clients of food-aid programs. Improved agricultural performance may also contribute to a higher level of capacity utilization in the industrial sector by generating foreign-exchange reserves with which to acquire industrial inputs.

KENYA'S POLICY REFORMS

Internal governmental studies of Kenya's balance-of-payments crisis began as early as 1972, and, by 1973, Kenyan officials had themselves concluded that import substitution was contributing to the country's acute shortage of foreign exchange. Governmental officials became virtually unanimous in their conviction that corrective measures had to be undertaken to stimulate the growth of exports.[4] The first specific action was the 1974 passage of the Local Manufactures (Export Compensation) Act, initiating a program to increase exports by providing financial subsidies to manufacturers who exported certain specified commodities. The first effort in this direction did not prove immediately effective, inasmuch as the subsidies required to stimulate exports were well beyond the available budgetary resources.

The government quickly followed the Export Compensation Act with a series of additional measures.[5] A sales tax was levied to increase the government's tax revenues, facilitating higher export subsidies without increasing the level of effective protection, as increased tariffs would have done. The government also undertook a major tariff reform, designed to move the country away from a strategy of import substitution by reducing the level of industrial protection.[6] Import restrictions were removed or lowered on a wide variety of goods, and tariffs were increased on certain kinds of machinery so as to discourage further capital investment in the import-substituting sector. The government also discontinued a variety of other protective practices, including the famous "letter of no objection," that, in effect, gave local manufacturers a veto over potentially competitive imports.[7]

It is not the point of this chapter to provide an exhaustive description of the Kenyan government's efforts at policy reform after 1975. Those efforts have been systematically and favorably described by the World Bank, in a published study of the Kenyan economy.[8] The central theme in this analysis is the strength of the political impulse toward economic policy reform generally, and, in particular, toward the implementation of policies favorable to the agricultural sector. This impulse was so strong that the Kenyan government was prepared to implement policy changes that ran counter to the interests of its urban constituents.

Four Policy Risks

The Kenyan policy landscape between 1975 and 1981 contains a great many examples illustrating this point. But there are four examples of policy changes that demonstrate with particular clarity the government's willingness to offend the economic interests of important urban clienteles: (1) wages policy; (2) interest-rate policy; (3) fiscal policy; and (4) exchange-rate policy and commodity pricing.

Perhaps the most obvious of the government's steps to alter the country's urban-rural economic balance was its introduction, in 1980, of a wages policy. The purpose of this policy was to dampen inflationary pressures by suppressing demand; its operational principle was to keep salary increases below the rate of inflation. Since wage earners are overwhelmingly urban, rather than rural, the burden of this policy fell disproportionately on the country's urban population. Although the wages policy affected, to some degree, all urban wage earners, it fell with particular weight on the shoulders of middle- and upper-level governmental employees, whose support is generally considered of critical importance for long-term political stability.

The second change was in Kenya's interest-rate policy. Urban consumers, especially those in the middle and working classes, tend to favor low interest rates because these are conducive to inexpensive credit, and hence to higher levels of personal consumption of items commonly bought through loans, such as automobiles and houses. Cheap credit is less important to peasant smallholders, who tend not to borrow for personal consumption but only to finance part of the costs of the planting and growing seasons. As a result, governments that want to appeal to their urban clienteles tend to favor negative interest rates, which in effect subsidize urban consumption. After 1975, the Kenyan government recognized that positive interest rates help stimulate development by encouraging savings and investment, while negative interest rates dampen development by encouraging excessive consumer borrowing. To help stimulate economic growth, the government initiated a series of interest-rate increases, doubling the interest rate on savings deposits from 5 to 10 percent in 1980.

The third measure concerns the government's fiscal policy. Urban dwellers have a greater interest in budget deficits than do their rural counterparts, for these tend to finance governmental activities that are primarily urban in character, including educational and medical services and the expansion of governmental employment. Not only do peasant smallholders benefit less from social services or governmental job creation, but they tend to suffer when budget deficits contribute to a rate of inflation that is greater than increases in producer prices. The urban stake in budget deficits becomes most apparent when governments seek to reduce expenditures, either by lowering services or by increasing taxes. Thus, a government whose policies are at all guided by the socioeconomic interests of urban residents will tend to engage in deficit budgeting. In this respect, as in many others, however, the Kenyan government undertook serious and concrete reform, initiating stringent controls on expenditures and a series of measures to increase tax collections.

The clearest examples of a tradeoff between urban and rural interests, however, are exchange-rate policy and the pricing of food staples. There is overwhelming evidence that overvalued currency favors urban populations, whose incomes consist principally of wages, while penalizing rural producers, whose incomes consist of the return on commodities. For this reason, no single step is as vital to agricultural recovery as currency devaluation. But no single step is nearly as fraught with political peril. African governments that seek to stay in power have generally been inclined to overvalue their currency and suppress the prices of food staples. As part of its overall process of policy reform, however, the Kenyan government initiated a program of phased devaluations, lowering the official exchange rate of the Kenya shilling by about 20 percent in 1981 alone. It also initiated a series of producer-price increases for maize, thereby further aggravating its urban constituents by raising the price of food.

The 1982 Coup Attempt

Against the background of these and other similar policy changes, it is not at all surprising that Kenya experienced a nearly successful coup attempt in the summer of 1982, nor that this effort apparently gained the momentary support of some of Nairobi's urban social groups, especially students, and large numbers of the urban poor, many of whom reside in slum areas on the edge of the city. Indeed, the only surprising feature of the 1982 coup attempt was that it failed—precisely because it did not gain widespread urban support. Initiated by one unit of Kenya's military, the air force, it failed completely, for example, to gain the support of the army, which was eventually instrumental in suppressing it. Nor did the coup attempt enjoy any visible measure of support among other governmental employees, such as teachers, civil servants, or transportation and postal workers—groups whose role has often been critically important in successful military coups elsewhere in Africa. Although the coup effort did enjoy some support among university students, it was not supported by university faculty members. Perhaps most importantly, the coup effort failed to gain any measure of support among the country's dissident political leaders.

The critical question, then, is: What deterred social groups that had been seriously pinched by the government's economic policy from supporting an attempt to overthrow it? The only persuasive explanation is that though all these groups had been adversely affected by measures that were part of a policy program designed to trigger agricultural growth by reducing urban consumption, they had sufficiently invested in the countryside to benefit from policies that were improving the income of rural producers. Not only had large numbers of politicians and high-ranking civil servants become farm owners, but, by the early 1980s, many had also invested in secondary businesses that depended on rural prosperity. Among these various businesses are beer and soft drink distributorships, tractor and farm vehicle dealerships, service firms and supply companies for agricultural inputs, and trucking companies. Although the owners of many of these firms resided in the city and, indeed, were partly dependent on wage income, their rural investments had created a deep countervailing interest in the economic well-being of the Kenyan rural sector. This interest not only explains their refusal to support an urban-based coup attempt, but their broad assent to the government's economic program.

STRUCTURAL ADJUSTMENT IN KENYA AND TANZANIA

The Kenyan government's policy position after 1980 has been fully detailed in Sessional Paper no. 4 of that year, *On Economic Prospects and Policies*. The significance of this document far transcends its somewhat mundane description of policy changes: it has been described by its supporters as a "friendship treaty" with the World Bank, and by its detractors as a "surrender agreement." Both labels confirm the extent to which the government of Kenya has aligned its internal policy framework with the recommendations made since 1975 by World Bank and IMF economists. In the current parlance of development studies, these alignments are commonly referred to as "structural adjustment." The most important political feature of structural adjustment in Kenya is that it did not have to be imposed on the country from outside, by international lending institutions using financial leverage to induce policy reforms by a reluctant and mistrustful government.

Kenya's implementation of structural adjustment had begun as early as the mid-1970s and sprang principally from the economic interests of its landholding elites. Its early implementation was thus the result of the policy needs of powerful internal social groups. By the early 1980s, when the bank was intensifying its program of structural-adjustment lending throughout Africa, Kenya's economic policies were already very close to the bank's broad prescriptions. Although there have been occasional and sometimes intense disagreements about particular issues, such as whether the NCPB should be dissolved, Kenya has generally enjoyed a high degree of credibility with bank officials. The generally good relations between Kenya and the bank grow out of a consensus on fundamental issues of economic management, such as exchange-rate policy, monetary and fiscal policy, trade and tariff administration, and the role of the private sector.

The contrast with Tanzania could not be greater. During the decade 1975 to 1985, Tanzania's relations with the World Bank and the IMF were deeply strained. Negotiations over economic policy were not only protracted but were conducted in an atmosphere of deep mistrust and political animosity. Agreements concerning policy reform were arrived at only with the utmost difficulty, to be suspended as one or another party found cause to consider the agreement void. At one point in the early 1980s, the atmosphere of tension between the World Bank and the government of Tanzania became so intense that it was impossible to conduct direct negotiations. An intermediary body, called the Tanzania Advisory Group Secretariat, had to be created to continue the process of policy dialogue. Although the membership of this group had been agreed to by both parties and consisted largely of academic economists who were known to be sympathetic to Tanzania's economic programs, its recommendations got a mixed reception. The response of the Tanzanian government at that time was to make a strong official commitment to policy reform but to be painstakingly slow in the implementation of major policy changes.

This sort of ambiguity has been the hallmark of Tanzania's posture on policy reform throughout the 1980s. The government has consistently tended to state its official commitment to the principle of policy reform and to announce specific measures, while delaying or providing only partial implementation. Thus, though the government officially announced a program of structural adjustment after receiving the report of the advisory group, World Bank officials report with frustration that implementation of its recommendations has been slow. When the government of Tanzania signed an agreement with the IMF in the late summer of 1986, this pattern repeated itself. There was some progress toward the implementation of the measures provided for in the agreement, but others remained pure declarations of intent.

Between August 1986 and May 1987, for example, the Tanzanian currency was devalued approximately 300 percent, from U.S. $1 = Shs.(T) 17 to approximately U.S. $1 = Shs.(T)50. But this fell far short of the devaluation recommended by the IMF and left the official rate still at only about one-fourth the unofficial rate. Import restrictions were also somewhat liberalized, allowing "own-financed imports." That is, individuals in possession of foreign exchange were given permission to bring a wide variety of goods into the country. The government also increased agricultural producer prices, but there remains considerable doubt that these increases approach the country's rate of inflation. Similarly, the government announced its intention to force the country's dozens of parastatal corporations to operate more efficiently, but few measures in this direction have actually been taken. Most importantly, there has been almost no progress toward implementation of the government's long-standing commitment to restore the country's once flourishing system of producer cooperatives and to allow these cooperatives to take over such economically critical functions as the marketing of agricultural commodities.

The constant fluctuation between official pronouncements of policy adjustment and painfully slow implementation demonstrates the extreme fragility of the impetus toward policy reform and may also be taken as an indication of deep political conflict in Tanzania. In the absence of a domestic social class with vested interests in policies promoting economic growth, the internal impetus toward policy change is extremely weak, found largely among a small number of high-ranking administrators and political leaders in only two ministries, finance and agriculture. These two ministries are pitted against virtually the whole Tanzanian officialdom, including the national political party. Tanzanian bureaucrats and party officers at all levels have benefitted from policies that promote urban welfare at the expense of rural development and that create a virtually limitless panorama of rent-seeking opportunities.

The Tanzanian state has become more and more corrupt, as politically connected individuals, caught in an inflationary squeeze, have converted their offices into sources of patronage and personal gain. Tanzania toward the end of the 1980s had become a strange mutation of the rent-seeking state: Its policies could be understood not so much as a matter of maximizing state revenues, but as a vehicle through which political and administrative office-holders could maximize their own financial well-being. The all-pervasiveness of opportunities for such maximization provides a powerful explanation for the failure of genuine policy reform in Tanzania thus far. It may also reveal a universal law of political behavior: Given the opportunity to decide, persons in positions of authority will consistently choose to retain the perquisites of power, as the leaders of a failing economic system, rather than to surrender these as the price of economic recovery.

TANZANIA'S ECONOMIC RECOVERY PROGRAM

Tanzania's agricultural performance between 1966 and 1985 provides a textbook example of the destructive effects of inappropriate policies. The policy framework implemented since the late 1960s offers a perfect illustration of the policy mistakes outlined by Elliot Berg in *Accelerated Development in Sub-Saharan Africa*.[9] For nearly twenty years, Tanzania overvalued its currency, suppressed real producer prices below shadow-market levels, tolerated gross inefficiencies and abuses in its parastatal corporations, and engaged in an industrial strategy that depleted the agricultural sector's capital. Although Tanzania was buffeted by a series of international economic shocks, the evidence suggests that policy misjudgments were a far greater factor in accounting both for the precipitous declines in agricultural exports and the ultimate failure of its strategy of food self-sufficiency to eliminate high volumes of grain imports. While it is uncertain whether Tanzania can reestablish a positive rate of growth unless the world-market prices of its principal exports improve, it seems certain beyond any doubt that it will be unable to take advantage of any growth opportunities unless it implements the policy reforms contemplated in the Economic Recovery Program.

It is convenient to date the beginning of Tanzania's commitment to policy reform from the inauguration of President Mwinyi in the late fall of 1985. But in fact there were strong indications of a change in economic mood at least three years before the presidential succession. As early as 1982, for example, the Ministry of Planning and Economic Affairs had published a study that stressed the need for greater economic incentives for agricultural producers, for reducing the government's large budget deficits, and for greater prudence in the management of the country's money supply.[10] In 1983, the government began to implement some of the recommendations of this study and initiated a modest program of trade liberalization, allowing individual Tanzanians with foreign-exchange accounts far greater latitude in importing such economically vital goods as pickup trucks, buses, and plant machinery. These changes were rather modest and piecemeal in character. Their significance lay in the extent to which they revealed the gradual emergence of reformist sentiment within the government, rather than in their impact on the vitality of the nation's economy. Since the July 1986 agreement, however, Tanzania has been committed to a process of comprehensive and far-reaching policy change. The Economic Recovery Program contemplates significant policy changes in the areas discussed below.

Currency Devaluation

The policy reform of utmost importance in the minds of everyone concerned to stimulate economic growth in Tanzania, both Tanzanian officials and representatives of external donor organizations, has been policy reform. Despite a 33-percent devaluation in the summer of 1984, the Tanzanian shilling remained drastically overvalued and, as Table 5.1 shows, was openly traded on the streets of Dar es Salaam at more than ten times its official value throughout 1984 and 1985. Since that time, the shilling has been successively devalued, and as of early 1988 its official rate is Shs.(T) 90 per U.S. $1, about one-fifth its value three years earlier. As importantly, the government has officially committed itself to further devaluations in order to reduce the remaining discrepancy between the official and parallel market rates, a goal that could require an exchange rate as low as Shs.(T) 150 per U.S. $1.

Trade Liberalization

A second major building block in the present government's program of policy reform is trade liberalization—the gradual removal of restrictions on the import and export of all categories of goods, consumer items as well as industrial and agricultural inputs. The liberalization of trade can be expected to serve a variety of purposes vital to economic recovery. First and foremost, it is vital to the effectiveness of currency devaluation, since it helps eliminate one of the most powerful motivations for exchanging currency illegally: If desired consumer goods become available in local shops, there is less reason to engage in illegal transactions for foreign currency with which to obtain them. No amount of devaluation is likely to produce a stable exchange rate if citizens can obtain the goods they desire only in foreign markets.

Trade liberalization is also vital as a stimulus for increased agricultural production. By the late 1970s, some firsthand observers of the Tanzanian rural sector had come to believe that the root cause of diminished production levels had less to do with low producer prices than with the fact that Tanzanian farmers could purchase very little with the shillings they did obtain.[11] In economic parlance, this is referred to as excessive liquidity, meaning that many Tanzanian farmers had ample supplies of cash given the meager stock of consumer goods available, and, therefore, little incentive for the added income that increased production might bring about.

Trade liberalization is also indispensable to stop the hemorrhaging of foreign-exchange that takes place when agricultural goods are smuggled out of the country in order to obtain goods that cannot be purchased locally. There is little doubt that a sizable proportion of Tanzania's annual coffee harvest has, in recent years, been quietly crossing into Kenya, as part of a complex bartering process to acquire goods that are locally unavailable. Not only has Tanzania lost the hard currency that legal sale of this commodity might have realized, but also the value of the imported inputs used in its production. Without trade liberalization, then, Tanzania would continue to endure an economic impasse. Its domestic production of consumer goods had been drastically reduced by shortages of foreign exchange, making it all but impossible to import the necessary industrial inputs of factory machinery, spare parts, and raw materials. But trade barriers erected to sustain its import-substituting industries had virtually eliminated imported supplies, thereby contributing to excessive shilling liquidity in the rural areas. The end result was that Tanzania's economy was stagnating at low levels of both consumption and production.

Price Reform

According to the Economic Recovery Program agreed to between the Tanzanian government and the IMF in July 1986, producer prices for agricultural commodities will be allowed to rise dramatically, by about 5 percent per year over inflation. In addition, private traders will be allowed to purchase and sell many of the country's most important commodities, including maize. Price reform may already have begun to yield impressive results, including the reestablishment of self-sufficiency in maize and, most dramatically, a 100-percent increase in cotton production between 1986 and 1987. Sisal production has also begun to recover as the area planted to this crop increased by about 65 percent during this same period.[12] While other exports, including coffee and cashew nuts, have been slower to register such increases, this may be attributable to the fact that, as tree crops, they require several years before production responds to a more favorable economic environment.

Parastatal Reforms

The fourth area of policy reform has to do with the role and financing of the country's agricultural parastatals. Under the terms of the Economic Recovery Program, private traders are now given far greater latitude to buy agricultural commodities directly from farmers, for resale in the cities and towns. The principal commodity affected by this change thus far has been maize, and there seems little doubt that the increased role of the private sector has much to do with the dramatic increase in the level of domestically produced marketed maize. The recovery program provides for a substantial broadening of the role of the private sector in the export area as well. Among other changes, it eliminates the parastatals' monopoly of the country's export trade by permitting both privately owned estates and producer cooperatives to act as exporters. Perhaps most importantly, Tanzania is officially committed to the revival of its producer cooperatives, banned in 1976 on the grounds of inefficiency and corruption. The operative idea is that competitive pressure from the cooperatives as well as from the private sector, combined with the phased reduction of government subsidies, is expected to compel the agricultural parastatals to operate in a more efficient and responsible manner.

The Balance of Payments

A host of questions has been raised about whether these reforms are likely to lead to a sustained economic recovery. As of this writing, it is far too early to provide a plausible or systematic response to questions of Tanzania's economic future. There is little doubt that some of the early indications are encouraging and suggest that important economic changes have begun to take place. In 1987, for example, Tanzania was able to attain a modest increase in per-capita income for the first time in many years. The recent increases in marketed production levels of maize and cotton have been astonishing for a country where annual declines seemed almost to be taken for granted, and these appear to portend comparable improvements in the production levels of other key agricultural commodities. Because of trade liberalization, moreover, Tanzanian shops now openly stock consumer goods that could be acquired only illicitly just a short time ago. Since currency devaluation has radically lessened the differential between the country's official and unofficial exchange rates, Tanzania may also have begun to stem the outflow of hard currency through illegal channels.

It would be tempting to conclude, on the basis of this fragmentary evidence, that policy changes have unleashed the beginnings of a far-reaching economic recovery. Such a conclusion would be premature: Implementation of the policy-reform package has proved to be a halting and laborious process. While the government has been able to implement policy reforms relatively quickly in some areas—such as currency devaluation, trade liberalization, and maize marketing—others—including restoration of the cooperative movement and fiscal improvements in the parastatal corporations—have been subject to political resistance. The painstaking and frustratingly piecemeal character of the reform process derives from and reveals much about the nature of the Tanzanian political system. Although a one-party state, Tanzania, like Kenya, had always exhibited a considerable degree of ideological diversity. It is not surprising that elements of the Tanzanian polity, identified with the former president, harbor deep doubts about the IMF program and use their positions within the system to resist it. The long-term prospects for policy reform in Tanzania depend entirely on the balance of political forces within the country, and this, in turn, depends on how well the present administration is able to address the sorts of economic problems that will inevitably arise in the changeover from a statist to a market-driven national economy.

One immediate issue is the country's staggering foreign debt. In early 1986, just before the Economic Recovery Program began, the debt-service ratio, as a percentage of export earnings, may well have reached 100 percent, as the country's total debt burden approached $3.6 billion. Under the terms of the IMF agreement, Tanzania has been given a temporary moratorium on debt payments and will not begin to resume debt servicing until the summer of 1989. The idea behind the debt moratorium is that the economy should be given breathing space for recovery, and that debt payments will be substantially easier once there is an upward economic trajectory.

The debt moratorium appears to be working splendidly. It permits the country to use its foreign-exchange earnings to finance the importation of desperately needed inputs for the industrial sector, the equipment and supplies needed to rebuild a badly deteriorated transportation infrastructure, and, perhaps most importantly, to import goods necessary to rejuvenate the agricultural sector. It has made all this possible while, at the same time, permitting the country considerable latitude to import the consumer goods necessary to provide material incentives for higher levels of production. The debt moratorium has also contributed to a new psychological atmosphere. As recently as 1984, the country was very much in the grips of a mood of economic defeatism. Today, this has clearly been replaced by an atmosphere of economic optimism about the future.

The difficult question is: What happens when Tanzania is required to resume some level of debt repayment? Much, of course, depends on the extent to which the country's creditors are prepared to continue a highly flexible approach to debt, in return for continuing policy reforms that encourage the private sector to play an important role in stimulating economic growth. Since Tanzania has begun to enjoy a much-improved image among donor agencies, such flexibility is not unlikely. But the possibility always exists that, if the country's creditors do insist on a high level of debt repayment, the sudden loss of foreign-exchange to debt servicing would severely hamper the process of economic recovery. Tanzania's next presidential election is scheduled for the fall of 1990, about one year after debt payments are scheduled to resume. If the process of economic recovery should falter at that critical juncture, the political ramifications would be considerable.

A second question has to do with the imminent potential for increased political resistance from elements of the state apparatus directly threatened by policy reform. One potential source of such resistance are the employees of parastatal corporations. Their resistance to economic liberalization could easily stiffen, if overstaffed government agencies were compelled by the new economic arrangements to begin laying off redundant employees. A case in point is the NMC. Now that private traders have taken over a great deal of the country's maize trade, the problem of overstaffing in this organization is more acute than ever. According to the new economic policy, however, parastatal bodies that incur losses will no longer be subsidized out of the government's budget and must seek ways to operate on the basis of the income they generate. If this policy is strictly imposed, the NMC and other parastatal bodies will be required to cut back substantially on staff size. Since the private sector is not yet sufficiently robust to absorb parastatal employees thus displaced, public-sector unemployment could occur and would have significant political ramifications.

Discontent within the public sector could also be seriously exacerbated by the high level of inflation that has accompanied the early stages of economic recovery. Although the shops and stores in Dar es Salaam have become a virtual cornucopia of consumer items that were practically unobtainable just a few years ago, the prices of these items have, in most cases, skyrocketed far beyond the reach of the average public-sector employee. The fivefold devaluation of the Tanzanian shilling has produced an equivalent increase in the shilling price of imported goods, and an almost equivalent increase in the cost of a host of domestically produced items. Even as this has occurred, the government has been compelled by the terms of its IMF agreement to maintain a strict ceiling on public-sector salary increases. Since these are now measurably below the country's annual rate of inflation, there has been a steady erosion of the purchasing power of government employees.

A final question is: How much breadth and depth will economic recovery be able to attain? There is much concern that a flood of imports will reduce the prospects of an economic recovery for domestic industries that had engaged in the production of items now being acquired from abroad. Will imported clothing, for example, make it difficult to revive the Tanzanian textile industry? To truly succeed in sparking a sustainable and broad-based pattern of economic growth, trade liberalization may need to be diluted with a measure of protection for potentially viable local industries. While there is little doubt that protectionism has allowed a number of Tanzanian industries to operate in an inefficient and costly manner, it is doubtful that the sudden and virtually complete removal of this protection will stimulate their economic maturity. Rather, protection may have contributed to long-term dependence on the importation of manufactured goods.

Tanzania has set in place the building blocks for an economic-recovery policy. But a variety of political and economic hurdles remain to be surmounted. There is considerable basis for optimism in the fact that the changes attained thus far have not precipitated deep political strain. But this cannot yet be interpreted to mean that Tanzania's policy-induced economic recovery is firmly in place.

NOTES

1. Bienefeld, "African State Policy," p. 7.

2. See, for example, Shamsher Singh, *Sub-Saharan Agriculture: Synthesis and Trade Prospects,* World Bank Staff Working Paper no. 608 (Washington, D.C., 1983), pp. 14–20. See also, The World Bank, The Outlook for Primary Commodities, World Bank Staff Commodity Working Paper no. 9 (Washington, D.C., 1983).

3. See Douglas R. Nelson, consultant, *The Political Structure of the New Protectionism,* World Bank Staff Working Paper no. 471 (Washington, 1981).

4. This discussion draws heavily upon Patrick Low, "Export Subsidies and Trade Policy: The Experience of Kenya," *World Development* 10, no. 4 (1982), pp. 293–304.

5. The Kenyan government outlined these measures and the reasons for them in an extremely important document: *On Economic Prospects and Policies,* Sessional Paper no. 4 (Government Printer, 1975).

6. This material is drawn from Cheryl Christensen, *et al.,* "Agricultural Development in Africa: Kenya and Tanzania," ed. Randall B. Purcell, and Elizabeth Morrison, *U.S. Agriculture and Third World Development: The Critical Linkage* (Lynne Rienner Publishers, Boulder, 1987), pp. 53–72.

7. The "letter of no objection" meant that an importer seeking to bring in manufactured goods had to receive letters from all local manufacturers whose sales might be affected, stating that they had no objection.

8. The World Bank, *Kenya: Growth and Structural Change*, vol. 1 (Washington, D.C., 1983), pp. 95–105.

9. The World Bank, *Accelerated Development in Sub-Saharan Africa: An*

Agenda for Action (Washington, D.C., 1981).

10. Tanzania, *Structural Adjustment*.

11. The author is indebted to USAID economist Alberto Ruiz de Gamboa for this observation.

12. Peter Mathsson, "Tanzania's Green Gold," *World Food Program Journal* 3 (July-September 1987), p. 5.

Bibliography

Abernethy, David B. "Bureaucratic Growth and Economic Decline in Sub-Saharan Africa." In *Africa's Development Crisis: The World Bank Response,* edited by Stephen Commins. Boulder and London: Lynne Rienner, 1988.

Amin, Samir. *Accumulation on a World Scale.* 2 vols. New York and London: Monthly Review Press, 1974.

Baker, Randall. "Linking and Sinking: Externalities and the Persistence of Destitution and Famine in Africa." In *Drought and Hunger in Africa,* edited by Michael H. Glantz. Cambridge: Cambridge University Press, 1987.

Baran, Paul A. *The Political Economy of Growth.* New York and London: Monthly Review Press, 1957.

Barkan, Joel D. "Urban Bias, Peasants and Rural Politics in Kenya and Tanzania." Occasional paper no. 1. Department of Political Science, University of Iowa, 1983.

———. "Comparing Politics and Public Policy in Kenya and Tanzania." In *Politics and Public Policy in Kenya and Tanzania,* edited by Joel D. Barkan. New York: Praeger, 1984.

———, ed. *Politics and Public Policy in Kenya and Tanzania.* New York: Praeger, 1984.

Barker, Jonathan. "The Debate on Rural Socialism in Tanzania." In *Towards Socialism in Tanzania,* edited by Bismarck U. Mwansasu and Cranford Pratt. Toronto: University of Toronto Press, 1979.

Bates, Robert H. "The Politics of Food Crises in Kenya." In *The Political Economy of Kenya,* edited by Michael G. Schatzberg. New York, Westport, and London: Praeger, 1987.

———. *Markets and States in Tropical Africa: The Political Basis of Agricultural Policies.* Berkeley and Los Angeles: University of California Press, 1981.

Belassa, Bela. "Policy Responses to External Shocks in Sub-Saharan African Countries." *The Journal of Policy Modeling* 5 (January 1983): 75–105. Reprint. World Bank Reprint Series no. 270.

Berg, Robert J., and Jennifer Seymour Whitaker, eds. *Strategies for African Development.* Berkeley and Los Angeles: University of California Press, 1986.

Bienefeld, Manfred. "Analyzing the Politics of African State Policy: Some Thoughts on Robert Bates' Work." *Institute for Development Studies Bulletin* 17 (January 1986): 6–11.

Blundell, M. *So Rough a Wind: The Kenya Memoirs of Sir Michael Blundell.*

London: Widenfeld and Nicolson, 1964.

Brett, E. A. *Colonialism and Underdevelopment in East Africa: The Politics of Economic Change.* London: Heinemann, 1973.

Browne, Robert S., and Robert J. Cummings. *The Lagos Plan of Action vs. the Berg Report: Contemporary Issues in African Economic Development.* Lawrenceville, VA: Brunswick, 1984.

Chege, Michael. "The Political Economy of Agrarian Change in Central Kenya." In *The Political Economy of Kenya,* edited by Michael G. Schatzberg. New York, Westport, and London: Praeger, 1987.

Chenery, Hollis. *Structural Change and Development Policy.* London, New York, and Toronto: Oxford University Press, 1979.

Chidzero, B. T. G. *Tanganyika and International Trusteeship.* London, New York, and Toronto: Oxford University Press, 1961.

Christensen, Cheryl, Michael Lofchie, and Larry Witucki. "Agricultural Development in Africa: Kenya and Tanzania." In *United States Agriculture and Third World Development: The Critical Linkage,* edited by Randall B. Purcell and Elizabeth Morrison. Boulder and London: Lynne Rienner, 1987.

Cliffe, Lionel. *One Party Democracy.* Nairobi: East African Publishing House, 1967.

——. "The Political System." In *One Party Democracy,* edited by Lionel Cliffe. Nairobi: East African Publishing House, 1967.

Cliffe, Lionel, and Peter Lawrence. "Agrarian Capitalism and Hunger." *Review of African Political Economy* 15/16 (1979): 1–3.

Cohen, Benjamin. *The Question of Imperialism.* New York: Basic Books, 1973.

Collier, Paul, and Deepak Lal. "Why Poor People Get Rich: Kenya 1960-79." *World Development* 12 (October 1984): 1007–1018.

Commins, Stephen, Michael Lofchie, and Rhys Payne. *Africa's Agrarian Crisis: The Roots of Famine.* Boulder: Lynne Rienner, 1986.

De Wilde, John C. *Agriculture, Marketing and Pricing in Sub-Saharan Africa.* Los Angeles: Crossroads Press for African Studies Association and University of California, Los Angeles African Studies Center, 1984.

Ellis, Frank. *Agricultural Producer Pricing in Tanzania 1970–1979: Implications for Agricultural Output, Rural Incomes, and Crop Marketing Costs.* Economic Research Bureau Paper no. 80.3. Dar es Salaam: University of Dar es Salaam, 1980.

——. "Agricultural Price Policy in Tanzania." *World Development* 10 (April 1982): 263–277.

Emmanuel, Arghiri. *Unequal Exchange: A Study of the Imperialism of Trade.* New York and London: Monthly Review Press, 1972.

Frank, André Gunder. *Capitalism and Underdevelopment in Latin America.* New York and London: Monthly Review Press, 1967.

Franke, Richard, and Barbara Chasin. *Seeds of Famine: Ecological Destruction and the Development Dilemma in the West African Sahel.* Montclair, NJ: Allanheld Osmun, 1980.

Gamboa, Alberto Ruiz de. "Resource Allocation and the Agricultural Sector." Photocopy. Dar es Salaam, n.d.

Gerrard, Christopher, and Greg Posehn. "Government Interventions and Food Grain Markets in Kenya: An Update." Photocopy. 1985.

Ghatak, Subrata, and Ken Ingersent. *Agriculture and Economic Development.*

Baltimore: Johns Hopkins University Press, 1984.

Glantz, Michael H., ed. *Drought and Hunger in Africa*. Cambridge: Cambridge University Press, 1987.

Gordon, David F. *Decolonization and the State in Kenya*. Boulder and London: Westview Press, 1986.

Grosh, Barbara. *Agricultural Parastatals Since Independence: How Have They Performed?* Institute for Development Studies. Working Paper no. 435. Nairobi: University of Nairobi, 1986.

Harberger, Arnold C., ed. *World Economic Growth: Case Studies of Developed and Developing Nations*. San Francisco: Institute for Contemporary Studies, 1984.

Hart, Keith. *The Political Economy of West African Agriculture*. Cambridge: Cambridge University Press, 1982.

Hopkins, Raymond. "Food Aid: Solution, Palliative or Danger for Africa's Food Crisis." In *Africa's Agrarian Crisis: The Roots of Famine,* edited by Stephen Commins, Michael Lofchie, and Rhys Payne. Boulder: Lynne Rienner, 1986.

Hyden, Goran. *Beyond Ujamaa: Underdevelopment and an Uncaptured Peasantry*. Berkeley and Los Angeles: University of California Press, 1980.

Jabara, Cathy L. "Agricultural Pricing Policy in Kenya." *World Development* 13 (May 1985): 611–626.

Jackson, Tony. *Against the Grain: The Dilemma of Project Food Aid*. Oxford: OXFAM, 1982.

Jones, William O. *Marketing Staple Food Crops in Tropical Africa*. Ithaca and London: Cornell University Press, 1972.

Katona, Emil. "Planning and Policy Making: Factors Affecting the Recovery of the Agricultural Sector in Tanzania." Photocopy. n.d.

Keene, Monk and Associates, Inc. "Agricultural Parastatals." Photocopy. Alexandria, VA, September 1984.

Lele, Uma. "Tanzania: Phoenix or Icarus?" In *World Economic Growth: Case Studies of Developed and Developing Nations,* edited by Arnold C. Harberger. San Francisco: Institute for Contemporary Studies, 1984.

Leo, Christopher. *Land and Class in Kenya*. Toronto: University of Toronto Press, 1984.

Leonard, David K. "Class Formation and Agricultural Development." In *Politics and Public Policy in Kenya and Tanzania,* edited by Joel D. Barkan. New York: Praeger, 1984.

Leys, Colin. *Underdevelopment in Kenya: The Political Economy of Neo-Colonialism*. Berkeley and Los Angeles: University of California Press, 1974.

Leys, Roger, ed. *Dualism and Rural Development in East Africa*. Copenhagen: Institute for Development Research, 1973.

Lipton, Michael. *Why Poor People Stay Poor: Urban Bias in World Development*. Cambridge, MA: Harvard University Press, 1976.

Low, Patrick. "Export Subsidies and Trade Policy: The Experience of Kenya." *World Development* 10 (April 1982): 293–304.

Mathsson, Peter. "Tanzania's Green Gold." *World Food Program Journal* 3 (1987): 3–5.

McHenry, Dean E., Jr. *Ujamaa Villages in Tanzania: A Bibliography*. Uppsala: Scandinavian Institute of African Studies, 1981.

———. *Tanzania's Ujamaa Villages: The Implementation of a Rural Development Strategy*. Berkeley: Institute of International Studies, 1979.

Middleton, John, and Greet Kershaw. *The Kikuyu and Kamba of Kenya.* London: International African Institute, 1965.

Migot-Adhola, S. E. "Rural Development Policy and Equality." In *Politics and Public Policy in Kenya and Tanzania,* edited by Joel Barkan. New York: Praeger, 1984.

Miller, Norman N. *Kenya: The Quest for Prosperity.* Boulder: Westview Press, 1984.

Morgan, E. Philip. "The Project Orthodoxy in Development: Reevaluating the Cutting Edge." *Public Administration and Development* 3 (1983): 329–339.

Mwansasu, Bismarck U., and Cranford Pratt, eds. *Towards Socialism in Tanzania.* Toronto: University of Toronto Press, 1979.

Ndulu, Benno. "The Current Economic Stagnation in Tanzania: Causes and Effects." Photocopy. African Studies Center, Boston University, n.d.

Njonjo, Apollo. "The Africanisation of the White Highlands: A Study of Agrarian Class Struggles in Kenya 1950–1974." Ph. D. diss., Princeton University, 1977.

Republic of Kenya. *African Socialism and Its Application to Planning in Kenya.* Sessional Paper no. 10. Nairobi: Government Printer, 1965.

————. *On Economic Prospects and Policies.* Sessional Paper no. 4. Nairobi: Government Printer, 1975.

————. *Development Plan 1984–1988.* Nairobi: Government Printer, [1984].

————. Ministry of Finance and Planning. *Economic Survey 1984.* Nairobi: Government Printer, 1984.

————. Ministry of Finance and Planning. *Economic Survey 1985.* Nairobi: Government Printer, 1985.

————. Ministry of Planning and National Development. Central Bureau of Statistics. *Statistical Abstract 1985.* Nairobi, n.d.

Roemer, Michael. "Economic Development in Africa: Performance Since Independence, and a Strategy for the Future." *Daedalus* (Spring 1982): 125–148.

Rothchild, Donald. *Racial Bargaining in Independent Kenya: A Study of Minorities and Decolonization.* London, New York, and Toronto: Oxford University Press, 1973.

Rwegasira, Delphin. "Exchange Rates and the External Sector." *Journal of Modern African Studies* 22 (March 1984): 451–467.

Schatzberg, Michael G. *The Political Economy of Kenya.* New York, Westport, and London: Praeger, 1987.

Seidman, A. W. "Comparative Development Strategies in East Africa." *East Africa Journal* 7 (April 1970): 13–18.

————. "The Dual Economies of East Africa." *East Africa Journal* 7 (May 1970): 6–20.

————. "The Agricultural Revolution." *East Africa Journal* 7 (August 1970): 21–36.

Sharpley, Jennifer. "External Versus Internal Factors in Tanzania's Macro-Economic Crisis." Photocopy. 1984.

Shivji, Issa. *Class Struggles in Tanzania.* New York and London: Monthly Review Press, 1976.

Sklar, Richard. "Democracy in Africa." Presidential Address. Annual Meeting of the African Studies Association. University of California, Los Angeles, 1982.

————. "Developmental Democracy." *Comparative Studies in Society and History* 29 (April 1987):

Stavenhagen, Rodolfo. *Social Classes in Agrarian Societies.* Garden City, NY:

Doubleday, 1975.

Stewart, Frances. *Planning to Meet Basic Needs*. London and Basingstoke: Macmillan, 1985.

Sunding, David. "Supply Response and the Impact of Marketing Boards on Agricultural Production in Kenya's Rift Valley." Photocopy. Berkeley, 1985.

Swainson, Nicola. *The Development of Corporate Capitalism in Kenya 1918–1977*. Berkeley and Los Angeles: University of California Press, 1980.

Timberlake, Lloyd. "Guarding Africa's Renewable Resources." In *Strategies for African Development*, edited by Robert J. Berg and Jennifer Seymour Whitaker. Berkeley and Los Angeles: University of California Press, 1986.

Truman, David B. *The Governmental Process: Political Interests and Public Opinion*. New York: Alfred A. Knopf, 1959.

Turnbull, Colin. *The Mountain People*. New York: Simon and Schuster, 1972.

United Nations. Food and Agricultural Organization. *Food Situation in African Countries Affected by Emergencies: Special Report*. December 16, 1985.

——. International Labor Office. Jobs and Skills Program for Africa. *Basic Needs in Danger: A Basic Needs Oriented Development Strategy for Tanzania*. Addis Ababa: International Labor Office, 1982.

United Republic of Tanzania. Ministry of Planning and Economic Affairs. *Structural Adjustment Programme for Tanzania*. Dar es Salaam, 1982.

——. Ministry of Agriculture. Marketing Development Bureau. *Estimates of 1981/82 Import Requirements for the Production, Processing and Marketing of Major Crops in Mainland Tanzania*. Working paper prepared by M. G. G. Schluter and M. A. Sackett. Dar es Salaam, 1982.

——. Ministry of Agriculture. Project Planning and Marketing Bureau. *Crop Authorities: Financial Position and Financial Performance*. Dar es Salaam, 1983.

United States. Department of Agriculture. Economic Research Service. *Food Problems and Prospects in Sub-Saharan Africa: The Decade of the 1980's*. Foreign Agricultural Research Report no. 166. August 1981.

United States Agency for International Development. *Resource Allocation and the Agricultural Sector*. By Alberto Ruiz de Gamboa. Dar es Salaam: USAID, n.d.

——. The *Consumption Effects of Agricultural Policies in Tanzania*. Study prepared by Andrew G. Keeler, Grant M. Scobie, Mitchell A. Renkow, and David L. Franklin. Sigma One Corporation, 1982.

——. *Assessment of Exchange Rate Policy in Kenya*. By K. Toh. Nairobi: USAID, 1986.

Vos, Anton de. *Africa, the Devastated Continent?* The Hague: Dr. W. Junk b.v. Publishers, 1975.

Wallerstein, Immanuel. *The Modern World System*. New York and San Francisco: Academic Press, 1974.

Watts, Michael. *Silent Violence: Food, Famine and Peasantry in Northern Nigeria*. Berkeley and Los Angeles: University of California Press, 1983.

World Bank. *Accelerated Development in Sub-Saharan Africa: An Agenda for Action*. Washington, DC: The World Bank, 1981.

——. *Commodity Trade and Price Trends*. Baltimore and London: Johns Hopkins University Press, 1985.

——. *Control, Accountability, and Incentives in a Successful Development Institution: The Kenya Tea Development Authority*. By Geoffrey Lamb and Linda

Muller. Washington, DC: The World Bank, 1982.

——. *Exchange Rate Policies in Eastern and Southern Africa, 1965–1983.* By Ravi Gulhati, et al. World Bank Staff Working Papers, no. 720. Washington, DC: The World Bank, 1985.

——. *Kenya: Growth and Structural Change.* Vol. 1. Washington, DC: The World Bank, 1983.

——. *The Outlook for Primary Commodities.* World Bank Staff Working Papers, no. 9. Washington, DC: The World Bank, 1983.

——. *The Outlook for Primary Commodities 1984 to 1995.* Edited by Ronald Duncan. World Bank Staff Commodity Working Papers, no. 11. Washington, DC: The World Bank, 1984.

——. *The Political Structure of the New Protectionism.* By Douglas R. Nelson. World Bank Staff Working Papers, no. 471. Washington, DC: The World Bank, 1981.

——. *Sub-Saharan Africa: Progress Report on Development Prospects and Programs.* Washington, DC: The World Bank, 1983.

——. *Sub-Saharan Agriculture: Synthesis and Trade Prospects.* By Shamsher Singh. World Bank Staff Working Papers, no. 608. Washington, DC: The World Bank, 1983.

——. *Towards Sustained Development in Sub-Saharan Africa: A Joint Program of Action.* Washington, DC: The World Bank, 1984.

——. *The World Bank Atlas 1986.* Washington, DC: The World Bank, 1986.

——. *World Debt Tables: External Debt of Developing Countries.* Washington, DC: The World Bank.

——. *World Development Report 1984.* New York: Oxford University Press, 1984.

——. *World Development Report 1985.* New York: Oxford University Press, 1985.

Zeitlin, Irving. *Capitalism and Imperialism.* Chicago: Markham, 1972.

Index

230

About the Book and the Author

Much recent scholarship on Africa has concerned itself with continent-wide trends toward declining per capita food production of exportable agricultural commodities. While useful, such broad generalizations tend to overlook the wide variety in the agricultural performance of individual African countries. Professor Lofchie systematically compares Kenya and Tanzania, demonstrating the extent of this variety. Kenya's great successes in dramatically boosting the production of both food and exportable crops during the period of independence is throughly documented; Tanzania, conversely, is shown to have suffered precipitous declines in both crop categories. Lofchie traces the reasons for this variation to differences in policy toward the agricultural sector.

Micheal F. Lofchie is director of the African Studies Center and professor in the Department of Political Science at the University of California, Los Angeles.